DINNER *in* MINUTES

DINNER *in* MINUTES

Memorable Meals for Busy Cooks

By Linda Gassenheimer

Photography by Steven Mark Needham

CHAPTERS PUBLISHING LTD., SHELBURNE, VERMONT 05482

Published by
Chapters Publishing Ltd.
2031 Shelburne Road
Shelburne, Vermont 05482

Library of Congress Cataloguing-in-Publication Data

Gassenheimer, Linda
Dinner in Minutes / by Linda Gassenheimer
photography by Steven Mark Needham
p. cm.
Includes index
ISBN 1-881527-02-6 : $29.95. — ISBN 1-881527-03-4 : $19.95
1. Dinners and dining. 2. Quick and easy cookery. I. Title
TX737.G33 1993
641.5'55—dc20
92-36193
CIP

Trade distribution by
Firefly Books Ltd.
250 Sparks Avenue
Willowdale, Ontario
Canada M2H 2S4

Printed and bound in Canada by
Metropole Litho Inc.
St. Bruno de Montarville, Quebec

Designed by Hans Teensma/Impress, Inc.

Cover photograph: Lamb & Eggplant Kabobs (page 221)

*To Harold, whose patience and enthusiastic
love of good food encouraged me to create these recipes*

Contents

◆

Acknowledgments

♦

WHILE WORKING on this book, I realized that *Dinner in Minutes* has always been part of my life. How else could I feed my active family, enjoy my work and still have time to play? My sons and their friends' love and critical reviews of my cooking have made creating these meals enjoyable. James, John, Charles and Cami have been active advisors.

The book would not have been written without my husband, Harold, who waited for his dinner, helped clean up after it and spent many hours editing both the flavor and the text.

Dinner in Minutes began in the *Miami Herald* with the help of Food Editor Felicia Gressette. She encouraged me to write for her and to create my column when I had just arrived from London. She has become a great friend and inspiration.

Judith Weber, my literary agent, introduced me to the exciting world of cookbook authors here in the States. What would I have done without her expert guidance and perseverance!

Finding a perfect job when arriving back on these shores after 20 years in Europe was a wonderful stroke of good luck. Elizabeth Gardner Adams and her husband, Maurice, proprietors of Gardner's Markets, gave me the opportunity to work in the retail food business. Along the way, they supported my writing and became delightful friends.

Fred Tasker, wine columnist for the *Miami Herald*, adds to my readers' enjoyment with his witty and wise suggestions for my column. I appreciate his contribution to this book.

Rux Martin came to Florida for a visit and our friendship began. She's a delight to know and a tireless editor.

Publicists Lisa and Lou Ekus coined the word creativity. Their generous advice and encouragement have been of immeasurable help.

And to all my readers throughout the country who have written and called over the years, a very big thank you. You have helped shape my ideas and made the solitary task of writing a two-way street.

Linda Gassenheimer

Introduction

♦

"WHAT'S FOR DINNER?" That's the main question on my mind as the light changes and I am still in the same spot in traffic where I have been for the past 10 minutes. It's 5:15 at the end of a long day, and I have to pick up one child at track practice and the other is waiting at home. This book is for all the busy cooks who have ever agonized over the same question and who love good food but have limited time to prepare it.

After 25 years of juggling my crowded schedule with that of my family, I have developed a style of cooking that pleases us all. Going out to dinner on a regular basis or bringing home take-out wasn't an option in my family. With three hungry boys involved in sports, the amount of food would have broken the bank and might not have been good for us, even if we could have afforded it. Quick, healthful meals at home were what we needed.

This book began as a series of columns in the *Miami Herald*. Over the years, readers have responded with plenty of praise, suggestions, questions, occasional criticisms and, always, requests for more recipes. In writing this book, my goal was to offer my favorite fresh, tasty, healthful meals for a family of four that can be made in about 45 minutes or less, start to finish.

In my home, dinner preparation encompasses the time I turn on the light in my kitchen until the moment the plates are brought to the table. It also includes the telephone ringing and various members of my family wanting to discuss their day's activities with me—immediately. Of course, some people work faster than others in the kitchen, so a few of the dinners may take a bit longer at first, but all are doable at the end of the day on a tight timetable.

Dinner in Minutes doesn't mean broiled chicken every night. A week of menus in my house can include Thai shrimp, Italian pasta and bean soup, Mexican enchiladas, French veal in Madeira sauce and American barbecued pork. While living in London, I was fascinated by the wonderful selection of international restaurants. Tandoori chicken with fragrant Indian breads, Middle Eastern dishes and spicy Chinese food seemed everyday fare. When we moved to Miami, exciting new flavors exploded on my palate. Cumin and cilantro combined with hot peppers, fish right out of the sea and tropical fruits and vegetables opened a whole new world of cooking for me. Exciting as these cuisines are, they don't have to take all day to prepare.

SMART SHOPPING

FAST COOKING starts with smart shopping. Food shopping is as important in my schedule as preparing dinner. Running to several stores to find just the right vegetable or spice can be inconvenient. Most of the ingredients in this book can be found in one market. In some cases—for Thai and Vietnamese dinners in particular—special ingredients give a dish its distinctive ethnic flavor. Although your local supermarket may not carry these products, you can still make the recipes since I have given substitutes for hard-to-find items. In each case, the recipe will be delicious, if not absolutely authentic.

I was surprised to find that most readers identify my "Dinner in Minutes" column as the one with the shopping list. One woman told me that the list saves her both time and money since she buys only what she needs. By using the "Staples" section of the list, she no longer fills her cabinets with extraneous items. For many of the dinners here, you will already have many of the ingredients and need only buy a few fresh items. To help you plan your pantry, I have included a separate section listing the staples used in the book (see page 17).

As Executive Director of Gardner's Markets, a chain of specialty food stores in Miami, I field a lot of questions about buying food. "How many carrots (or onions or mushrooms) do I need for a cup?" "Your fresh tomatoes aren't ripe; can I use canned?" To anticipate problems like these, I have listed the ingredients in my shopping lists according to how much you will need or what you can substitute. In some cases, the list calls for a larger quantity than in the recipe because that is how the food is sold.

AN ORGANIZED KITCHEN

Everyone seems to have his or her own tricks for getting dinner on the table fast. Working in an efficient kitchen with clear countertops is important to me. The size doesn't matter. My English kitchen was about as large as a small pantry, and I still managed to prepare meals for 40 in it.

Everything in my kitchen has its spot and needs to be in it when I'm cooking. I don't want to stop and hunt for my potato peeler or garlic press. Knowing exactly where everything is means I can concentrate on making the meal. It also helps to have equipment within easy reach. Several important utensils in my kitchen hang from a pot rack. Other smaller items are divided among small jars or pitchers. One near my stove is filled with cooking spoons, forks and spatulas. A pottery crock on my work top has peelers and zesters, while another is filled with measuring spoons. If you prefer to have everything put away in drawers, make sure each drawer is designated for a certain type of utensil.

I cook on a gas stove, so I don't have to wait for it to warm up. When I do use an electric stove, I usually work with two burners on, one set on low, the other on high. That way I can switch the pans back and forth without waiting for the burner to adjust its temperature.

One of the biggest and most easily overlooked timesavers is to make sure the kitchen sink is free of dishes before you begin making dinner. Starting with a clear sink can shave off as much as 10 to 15 minutes from preparations. My family knows that finding the sink full when I get home from work is one of my pet peeves.

Recipes that involve peeling and chopping are time-consuming, so I have tried to keep these preparations to a minimum: potatoes are washed and the skins left on; foods are chopped or sliced in the food processor whenever possible; longer-cooking recipes in a dinner are started first and then the rest of the meal is prepared. The "Helpful Hints" given with each dinner will also speed your cooking.

HEALTHFUL MENUS

IN MY FAMILY, we love good food, but we also eat to stay healthy. Current nutritional guidelines recommend that we should limit our fat intake to no more than 30 percent of calories as an average. By carefully selecting ingredients and altering cooking methods where necessary, I have created recipes low in calories and fat. The fat content of these dinners as a percentage of total calories ranges from a low of 5 percent to a high of 35 percent. However, taste always remains the most important element. Using this book, you can select from menus full of ethnic flavors that are in line with nutritional recommendations.

Living in Miami means that we get lots of visitors. "Hi, we've just come for a little sun," old friends announce on the phone as soon as the weather turns cool up north. Unexpected friends for dinner usually calls for a tempting finish to the meal. For those times, I have developed a repertoire of quick desserts. They run the gamut from those that begin with prepared foods to pies and cakes that may appear elaborate but can be made in a relatively short time with little effort.

Every one of these dinners has been tested by my family, friends, relatives and anyone else who happened to stop by. One Sunday evening, the phone rang. "Are you testing any dinners tonight?" the voice on the other end asked.

"Sure, come on over," I answered. Literally two seconds later, the doorbell rang. Our friends were calling from their car in my driveway.

All of the dinners in this book have passed such ultimate tests. They had to be approved by three ravenous sons, a husband with a discriminating palate and by friends who travel in culinary circles. We have enjoyed them all and hope you will too.

———————————————

THE FOLLOWING GUIDELINES were used in determining the nutritional analysis for each menu:
   ♦ When a recipe offers a choice within the ingredient list, the first ingredient listed is the one incorporated in the analysis.
   ♦ When an ingredient is listed as "optional," it is always included in the analysis.
   ♦ Ingredients added "to taste" are not included in the analysis.
   ♦ Where a marinade is used, the liquid was measured before and after and only the amount absorbed is included in the analysis.

Timesavers

♦

PLANNING MEALS AND SHOPPING

♦ Make a list of about four dinners in advance. Because my family's schedule keeps changing, I find planning for the entire week difficult. Instead, I buy fresh ingredients that will keep at least four days in the refrigerator to go along with the staples I already have on hand.

♦ Shopping at the end of the day when the stores are crowded is tiring, especially if you have to go home and cook too. Keep a cooler in the trunk of your car so that you can shop before work or at lunch.

♦ Let your supermarket help you. Supermarket services available can include precut vegetables and fruit, prewashed salads and meats and poultry cut for stir-frying. Some markets will shell shrimp for you.

♦ The quickest cuts to buy are fish fillets, boneless, skinless chicken and turkey breasts and veal cutlets. These need no trimming and cook in just minutes. Cuts of meat such as boneless veal and pork tenderloin are tender and readily absorb flavor, avoiding the need for long cooking times.

♦ Keep pasta, pizza shells and bottled or frozen sauces on hand for emergency dinners. You can add practically anything in the refrigerator to the sauce for a quick dinner when you haven't had time to plan or shop.

♦ Freeze good-quality, freshly grated Parmesan cheese. It can be measured without defrosting and will quickly reach room temperature. Buy it in one piece and ask your market to grate it for you or chop it in your food processor.

MEAL PREPARATION

♦ Read the entire recipe through before beginning. Start water boiling or preheat the oven first, then gather all your ingredients together.

♦ Chop dry ingredients such as nuts or bread crumbs in a food processor first. Then you can chop wet foods such as onions without having to wash the processor bowl.

♦ If onions or garlic are used in two recipes for the same dinner, chop them all at one time and divide into appropriate portions.

♦ If a recipe freezes well and you have some extra time, make double and freeze half for another meal.

EQUIPMENT

♦ Keep as much equipment within easy reach as possible. Put your food processor on the counter. If it is stored away, it will never be used.

♦ Chop and slice as much as you can in your food processor. I find the chopping blade, grating disk, thick slicer and thin slicer invaluable.

♦ Use your microwave to its best advantage. It's great for small amounts of food, but for large quantities, it can take longer than conventional methods. One asset: whatever dish goes in my microwave also can go in the dishwasher, saving on clean-up time.

♦ Nonstick cooking pans eliminate the need for a lot of fat and are also easy to clean. I use the type that will go in the dishwasher and can stand up to metal cooking spoons and forks.

♦ Use a salad spinner to rinse and dry vegetables quickly.

♦ Replace vegetable peelers often. Like knives, they need to be sharp to work efficiently. If you still have one from five years ago, invest in a new one.

♦ Use a garlic press with large holes for chopping ginger or garlic.

♦ Use pans with handles that are ovenproof to save dirtying another pan when sautéing and baking in the same recipe.

♦ If you keep two or three chopping boards available, you won't have to stop and wash a board while cooking. I prefer those that are dishwasher-safe. I also like a medium-size one that can be easily moved around so I can chop all my vegetables on it and carry them straight to the stove.

♦ You really only need three sharp knives on hand. For most cutting tasks, a 13-inch and an 8-inch knife are sufficient. Additionally, a stainles-steel serrated knife is perfect for cutting fruit or tomatoes.

TECHNIQUES

♦ Poaching, sautéing, broiling and stir-frying are the best methods for cooking food quickly.

♦ When stir-frying, place all the prepared ingredients on a plate or chopping board in order of use. You won't have to keep looking at the recipe to see which ingredient to add next.

♦ Keep a couple of unopened cans of low-sodium chicken stock in the refrigerator. The fat will harden and can easily be skimmed off.

♦ Mix dressing in the bottom of your salad bowl, then add the salad and toss, to avoid using extra mixing bowls. If you want to save some dressing for another meal, mix it separately and add it to the individual portions as they are served.

♦ Salted water takes longer to boil, so bring the water to a boil first and then add salt when cooking pasta or rice.

♦ For quick fluffy rice, cook it like pasta in a lot of boiling water. It will roll in the water and take only about 10 minutes to cook. Fresh pasta and couscous can also be prepared in much less time.

♦ The sauce made by reducing the juices of meat or fish can be served over rice or pasta. It saves making a second sauce or adding extra fat to moisten the starch. Serving the main dish over the rice or pasta works the same way.

Staples

♦

A WELL-STOCKED PANTRY makes weekly food shopping much easier. With these staples on hand, I need only a few fresh items to make dinner.

BASICS

all-purpose unbleached flour
cornstarch
brown sugar
sugar
confectioners' sugar
baking powder
unsweetened cocoa powder
raisins

tea
coffee
cornmeal
salt
black peppercorns

SPICES

FREQUENTLY USED
bay leaf
thyme
ground cumin
ground cinnamon
rosemary
oregano
whole or ground nutmeg

SELDOM USED
curry powder
saffron or turmeric
dry mustard
chili powder
sage
poppy seeds
tarragon
ground cayenne
ground coriander
ground cardamom
ground allspice
caraway seeds
cinnamon stick
vanilla extract or bean

DRY GOODS

long-grain white rice
white basmati rice
Arborio rice
Valencia-style rice
dried linguine or fettuccine
orzo
penne

quick-cooking barley
lentils
couscous (precooked)
plain bread crumbs
plain cracker crumbs

CANNED OR BOTTLED GOODS

whole tomatoes

crushed tomatoes

tomato sauce

tomato paste or puree

canned chicken stock

cannellini beans

red kidney beans

white navy beans

black beans

tuna packed in water

nonfat mayonnaise

honey

Dijon mustard

honey mustard

crunchy peanut butter (seldom used)

OILS

canola oil

olive oil

peanut oil

sesame oil

vegetable-oil cooking spray

VINEGARS

cider vinegar

balsamic vinegar

sherry-wine vinegar

Oriental rice vinegar

white vinegar

white-wine vinegar

red-wine vinegar

CONDIMENTS

FREQUENTLY USED

Worcestershire sauce

Tabasco or other hot pepper sauce

low-sodium soy sauce

low-sodium Tamari sauce

nonfat mayonnaise

SELDOM USED

ketchup

oyster sauce

capers

fish sauce (*nuoc mam* or *nam pla*)

maple syrup

horseradish

DAIRY

butter, unsalted butter, or margarine

skim milk

nonfat plain yogurt

eggs

Parmesan cheese (can be grated and frozen)

PRODUCE

lemons
limes
onions
garlic
carrots
fresh orange juice

WINES AND BEER

dry white wine
dry red wine
dry sherry
medium sherry
canned or bottled beer
white rum
whiskey
dry vermouth
Cognac or brandy

General Helpful Hints

♦

SHOPPING FOR AND SELECTING STAPLES

Defatted Chicken Stock
♦ Defatted, low-sodium chicken stock is an excellent substitute for oil in sauces, salad dressings and sautés.
♦ Low-sodium chicken stock is readily available in most supermarkets. I keep a couple unopened cans in the refrigerator. When I need them, the fat has already hardened and can easily be skimmed off.

Dried Herbs
♦ If you use dried herbs, make sure they are no more than six months old. They lose their flavor and can become bitter if kept too long.

SHOPPING FOR AND SELECTING PRODUCE, POULTRY, FISH AND MEAT

Tomatoes
♦ If you don't have ripe tomatoes on hand, use canned whole tomatoes. They will give a better result than will out-of-season tomatoes, which have little flavor.
♦ Buy vine-ripened tomatoes when available, and store them at room temperature. Cold kills the flavor of tomatoes, hampers ripening and turns them mushy. Place them in a paper bag to help speed the ripening process.

Fresh Poultry
♦ I have called for white meat only, because this is the lowest-fat cut. Sometimes the skin is left on while cooking to keep the meat moist, but it is always removed before serving.

Fresh Fish
♦ It is easier to tell if a fish is fresh when you buy it whole rather than already cut into fillets:
  —the eyes should be bright
  —the gills red
  —the flesh firm, and a finger pressed on the flesh should not leave
   an impression.

Fresh Shrimp
♦ Buy preshelled shrimp whenever possible. Many markets sell it or will shell it for you for a small charge. I find the slightly higher cost is worth the time saved.

Fresh Beef

♦ Round steak is low in fat. If using ground beef, it is worth asking the meat department to grind a piece of round steak for you, if it is not already on display.

SPECIAL EQUIPMENT

Nonstick Pans

♦ Nonstick pans are a great help in lowering the amount of fat needed in cooking.

♦ Use a good-quality nonstick pan. There are several brands that can stand up to metal utensils and that can be washed in the dishwasher.

COOKING TECHNIQUES

Cooking Onions

♦ Sautéing onions until they are golden removes bitter juices and caramelizes them. Cooking them in a little defatted chicken stock or water in a nonstick pan will accomplish this without adding fat.

Chopping Fresh Ginger

♦ A quick way to chop ginger is to peel, cut into chunks and press through a garlic press with large holes. Hold it over the bowl or food as you press to catch the juices.

Grilling

♦ Turn the grill or broiler on to preheat when you start your dinner.

♦ Preheat a gas grill or broiler for 10 minutes.

♦ Start a charcoal fire 30 minutes ahead.

Cooking Fish

♦ A fish that is 1 inch thick should take about 10 minutes to cook. If the fish is thicker or thinner, adjust the cooking time using the 10-minute rule as a guideline.

♦ Do not overcook fish. It will continue to cook after it is removed from the heat.

♦ To broil fish: Coat with a little oil or vegetable-oil cooking spray before cooking. This will protect it from burning and will help retain moisture.

♦ Place fish 3 to 4 inches from the broiling surface. This is just close enough to cook efficiently without burning.

Cooking Pasta

♦ Always use a large pot. Pasta needs room to move as it cooks.

♦ Be sure to bring water to a rolling boil.

♦ Add all the pasta at once and stir once to keep it from sticking to the pan.

♦ Test it a few minutes before it is supposed to be done. It should be cooked through but still firm.

♦ Drain immediately, tossing briskly two or three times, and dress with sauce immediately.

Cooking Rice
♦ Cook like pasta in a lot of boiling water. It will roll in the water and take only about 10 minutes.

Wok Cooking
♦ Make sure the wok or skillet is very hot before adding the ingredients.
♦ Add a few ingredients at a time. If too many are added at once, the heat of the pan will be lowered and the food will steam rather than become crisp.

Special Meals and Wine Recommendations

◆

POULTRY DINNERS

Sherry-Soused Chicken ◆ Brown Rice & Sugar Snap Peas

Drink dry sherry with this—either a crisp, rich fino or a slightly salty manzanilla. Careful, though: these have 14 to 15 percent alcohol, compared to 12 percent in most table wines. Or, try a dry, rich, full-bodied French white Rhône wine or a Sémillon from Washington State.

Chicken Pizzaioli ◆ Sautéed Potatoes ◆ Fennel Salad

To match the tomato sauce and the savory richness of garlic and oregano, try a high-acid Italian Chianti or an equally crisp white Italian Gavi.

Game Hens in Red Wine ◆ Hot Buttered Noodles ◆ Endive & Watercress Salad

Serve with Beaujolais Nouveau. Or, to save money and get the same effect, try one of the California nouveau Gamays.

FISH & SEAFOOD DINNERS

Pernod Shrimp ◆ Tarragon Rice

Match the strength of flavor of the cream sauce with a big, rich, fruity Chardonnay from California or Australia, or contrast it with a lean, crisp Chardonnay from France's Macon region. To splurge, try a French Mersault.

Scallops in Light Wine Sauce ◆ Rice With Mushrooms

A too-rich or too-fruity wine would overpower the scallops' delicate flavor and texture. Instead, match those qualities with a dry Italian Pinot Grigio or a light, bone-dry French Muscadet.

Barbecued Balsamic Swordfish ◆ Hot Arugula (or Watercress) Pasta

The firmness and full flavor of the swordfish, especially when barbecued with balsamic vinegar, makes red wine a suitable choice. Try a soft, fruity Pinot Noir. Or, if you prefer a more traditional white wine, try a steely Sauvignon Blanc.

BEEF DINNERS

Steak au Poivre ♦ Leeks Vinaigrette ♦ Roasted Garlic Potatoes
With steak, you can always drink a California Cabernet Sauvignon. But with this peppery version, one of the new California Merlots may be preferable. They have a savory, peppery flavor themselves, and some have Cabernet Sauvignon added for firmer body. If it's a special occasion, go all out with an expensive French Bordeaux from the Pomerol district.

Grilled Stuffed Steak ♦ Pepper Jelly Succotash
To complement not only the full-flavored beef and mushroom stuffing but the spiciness of the jalapeño-laced succotash, try a zingy, spicy California Zinfandel.

LAMB DINNERS

Lamb With Lemon Sauce ♦ Roasted French Fries ♦ Green Beans Vinaigrette
Serve with a traditional Spanish choice: a soft, rich, deeply-perfumed red Rioja.

VEAL DINNERS

Veal Gorgonzola ♦ Italian Rice & Peas ♦ Radicchio & Radish Salad
A red Italian Docetto has the fruitiness and bitter-almond edge to stand up to this meal. Or you could try one of the firm, intense white wines from southern Italy—a Greco di Tufo, with the flavor of toasted almonds, or a Fioano di Avellino, which has hazelnut undertones. If these are unavailable, serve a California Sauvignon Blanc.

Veal Medallions in Madeira Sauce ♦ Kumquats & Rice
The rich flavor of the Madeira sauce calls for a firm, rich Cabernet Sauvignon from California, Australia or Chile. If you want a white wine, try a Gewürztraminer—either an intense, bone-dry one from France's Alsace or a fruitier one from California.

Wine suggestions were provided by Fred Tasker, whose weekly wine column in the Miami Herald *is carried in newspapers across the country.*

CHAPTER I

Soup, Rice & Pasta Dinners

Soup, Rice & Pasta Dinners

◆

Pasta & Bean Soup
Italian Lettuce Salad
Herbed Bread

Shopping List

1 small bunch celery
2 jalapeño peppers
1 bunch fresh basil or flat-leaf parsley
1 bunch fresh parsley
1 small bunch fresh oregano or dried
1 small head romaine lettuce
2 small Belgian endives
2 small heads radicchio
1-ounce piece Parmesan cheese
2 cans cannellini beans (19 ounces each)
1 French baguette

Staples

garlic
2 cans whole tomatoes (28 ounces each)
small pasta (acini di pepe, orzo or riso)
olive oil
balsamic or red-wine vinegar
2 cans chicken stock (14½ ounces each)
salt
black peppercorns

Helpful Hints

♦ *For a vegetarian meal, substitute vegetable stock for chicken stock.*

♦ *Use up the last bits of pasta left in various opened boxes.*

♦ *Canned Great Northern beans may be substituted for cannellini beans.*

I CREATED THE MAINSTAY of this meal, Pasta & Bean Soup, for my son and his college friends who needed something filling and delicious when they returned from rowing crew at night. Their other requirements: The dish had to be made from staples, it had to be vegetarian, and it had to simmer while they showered and be ready when they came back to the kitchen.

If you, like my son, are pressed for time, serve the soup on its own with some crusty bread, and use any type of salad greens you have on hand with your favorite bottled dressing.

Serves 5.

THIS MEAL CONTAINS A TOTAL OF 758 CALORIES PER SERVING WITH 26 PERCENT OF CALORIES FROM FAT.

⏳ Countdown

♦ *Preheat broiler for bread.*
♦ *Start soup.*
♦ *While soup cooks, make salad.*
♦ *Prepare bread.*

PASTA & BEAN SOUP

KNOWN AS *pasta e fagioli*, this may be Italy's most famous soup, after minestrone. The combination of pasta and beans is satisfying and inexpensive as well as nutritionally correct. My son would probably leave out the fresh basil, but the addition of fresh herbs perks it up considerably.

2	19-ounce cans cannellini beans
2	28-ounce cans whole tomatoes
6	stalks celery, diced
4	medium cloves garlic, crushed through a press
2	medium jalapeño peppers, seeded and chopped
4	cups defatted chicken stock
¼	cup olive oil
8	ounces or 1 cup pasta (any small size or leftover pieces)
1	cup chopped fresh basil or flat-leaf parsley
	Salt and freshly ground black pepper to taste
¼	cup freshly grated Parmesan cheese

Drain and rinse beans. Place beans, tomatoes and their liquid, celery and garlic in a large pot. Add jalapeño peppers and chicken stock. Cover and bring to a boil. Simmer for 15 minutes, breaking up tomatoes with the side of a spoon. Add oil, pasta and basil and return to a boil. Boil, uncovered, for about 10 minutes, or until pasta is cooked. Add salt and pepper to taste.

Serve in large soup bowls and pass Parmesan to sprinkle on top.

ITALIAN LETTUCE SALAD

THERE ARE NO TOMATOES in this salad, making it a good choice for a midwinter supper. Instead, lively color is provided by the crisp, contrasting leaves of the deep-red radicchio, green romaine and pearly white endive. Radicchio and endive, incidentally, are particularly quick greens to prepare for salad since they are so easy to wash.

Helpful Hint

♦ *Belgian endive will turn brown if soaked with water. Either wipe it with a damp paper towel or pass it briefly under water and dry.*

2   small heads radicchio
1   small head romaine lettuce
2   small Belgian endives
2   tablespoons balsamic or red-wine vinegar
1   tablespoon olive oil
    Salt and freshly ground black pepper to taste

Wash and dry radicchio and romaine. Tear into bite-size pieces. Wipe endives with a damp paper towel and slice into ¼-inch pieces. Mix vinegar, oil, salt and pepper together in a salad bowl. Add lettuce leaves to the bowl and toss.

HERBED BREAD

THE GARLIC doesn't overpower this simple bread topping, and its taste is freshened by the addition of herbs. If using dried oregano, add it to the parsley when chopping; the moisture from the parsley will help release the flavor of the oregano.

1   French baguette
1   tablespoon olive oil
4   medium cloves garlic, crushed through a press
2   tablespoons chopped fresh parsley
4   teaspoons chopped fresh oregano or 1 teaspoon dried

Preheat broiler. Cut bread in half lengthwise. Mix oil, garlic and herbs together. Spoon over center of bread. Place on a baking sheet lined with foil and broil 5 minutes, or until crisp and golden.

White Bean Vichyssoise

Red Pepper Pizza

THIS SOUP is a favorite on those nights when we don't feel like a huge meal but want something satisfying. Light yet filling, it is made with canned beans, and it can be served hot or at room temperature, accompanied by a colorful French-bread pizza. If you're pressed for time, just buy a French baguette, cut it in half, sprinkle with Parmesan cheese and toast in the oven.

Serves 4.

THIS MEAL CONTAINS A TOTAL OF 724 CALORIES PER SERVING WITH 16 PERCENT OF CALORIES FROM FAT.

⧖ Countdown

♦ *Preheat oven to 350 degrees F for pizza.*
♦ *Start soup and sauté leeks for soup.*
♦ *While leeks sauté, sauté onions for pizza.*
♦ *Finish soup.*
♦ *While soup is cooking, complete pizza.*

WHITE BEAN VICHYSSOISE

ON A TRIP to New York City, I stopped at the Union Square Café and tasted a delicious vichyssoise with white beans and leeks. I have adapted their recipe to make a quick soup. If you prefer a soup with a very smooth consistency, strain the pureed mixture through a wire-mesh sieve.

4	teaspoons dry white wine
4	medium cloves garlic, crushed through a press
2	tablespoons butter or margarine
2	medium leeks, well washed and sliced
2	stalks celery, sliced
2	19-ounce cans cannellini beans
2	14½-ounce cans defatted chicken stock
2	teaspoons each chopped fresh rosemary, thyme, sage or ½ teaspoon each dried
2	bay leaves
	Salt and freshly ground black pepper to taste
2	tablespoons chopped fresh chives or scallions for garnish

Heat white wine in a small nonstick skillet. Add garlic and cook over a low flame without browning it, for 10 minutes. Meanwhile, heat butter in a medium-size nonstick saucepan. Add leeks and celery and sauté gently until wilted and

Shopping List

2 leeks
2 stalks celery
3 red peppers
1 small bunch each fresh rosemary, thyme, sage; or dried
1 small bunch fresh chives or scallions
1-ounce piece Parmesan cheese
8 pitted black olives
1 small tin anchovies
2 cans cannellini beans (19 ounces each)
1 French baguette

Staples

onions (2)
garlic
bay leaves
butter or margarine
dry white wine
3 cans chicken stock (14½ ounces each)
salt
black peppercorns

Helpful Hints

♦ *Crush garlic for both dishes and divide accordingly.*

♦ *To remove all the grit hiding in the leek stalks, cut them in half lengthwise and in half again and rinse well under running water. Cook until sweet and just lightly colored. This will take about 10 minutes of slow cooking.*

♦ *Cannellini beans are large, white Italian kidney beans found in the canned bean or Italian-products section of supermarkets. Be sure to drain them and rinse well to remove any tinny taste.*

lightly colored, about 10 minutes. Drain and rinse beans. Add to leek mixture along with chicken stock, herbs and bay leaves. Add garlic mixture and simmer 15 minutes. Add salt and pepper to taste. Remove bay leaves. Puree in a blender or food processor. Serve warm or at room temperature with a sprinkling of chives or scallions as a garnish.

♦ *If you use dried herbs, make sure they are no more than 6 months old. They lose their flavor and can become bitter.*

RED PEPPER PIZZA

WITH ITS BLACK OLIVES, red bell peppers, garlic and anchovies, this pizza combines the sweet, salty and sharp flavors that are characteristic of Mediterranean cooking, providing the perfect counterpart to the mild bean soup.

Helpful Hints

♦ *Buy pitted olives.*

♦ *Buy good Parmesan and ask the store to grate it for you, or cut it into pieces and chop in a food processor.*

¼	cup defatted chicken stock
1	medium onion, sliced thinly
3	medium red bell peppers, sliced thinly
2	medium cloves garlic, crushed through a press
1	French baguette
4	anchovy fillets, cut in half
8	good-quality black olives, pitted and quartered
1	tablespoon chopped fresh thyme or ½ tablespoon dried
¼	cup freshly grated Parmesan cheese
	Salt and freshly ground black pepper to taste

Preheat oven to 350 degrees F. Heat chicken stock in a nonstick skillet and add onion. Cook 5 minutes and add red peppers and garlic. Cook 10 more minutes. Onion should be golden and peppers soft. Slice baguette in half lengthwise and place each half, crust-side down, on a baking tray lined with foil. Spoon red pepper mixture evenly over both halves. Scatter anchovy and olives evenly on top. Sprinkle with thyme, Parmesan, salt and pepper to taste. Place in oven for 5 minutes, or until bread is toasted and cheese begins to brown.

Italian Fish Soup

Romaine & Bean Salad

Crusty Bread

Shopping List

1 pound yellowtail, grouper, cod halibut, swordfish or flounder
¼ pound clams (about 4)
6 ounces shrimp (8 large)
2 stalks celery
2 carrots
1 head romaine lettuce
1 small bunch fresh parsley
1 pound plum tomatoes or canned
2 bottles clam juice (8 ounces each)
1 small tin anchovy fillets
1 can cannellini beans (19 ounces)
1 loaf Italian bread

Staples

lemon
onion
garlic
butter or margarine
Dijon mustard
olive oil
dry white wine
chicken stock
salt
black peppercorns

Helpful Hints

♦ *Any type of nonoily fish that will hold its shape when cooked can be used. Of course, the fresher the fish, the better.*

♦ *If plum tomatoes are not in season, use good-quality canned, drained tomatoes.*

♦ *To devein shrimp, remove shells and slit shrimp down the back; remove black vein. Rinse and drain.*

THOUGH IT'S amazingly easy to prepare, this aromatic fish soup is a meal to anticipate, for it retains the individual flavors of fish, clams and shrimp. A simple salad of soft-textured beans on crunchy lettuce and a crusty loaf of bread rounds it out. *See photograph, page 102.*

    Serves 4.

THIS MEAL CONTAINS A TOTAL OF 842 CALORIES PER SERVING WITH 24 PERCENT OF CALORIES FROM FAT.

⧗ Countdown

♦ *Preheat oven to 450 degrees F for bread.*
♦ *Start soup.*
♦ *While soup cooks, prepare bread.*
♦ *Make salad.*

ITALIAN FISH SOUP

EVERY COASTAL TOWN in Italy has its own fish soup based on the types of fish found in that area. I've simplified and adapted the basic recipe, using the varieties available in this country.

¼	cup olive oil
2	medium carrots, chopped
2	stalks celery, chopped
1	medium onion, chopped
2	medium cloves garlic, crushed through a press
2	anchovy fillets
2	fresh parsley sprigs
1	pound yellowtail, grouper, cod, halibut, swordfish or flounder fillets
2	cups dry white wine
4	clams, in shell (little necks, cherrystones or steamers)
1	pound plum tomatoes (about 4 medium) or canned, drained
2	cups bottled clam juice
½	teaspoon salt
¼	teaspoon freshly ground black pepper
8	large shrimp, shelled and deveined

Heat oil in a large saucepan and add carrots, celery, onion, garlic, anchovy and parsley. Gently sauté ingredients until onion turns golden, about 10 minutes. Do not let vegetables burn.

Cut fish fillets into 3-inch pieces and add to pan. Carefully stir in wine, trying not to break up fish. Simmer gently for 5 minutes to slightly reduce wine. Scrub clam shells. Add clams in their shells, tomatoes and clam juice to the pan. Season with salt and pepper. Bring soup to a boil, add shrimp, lower the heat and simmer for 5 minutes. Check seasoning and add more if necessary. Serve in large soup bowls.

CRUSTY BREAD

- 1 loaf unsliced Italian bread
- 1 tablespoon melted butter

Preheat oven to 450 degrees F. Place bread on a piece of foil and brush with melted butter. Bake in the oven for 5 to 10 minutes, or until crusty.

ROMAINE & BEAN SALAD

To SAVE clean-up and preparation time, mix the dressing in the bottom of your salad bowl and toss the beans and lettuce right in the bowl.

- 1 tablespoon fresh lemon juice
- 1 teaspoon Dijon mustard
- 2 tablespoons defatted chicken stock
- 2 teaspoons olive oil
  Salt and freshly ground black pepper to taste
- ½ head romaine lettuce
- 2 cups cannellini beans

Helpful Hint

♦ *Cannellini beans are readily available in the bean or Italian-products section of the supermarket. You can substitute any type of canned beans you like.*

Whisk lemon juice and mustard together in the bottom of a salad bowl. Add chicken stock and oil and whisk until blended. Add salt and pepper to taste. Break lettuce in half, then quarters, so that each quarter has some of the inner and outer leaves. Wash, dry and tear into bite-size pieces. Drain cannellini beans. Rinse under cold water and drain again. Toss beans in salad dressing and then add lettuce. Toss all ingredients together.

Get-Together Rice

Chicken & Mushroom Soup

Shopping List

*½ pound boneless, skinless
    chicken breast
6 ounces lean ham
1 bunch scallions
¼ pound fresh snow peas
½ pound fresh mushrooms
1 small package fresh bean sprouts
1 bunch watercress
1 small bunch fresh parsley
2 cans chicken stock
    (14½ ounces each)*

Staples

*onion
long-grain white rice
sugar
low-sodium soy sauce
sesame oil
canola oil
dry sherry
salt
black peppercorns*

Helpful Hints

♦ *It's best to have all ingredients chopped and placed in proper cooking order on a cutting board or plate before you start to cook.*

♦ *Make sure the wok or skillet is very hot before adding ingredients.*

♦ *In a food processor, slice vegetables first and then chop parsley without washing the processor bowl. Don't bother to wash the bowl before slicing mushrooms for soup.*

IN THE SAME AMOUNT of time that you can get Chinese take-out, which often has a gluey sauce, you can make this fried rice and soup. The sauce on the rice is light, and the vegetables stay crunchy. This dinner is the perfect excuse to celebrate Chinese New Year, which falls at the end of January or the beginning of February, depending on the year.

    Serves 4.

THIS MEAL CONTAINS A TOTAL OF 683 CALORIES PER SERVING WITH 19 PERCENT OF CALORIES FROM FAT.

⧗ Countdown

♦ *Slice chicken for soup and begin marinating.*
♦ *Cook rice and prepare vegetables for Get-Together Rice.*
♦ *Complete soup.*

GET-TOGETHER RICE

THIS RECIPE was given to me by a delegate to the All-China Women's Federation who visited me. It is a simplified version of a traditional Shanghai dish that her family serves on the New Year. The many ingredients are supposed to symbolize the union of families during the holiday.

1½	cups uncooked long-grain white rice
2	tablespoons canola oil, *divided*
¼	medium onion, chopped
4	sliced scallions
6	ounces diced lean ham (1½ cups)
1	cup snow peas, trimmed, cut in half
1	cup fresh bean sprouts
¼	cup dry sherry
4	teaspoons low-sodium soy sauce or more to taste
2	teaspoons sugar
¼	cup chopped fresh parsley
	Salt to taste

Fill a medium-size saucepan with 2 to 3 quarts water and add rice. Bring water to a boil and let rice boil freely, uncovered, for about 10 minutes, or until cooked through. Drain and stir in 1 tablespoon oil. While rice is cooking, wash and cut vegetables and ham. Mix sherry, soy sauce and sugar together. Heat a wok or skillet and add remaining 1 tablespoon oil. When it is smoking, add onion and stir-fry for 1 minute. Add scallions and continue to fry for another ½ minute. Add ham, snow peas, bean sprouts and rice and stir-fry for 3 minutes. Push ingredients aside, making a hole in the center, and add soy sauce mixture. Tossing all ingredients together, continue to fry another 4 to 5 minutes. Add parsley and toss. Taste for seasoning. Add salt if necessary.

CHICKEN & MUSHROOM SOUP

Soup is generally served in the middle or at the end of a Chinese meal rather than at the beginning as in the West. Clear stock or boiling water is added to whatever is left from the main dish, and the mixture is quickly heated and served as an instant soup.

½	pound boneless, skinless chicken breast
¼	cup low-sodium soy sauce
4	cups defatted chicken stock
1	bunch watercress leaves, washed
½	pound mushrooms, washed and sliced (about 2 cups)
¼	cup dry sherry
2	teaspoons sesame oil
	Salt and freshly ground black pepper to taste
2	scallions, sliced

Thinly slice chicken breast and marinate in soy sauce for 15 minutes. Bring chicken stock to a rolling boil; add chicken. Cut off stems of watercress and discard. When soup starts to boil again and chicken floats to the top, add watercress leaves and mushrooms. Remove from heat and stir in sherry and sesame oil and taste for seasoning. Add salt and pepper, if necessary. Serve in individual soup bowls and sprinkle scallions on top.

Helpful Hints

♦ *Wash watercress by immersing it in a bowl of water. Let stand a couple of minutes, then lift out of bowl. Sand and dirt will be left behind.*

♦ *Slice mushrooms in a food processor.*

Green Peppers Stuffed With Rice & Tuna

Chick-Pea & Arugula Salad

THE ARRIVAL OF big, sweet bell peppers in the market is my cue that it's time to make this quick and easy light supper. Serve with a salad of warm garlicky beans over arugula or romaine lettuce, with bread and a glass of chilled Chardonnay.
 Serves 4.

THIS MEAL CONTAINS A TOTAL OF 655 CALORIES PER SERVING WITH 15 PERCENT OF CALORIES FROM FAT.

⧗ Countdown

- *Put water for peppers on to boil.*
- *Preheat oven to 400 degrees F for peppers.*
- *Prepare peppers.*
- *While peppers are baking, warm bread and make salad.*

GREEN PEPPERS STUFFED WITH RICE & TUNA

No ANTIPASTO TABLE in Italy is complete without stuffed zucchini, mushrooms, peppers or even onions. This dish combines two Italian favorites, firm green peppers and good-quality canned tuna. Both the stuffed peppers and the salad may be served warm or at room temperature.

4	medium green bell peppers or a mixture of 4 green, yellow or red bell peppers
½	cup uncooked long-grain white rice
¾	cup defatted chicken stock, *divided*
½	medium onion, sliced
2	medium cloves garlic, crushed through a press
2	cups crushed canned tomatoes
	Salt and freshly ground black pepper to taste
2	6⅛-ounce cans water-packed solid white tuna
1	cup chopped fresh basil or 1 cup fresh parsley chopped together with 1 teaspoon dried oregano
2	teaspoons olive oil
1	loaf Italian bread

Preheat oven to 400 degrees F. Bring a large pot with 3 to 4 quarts of water

Shopping List

*4 medium green bell peppers or a
 mixture of 4 green, yellow or
 red bell peppers
1 bunch fresh basil or mixture of
 fresh parsley and dried oregano
2 bunches fresh arugula or 1 head
 romaine
1 loaf Italian bread
2 cans water-packed solid white
 tuna (6⅛ ounces each)
2 cans chick-peas (27 ounces each)*

Staples

*long-grain white rice
onion
garlic
1 can crushed tomatoes (19 ounces)
balsamic vinegar
olive oil
chicken stock
salt
black peppercorns*

Helpful Hints

- *Crushed garlic is used in both recipes. To save time, crush all the garlic at once using a garlic press.*

- *Use a combination of red, yellow or green bell peppers for an attractive presentation.*

- *Good-quality tuna fish is important to this dish. Use a solid white tuna packed in water.*

to a boil. Place whole peppers in boiling water and simmer 4 minutes. Remove and immediately refresh under cold water.

Cook rice in boiling water, uncovered, for 8 to 10 minutes and drain. Heat ¼ cup chicken stock in a nonstick skillet and sauté onion and garlic 5 minutes. Add crushed tomatoes and cook 5 more minutes. Add salt and pepper to taste. Mix rice, tuna and basil together. Add olive oil. Taste and add salt and pepper as needed. Be careful: There may already be enough salt from tuna.

Cut peppers in half lengthwise and remove core and seeds. Place peppers in a small roasting pan or baking dish. It should be just large enough to fit them snugly together. Pour remaining ½ cup chicken stock into pan. Spoon rice stuffing into peppers. Spoon tomato sauce over peppers. Cover with foil and bake for 15 minutes. Peppers should be cooked through but still slightly crunchy.

Warm bread, slice and serve in a basket.

CHICK-PEA & ARUGULA SALAD

WHEN SAUTÉED, the ordinarily bland chick-peas become flavorful and slightly crisp. Use romaine lettuce if you don't have arugula.

4   teaspoons olive oil, *divided*
2   medium cloves garlic, crushed through a press
3   cups canned chick-peas, drained and rinsed
    Salt and freshly ground black pepper to taste
2   bunches fresh arugula or romaine
2   tablespoons balsamic vinegar
2   tablespoons defatted chicken stock

Heat 2 teaspoons oil in a small nonstick skillet and add garlic. Sauté 1 minute and add chick-peas. Sauté 2 to 3 minutes, or until chick-peas are warmed and slightly crisp on the outside. Add salt and pepper to taste. Set aside to cool for several minutes. Remove stems from arugula or break romaine into bite-size pieces and wash and dry well. Arrange on a serving plate and spoon chick-peas on top. Whisk vinegar and chicken stock together and add remaining oil. Blend well. Add salt and pepper to taste. Pour over chick-peas and arugula.

Penne Pasta Primavera

Toasted Bread With Goat Cheese

Shopping List

2 medium eggplants
2 medium zucchini
1 red bell pepper
1 green bell pepper
1 small bunch fresh basil
1 small bunch fresh oregano or
    dried
½ pint heavy cream
2-ounce piece Parmesan cheese
1 package garlic-herbed fresh goat
    cheese, plain fresh goat cheese or
    Bel Paese (4 ounces)
1 pound penne
1 French baguette

Staples

onion
garlic
1 can Italian plum tomatoes
    (28 ounces)
olive oil
salt
black peppercorns

Helpful Hints

♦ Substitute other thick types of
pasta such as small shells, ziti,
rigatoni or fusilli, if you like.

♦ Vegetables should be the same
size as the penne, but if you do not
have a special julienne blade on
your food processor, use a large
slicing blade or cut the vegetables
into thin slices with a knife.

♦ In a pinch, substitute flat-leaf
parsley chopped with 1 teaspoon
dried oregano for fresh basil.

FRESH VEGETABLES in a light tomato sauce make a richly flavored, filling vegetarian supper. It is complemented by a simple "pizza" made of toasted rounds of bread topped with fresh goat cheese. If pressed for time, serve warm French or Italian bread instead. *See photograph, page 99.*
    Serves 4.
THIS MEAL CONTAINS A TOTAL OF 831 CALORIES PER SERVING WITH 25 PERCENT OF CALORIES FROM FAT.

⧖ Countdown

♦ *Put water for pasta on to boil.*
♦ *Cut vegetables for pasta in a food processor with a julienne or French-fry blade.*
♦ *Prepare sauce for pasta.*
♦ *Preheat broiler for Toasted Bread.*
♦ *Cook pasta and make Toasted Bread.*

PENNE PASTA PRIMAVERA

ALTHOUGH Pasta Primavera was first invented at Le Cirque in New York City, the idea of combining fresh vegetables and pasta is a particularly Italian one. I first tasted this dish in one of my favorite restaurants tucked away in a corner of Venice. The sauce was made right at the table, so I suspected that it wouldn't be difficult to adapt to a tight deadline, and the aroma was so wonderful we couldn't wait to eat. Penne, little quill-shaped pasta, hold the sauce nicely.

4	teaspoons olive oil
1	medium onion, sliced
2	medium eggplants, unpeeled
2	medium zucchini
1	medium red bell pepper
1	medium green bell pepper
6	medium cloves garlic, crushed through a press
3	cups canned plum tomatoes
¼	cup heavy cream
	Salt and freshly ground black pepper to taste
1	pound penne
½	bunch fresh basil, torn into small pieces
½	cup freshly grated Parmesan cheese

Put a large pot with 3 to 4 quarts of water on to boil. Heat olive oil in a large nonstick skillet and add onion. Sauté gently 5 minutes. Wash eggplants and zucchini and, using a food processor, cut into very thin julienne strips, about 2 inches long and ⅛ inch thick. Cut peppers into similar-size strips. Add vegetables and crushed garlic to the pan with onion. Sauté 8 more minutes, stirring occasionally. Cut plum tomatoes into quarters and add to the pan with their juices. Lower heat to a simmer and continue to cook 5 more minutes. Add cream. Blend well and season with salt and pepper to taste.

When water comes to a boil, add pasta. Boil for about 10 minutes. Test to make sure pasta is cooked. It should be cooked through, but firm. Drain and place in a large serving bowl. Pour sauce over pasta. Sprinkle with basil and Parmesan. Taste and add more salt, pepper, basil or cheese if necessary.

TOASTED BREAD WITH GOAT CHEESE

THE ITALIANS like to cover sliced bread with other leftover foods and then heat them in a wood fire. The resulting crostini, or "little crusts," make a great side dish for this dinner.

1   **French baguette, sliced into about 12 rounds**
1   **teaspoon olive oil**
1   **4-ounce package garlic-herbed fresh goat cheese, plain fresh goat cheese or Bel Paese**
4   **teaspoons chopped fresh oregano or 2 teaspoons dried**

Preheat broiler or preheat oven to 400 degrees F. Slice bread on diagonal into ½-inch rounds. Brush with olive oil and spread with goat cheese. Place under broiler for 1½ minutes, or until cheese melts, or in oven for 5 minutes. Sprinkle with oregano and serve.

Helpful Hint

♦ *Any type of soft fresh goat cheese can be used. It has a creamy texture and a mild flavor with a slight tang. Local varieties are available in the dairy case of most supermarkets. (Avoid the aged French variety, which has a strong goaty taste.)*

Pesto Spaghettini

Tuscan Tomatoes

Shopping List

4 large ripe tomatoes
1 large bunch fresh parsley
1 large bunch fresh basil
1 small bunch fresh oregano or dried
1 small tin anchovy fillets
1 small bottle capers
1-ounce jar pine nuts
2-ounce piece Parmesan cheese
½ pound spaghettini
1 loaf crusty sourdough bread or Italian bread sticks

Staples

lemon
garlic
Dijon mustard
extra-virgin olive oil
chicken stock
plain bread crumbs
salt
black peppercorns

WHENEVER I am at my vacation home, I love to serve pasta with pesto sauce, because the parsley and basil are picked fresh from a nearby farm and the sauce is so easy to make. There are always a lot of family and friends around, and this meal can be made for a few or many. Serve it with crusty sourdough bread or Italian bread sticks and stuffed tomatoes.

Serves 4.

THIS MEAL CONTAINS A TOTAL OF 615 CALORIES PER SERVING WITH 27 PERCENT OF CALORIES FROM FAT.

⧖ Countdown

◆ *Put water for pasta on to boil.*
◆ *Preheat oven to 350 degrees F to warm bread.*
◆ *Prepare tomatoes.*
◆ *Cook pasta.*
◆ *While pasta boils, make pesto sauce in food processor.*

TUSCAN TOMATOES

RIPE TOMATOES filled with bread crumbs, capers and anchovies are the perfect accompaniment to the green-sauced pasta. This dish is a kind of Salade Niçoise stuffed into a tomato. It was inspired by a recipe given to me by Lorenza de Medici.

4	large ripe tomatoes
4	anchovy fillets
4	teaspoons capers, drained
4	tablespoons plain bread crumbs
2	tablespoons chopped fresh oregano or 2 teaspoons dried
2	tablespoons chopped fresh parsley, *divided*
1	tablespoon fresh lemon juice
2	teaspoons Dijon mustard
2	tablespoons defatted chicken stock
2	teaspoons extra-virgin olive oil
	Salt and freshly ground black pepper to taste

Helpful Hints

◆ *Cut a thin slice off the bottom of the tomato to help it sit flat on the plate.*

◆ *The top of the tomato is the stem end. Cut just below it to hollow the tomato.*

Cut off tops of tomatoes and, with a spoon, hollow out about one-third of tomato pulp. Place tomatoes on individual plates. Chop tomato pulp. Mash anchovy fillets and capers in a small bowl with a fork. Add chopped tomato, bread crumbs and oregano. Reserve 1 tablespoon parsley for garnish and mix remaining 1 tablespoon into stuffing. Whisk lemon juice and mustard together. Add chicken stock and oil. Add salt and pepper to taste. Moisten stuffing with some dressing. Fill tomatoes with stuffing; sprinkle some parsley on top and serve remaining dressing on the side.

PESTO SPAGHETTINI

THIS PESTO is unusual because it uses so little oil. Buy the best-quality extra-virgin olive oil you can find to give this sauce its fullest flavor.

2	cups fresh basil leaves
1	cup fresh parsley, preferably flat-leaf, stems removed
8	medium cloves garlic, crushed through a press
2	tablespoons pine nuts
½	teaspoon salt
2	tablespoons extra-virgin olive oil
½	cup freshly grated Parmesan cheese
⅓	cup plus 2 tablespoons water
½	pound spaghettini
1	loaf sourdough bread or Italian bread sticks

Put a large pot of 3 to 4 quarts water on to heat while you make the sauce. Preheat oven to 350 degrees F to warm bread. Wash and thoroughly dry basil and parsley leaves. Put basil, parsley, garlic, pine nuts and salt into the bowl of a food processor and process. With processor running, add oil. Transfer to serving bowl and add Parmesan and ⅓ cup plus 2 tablespoons water. Taste for seasoning, adding more salt if necessary. If you do not have a food processor, finely chop all ingredients by hand, place in bowl and blend in oil, cheese and water.

When water boils, add spaghettini and boil for about 10 minutes, or until pasta is cooked but still firm. Drain. Add to pesto sauce and toss.

Warm bread 5 minutes, or until crusty. Slice and serve with pasta.

Helpful Hint

♦ *Buy good-quality Parmesan cheese (the best is Parmigiano-Reggiano). Ask the store to grate it for you or it cut into small pieces and chop in food processor.*

Italian Stuffed Shells

Colorful Greens & Bean Salad

Shopping List

1 box frozen chopped spinach
   (10 ounces)
1 large head radicchio or red leaf
   lettuce
1 medium head escarole or other
   crisp lettuce
1 small bunch fresh parsley
1 small bunch fresh basil or flat-
   leaf parsley or chives, optional
1-pound carton part-skim ricotta
   cheese
2-ounce piece gruyère or Cheddar
   cheese
1 box jumbo pasta shells
   (12 ounces)
1 can Great Northern beans
   (19 ounces)

Staples

onion
garlic
bay leaves
ground nutmeg
sugar
nonfat plain yogurt
honey mustard
canned crushed or chopped
   tomatoes (36 ounces)
sherry-wine vinegar
olive oil
salt
black peppercorns

Helpful Hint

♦ Chop onion for sauce and
filling at the same time in a food
processor and divide as needed.

STUFFED PASTA SHELLS are a favorite of all age groups. I used to love them when I was young, because they "caught" the meat and sauce inside them. This is a colorful, tasty vegetarian dish. Since it freezes well, make double if you have time and freeze for emergencies. Serve with a crisp salad made with escarole and radicchio and canned Great Northern beans, or with any tossed green salad made from whatever greens you have on hand. Place a basket of warm rolls on the table.

Serves 4.

THIS MEAL CONTAINS A TOTAL OF 717 CALORIES PER SERVING WITH 21 PERCENT OF CALORIES FROM FAT.

Countdown

♦ Put water for pasta on to boil.
♦ Preheat oven to 400 degrees F for baking pasta.
♦ Start pasta sauce.
♦ While sauce simmers, make filling for pasta.
♦ Cook pasta shells and stuff them.
♦ While pasta bakes, make salad.

ITALIAN STUFFED SHELLS

PASTA IS VERY EASY TO COOK, but it does need to be watched so it doesn't turn mushy. One of my Italian friends always says, "Never leave the kitchen while the pasta is cooking; it can't take care of itself."

SAUCE

4	cups canned crushed or chopped tomatoes
½	medium onion, chopped (about 1 cup)
2	medium cloves garlic, crushed through a press
2	bay leaves
1	teaspoon sugar
	Salt and freshly ground black pepper to taste

FILLING

2	teaspoons olive oil
1	medium onion, chopped (about 2 cups)
1	10-ounce package frozen chopped spinach
2	teaspoons ground nutmeg
2	cups part-skim ricotta cheese
½	cup chopped fresh parsley

24   **jumbo shells**
2   **ounces grated gruyère or Cheddar cheese (about ½ cup)**

Preheat oven to 400 degrees F. Place a large pot with 3 to 4 quarts of water on to heat.

For sauce: Place tomatoes, onion, garlic and bay leaves in a saucepan and bring to a simmer. Cover and cook gently for 15 minutes. Add sugar and salt and pepper to taste. Remove bay leaves.

For filling: Heat oil in a small nonstick saucepan and sauté onion for 3 minutes. Add spinach and cook, covered, over medium heat until spinach is defrosted, about 5 minutes. Uncover and cook until liquid is evaporated. Add nutmeg. Mix ricotta and parsley together in a bowl. Add spinach mixture and blend well. Taste for seasoning and add nutmeg, salt or pepper to taste.

For pasta: Cook shells in boiling water for 12 minutes, or until tender but firm. Drain and run cold water over them.

To assemble: Spoon half the sauce into a small baking dish just large enough to hold shells in one layer. Fill each shell with a large teaspoon of spinach and ricotta mixture. Place shells on sauce in the baking dish. Spoon remaining sauce over shells and sprinkle cheese on top. Bake for 10 minutes, or until sauce is bubbly.

COLORFUL GREENS & BEAN SALAD

ESCAROLE, a curly large-leaf lettuce, and radicchio, a deep-red, white-veined leaf lettuce, make this salad colorful. I serve the dressing a lot, for I can whip it together in no time at all. It's nice and creamy. If I don't have time to put in basil or wine vinegar, I just mix the nonfat yogurt and honey mustard together. It doubles as a quick dip.

1   **19-ounce can Great Northern beans**
8   **large radicchio leaves or red leaf lettuce**
10 **large escarole leaves**
½   **cup nonfat plain yogurt**
4   **teaspoons honey mustard**
4   **teaspoons sherry-wine vinegar**
2   **tablespoons finely chopped fresh basil or flat-leaf parsley or chives,** *optional*
2   **medium cloves garlic, crushed through a press**

Drain and rinse beans, wash radicchio and escarole and dry well. Place in a salad dish. Mix yogurt and honey mustard together in a small bowl. Add vinegar, basil and garlic. Blend well. Spoon onto salad and toss well.

Helpful Hints

♦ *Any type of bean, such as kidney or cannellini, can be used.*

♦ *Substitute any type of crisp lettuce for escarole.*

Penne Pasta With Tuna Sauce

Green Bean Salad

THIS IS A PERFECT DINNER for a busy week when you haven't had time to go shopping. Most of the ingredients are already on your pantry shelf. Fresh green beans in a light vinaigrette complete this quick meal.

Serves 4.

THIS MEAL CONTAINS A TOTAL OF 799 CALORIES PER SERVING WITH 17 PERCENT OF CALORIES FROM FAT.

⧗ Countdown

- ♦ *Put water for pasta on to boil.*
- ♦ *Put water for green beans on to boil.*
- ♦ *Preheat oven to 350 degrees F for bread.*
- ♦ *Make pasta sauce.*
- ♦ *While sauce simmers, make salad.*
- ♦ *Finish pasta dish.*

PENNE PASTA WITH TUNA SAUCE

I CREATED THIS RECIPE one December evening when my refrigerator was packed with holiday food. Because I had most of the ingredients in the house, I didn't have to face the crowds out shopping or tax my already groaning refrigerator. The dish quickly became a year-round family favorite.

2	tablespoons olive oil
½	medium onion, chopped
4	medium cloves garlic, crushed through a press
6	anchovy fillets
1	28-ounce can whole tomatoes (about 3 cups)
2	6⅛-ounce cans water-packed solid white tuna
	Salt and freshly ground black pepper to taste
¾	pound penne
1	tablespoon butter or margarine
1	loaf Italian bread
¼	cup chopped fresh parsley

Preheat oven to 350 degrees F for bread. Heat oil in a nonstick skillet and add onion. Sauté until transparent, about 5 minutes. Add garlic and continue to cook until onion starts to brown. Drain and rinse anchovies. Add to onion. Crush them with a spoon. Add tomatoes. Simmer, covered, about 15 minutes, breaking up tomatoes with a spoon to form a sauce. Drain tuna and break into

Shopping List

1 pound green beans
1 small bunch fresh parsley
1 small tin anchovy fillets
1 loaf Italian bread
¾ pound penne

Staples

lemon
onion
garlic
1 can whole tomatoes (28 ounces)
butter or margarine
2 cans water-packed solid white tuna (6⅛ ounces each)
olive oil
salt
black peppercorns

Helpful Hint

♦ *Penne means quill, and this pasta is named for its shape—a short tube with ends cut on a diagonal. Any type of thick pasta, such as ziti, small shells, rigatoni or fusilli, can be used.*

large flakes. Add to sauce with a little salt and pepper to taste. Remember that anchovies and tuna are already salty, so be careful if you add salt. Simmer, uncovered, for 5 minutes. Juices will evaporate and sauce will thicken.

Cook penne in boiling water, stirring once. Boil until *al dente* or firm to the bite, about 10 minutes. Drain. Add butter and mix well.

Place bread in oven for 5 minutes, or until crusty on top. Add parsley to warm sauce and toss with pasta. Serve immediately.

GREEN BEAN SALAD

I LIKE MY GREEN BEANS crisp and crunchy. Blanching them keeps them beautifully green, and they can then be dressed with a light vinaigrette. I always make them like this if I'm having company. They are best served lukewarm or at room temperature.

1   **pound fresh green beans**
2   **teaspoons olive oil**
2   **tablespoons fresh lemon juice**
    Salt and freshly ground black pepper to taste

Trim green beans, cut in half and wash. Bring a pot of water to a boil and add beans. As soon as water returns to a boil, drain beans and rinse under cold water. This stops the cooking and sets the color. Place beans in a bowl and toss in oil. Add a little lemon juice and taste. Add more if needed. Add salt and pepper to taste. Toss again and serve.

Helpful Hint

♦ *If you do not have fresh green beans on hand, make any type of salad with your available vegetables.*

CHAPTER 2

Poultry Dinners

Poultry Dinners

◆

Sherry-Soused Chicken

Brown Rice & Sugar Snap Peas

THIS IS A DREAM DISH. You simply put the chicken into the sherry-mushroom sauce and leave it to simmer on its own. Thirty minutes later, you have a delicious dinner. I love the nutty flavor of brown rice, and the sweet sugar snap peas add color and crunch. If pressed for time, use long-grain white rice instead of brown. It cooks in about 10 minutes.

Serves 4.

THIS MEAL CONTAINS A TOTAL OF 680 CALORIES PER SERVING WITH 12 PERCENT OF CALORIES FROM FAT.

⌛ Countdown

♦ *Start rice first. It will need 30 minutes to cook after water has come to a boil.*
♦ *Soak dried mushrooms for Sherry-Soused Chicken in boiling water.*
♦ *Start cooking chicken.*
♦ *While chicken simmers, prepare sugar snap peas.*
♦ *Finish sauce for chicken.*

BROWN RICE & SUGAR SNAP PEAS

SUGAR SNAP PEAS, like snow peas, have edible pods. They are less fragile than snow peas and will last a couple of days in the refrigerator without getting limp.

1½	cups brown rice
¾	pound sugar snap peas (about 3 cups)
2	teaspoons butter or margarine
	Salt and freshly ground black pepper to taste

Fill a medium-size saucepan three-quarters full with cold water. Add rice. Cover and bring to a boil. As soon as water boils, remove lid and let boil for 30 minutes. Rice should be cooked through, but not soft. Boil 5 more minutes, if necessary. Drain. Meanwhile, trim strings from sugar snap peas. Cut pea pods in half, if large. Place in a microwave-safe bowl and cook on high for 1 minute. Or bring a small pot of water to a boil and add peas. As soon as water returns to a boil, drain. Toss cooked peas and butter with cooked rice. Add salt and pepper to taste.

Shopping List

4 chicken breasts (7 ounces each)
2 ounces wild mushrooms or
  ½ ounce dried
½ pound button mushrooms
¾ pound fresh sugar snap peas or
  snow peas or green beans
1 small bunch fresh parsley
3 ounces brown rice

Staples

lemon
garlic
butter or margarine
cornstarch
medium sherry
salt
black peppercorns

Helpful Hint

♦ *If sugar snaps are not available,*
use snow peas or green beans.

SHERRY-SOUSED CHICKEN

I DEVELOPED this recipe for my cooking classes in London. We could work on a more complicated first course and dessert while the chicken cooked on its own, giving us a tasty main course with very little effort.

2   ounces wild mushrooms (about 1 cup) or ½ ounce dried (½ cup)
4   7-ounce chicken breasts
¼   lemon
1   teaspoon butter or margarine
4   medium cloves garlic, crushed through a press
1   cup medium sherry
½   pound button mushrooms, sliced (about 2 cups)
1   teaspoon cornstarch
2   tablespoons water
    Salt and freshly ground black pepper to taste
2   tablespoons chopped fresh parsley for garnish

If using dried wild mushrooms, soak them in boiling water to cover. Rub chicken with lemon. Melt butter over medium heat in a heavy-bottomed casserole just large enough to hold chicken. When butter is melted, add chicken and turn it to coat with butter. Add garlic and sherry. Cover tightly and bring to a simmer. Cook slowly for 25 minutes. Wash and slice fresh mushrooms. Add fresh and drained dried mushrooms to chicken and continue to simmer. Remove chicken to a warm serving plate and cover with foil. Remove as much fat as possible from sauce. Mix cornstarch with water and pour into sauce. Bring to a simmer, stirring constantly. Remove skin from chicken and spoon sauce over top. Add salt and pepper to taste. Sprinkle with chopped parsley.

Helpful Hints

♦ *This method of poaching chicken keeps it moist. Leftover pieces will rewarm without drying. If you have time, make extra and serve it a second evening.*

♦ *Use a saucepan in which the chicken will fit snugly in one layer. If the pan is too large, the juices will evaporate instead of forming a sauce.*

♦ *Cook chicken on low flame. Sherry has a high sugar content and will burn if cooked on high heat.*

♦ *Slice mushrooms in a food processor fitted with a thick slicing blade. Remove and chop parsley in the same bowl without rinsing it.*

♦ *Sherry is categorized as dry, medium and sweet. Amontillado is my favorite medium sherry because of its nutty flavor, but any medium sherry will work here.*

Turkey Chili

Mexican Salad

Shopping List

12 ounces cooked turkey or
  14 ounces turkey tenderloin
  or breast meat
1 fresh lime
1 head iceberg lettuce
1 small red onion
2 medium tomatoes
1 small ripe avocado
4 jalapeño peppers
1 bunch fresh cilantro
1 container nonfat sour cream
  (8 ounces)
1 can or package frozen corn (11-
  ounce can or 10-ounce package)
1 can red kidney beans (19 ounces)
1 loaf sourdough bread or tortilla
  chips

Staples

yellow onions (2)
garlic
ground cinnamon
chili powder
ground cumin
Dijon mustard
1 can whole tomatoes (28 ounces)
canola oil
white vinegar
chicken stock
salt
black peppercorns

Helpful Hints

♦ Use leftover cooked turkey or
chicken to make a really speedy
meal.

♦ You can now buy baked tortilla
chips instead of fried ones. They
are very good and have less fat.

WHENEVER I have leftover roast turkey, I like to make it into something completely different so it becomes a special new meal. The spices here create some excitement, and chili fans love this variation on their treasured dish. It's so good, in fact, that I often buy turkey tenderloin just to make it. Corn and avocado create a colorful Mexican salad. If you are pressed for time, make a tomato and lettuce salad instead. Serve with sourdough bread warmed in the oven or tortilla chips.

   Serves 4.

THIS MEAL CONTAINS A TOTAL OF 769 CALORIES PER SERVING WITH 20 PERCENT OF CALORIES FROM FAT.

Countdown

♦ Preheat oven to 350 degrees F if serving bread.
♦ Cut turkey and marinate.
♦ Prepare chili.
♦ While chili simmers, make dressing and salad.

TURKEY CHILI

VINEGAR AND CUMIN counter the sweetness of the cinnamon, producing complexity of flavor without long simmering.

12	ounces cooked turkey or 14 ounces turkey tenderloin or breast (about 3 cups cubed)
¼	cup white vinegar
2	teaspoons ground cinnamon
½	cup defatted chicken stock
1	medium yellow onion, coarsely chopped (about 2 cups)
4	medium cloves garlic, crushed through a press
4	jalapeño peppers, seeded and chopped
1	19-ounce can red kidney beans
1	28-ounce can whole tomatoes
2	tablespoons chili powder
2	teaspoons ground cumin
	Salt and freshly ground black pepper to taste

GARNISH

¼	small yellow onion, chopped (about ½ cup)
1	cup nonfat sour cream
1	small bunch fresh cilantro, chopped

1   loaf sourdough bread or tortilla chips

Preheat oven to 350 degrees F for warming bread. Cut turkey into bite-size pieces (about ½-inch cubes). Place in a bowl and sprinkle with vinegar and cinnamon. Meanwhile, heat chicken stock in a nonstick saucepan and cook onion about 5 minutes. It should be transparent, not brown. Add turkey mixture and cook another 5 minutes. Add garlic and jalapeño peppers and cook 3 to 4 minutes. Drain and wash kidney beans and add to pan along with tomatoes, chili powder and cumin. Break up tomatoes with a spoon. Simmer gently 15 minutes. Add salt and pepper and taste for seasoning. Add more chili powder or cumin as needed.

Warm bread in oven 5 minutes; slice and serve in bread basket. Pass bowls of onion, sour cream and cilantro at the table to go with the chili.

MEXICAN SALAD

FINDING A RIPE AVOCADO on the day you want to use it is sometimes impossible. I usually ask the produce manager if he has any in the back that are too far gone to put out on display. If you can plan ahead, remove the stem from the narrow end of the avocado and place the avocado in a paper bag in a warm spot to help speed ripening.

Helpful Hint

♦ *If your avocado is still hard, substitute segments from 2 medium oranges or 1 large grapefruit.*

4   cups shredded iceberg lettuce
1   cup frozen corn, thawed, or canned, drained
¼   medium red onion, chopped (about ½ cup)
2   medium tomatoes
2   tablespoons fresh lime juice
2   teaspoons Dijon mustard
2   tablespoons defatted chicken stock
2   teaspoons canola oil
     Salt and freshly ground black pepper to taste
1   small ripe avocado, cubed (½ cup)

Toss lettuce, corn and onion together. Cut tomatoes into 8 wedges and then cut each wedge in half. Add to lettuce mixture. In a medium bowl, whisk lime juice and mustard together. Whisk in chicken stock and oil. Add salt and pepper to taste. Toss avocado in dressing. Spoon avocado and dressing over salad.

Jamaican Jerk Chicken

Glazed Plantains & Rice

Shopping List

*4 boneless, skinless chicken breast
  halves (5 ounces each)
1 small bunch fresh thyme or dried
2 medium-size ripe plantains or
  firm bananas
1 small jar hot jalapeño pepper
  jelly*

Staples

*onion
orange juice
brown sugar
ground nutmeg
ground allspice
sugar
long-grain white rice
canola oil
salt
black peppercorns*

Helpful Hints

♦ *Prepare jerk seasoning in the
food processor.*

♦ *The juice from the onion
provides enough liquid for the
marinade to bind the mixture so it
coats the chicken.*

AROUND THE MIDDLE of January when I've had enough of winter, I like to bring a little sunshine into the kitchen with Jamaican hot spices. The chicken, which gets its kick from lots of black pepper and some nutmeg, plays against the sweet and spicy starch of the plantains and rice.

Serves 4.

THIS MEAL CONTAINS A TOTAL OF 758 CALORIES PER SERVING WITH 18 PERCENT OF CALORIES FROM FAT.

⧗ Countdown

♦ *Make jerk seasoning and rub it on chicken.*
♦ *While chicken marinates, cook rice.*
♦ *While rice is cooking, sauté plantains.*
♦ *When rice dish is completed, sauté chicken.*

JAMAICAN JERK CHICKEN

"JERKING" is an ancient Jamaican method for preserving and cooking meat, thought to have been invented by the Arawac Indians native to that island. Today the men who prepare the meat and sell it to the markets are called "jerk men." They marinate the meat and slowly cook it over a pimiento (allspice) wood fire. Adapted for a busy schedule, this recipe uses a dry-rub marinade and boneless breasts, which are quickly sautéed in oil rather than barbecued slowly.

JERK SEASONING

2	tablespoons chopped onion
4	teaspoons chopped fresh thyme or 2 teaspoons dried
4	teaspoons sugar
2	teaspoons freshly ground black pepper
2	teaspoons salt
½	teaspoon ground nutmeg
¼	teaspoon ground allspice
4	5-ounce boneless, skinless chicken breast halves
2	tablespoons canola oil

For jerk seasoning: In a food processor or by hand, chop onion and mix with thyme, sugar, black pepper, salt, nutmeg and allspice. Remove all fat from chicken breasts and poke several holes in them. Spoon jerk seasoning over both sides of chicken and let marinate for 20 minutes.

Heat oil in a nonstick skillet and add chicken. Gently sauté on each side for 5 to 10 minutes, depending on the size of the chicken breasts.

GLAZED PLANTAINS & RICE

PLANTAINS look like oversized bananas but are firm and starchy. They are carried by most supermarkets. Jalapeño pepper jelly gives a sweet and pungent taste to this dish.

Helpful Hints

♦ *Ripe plantains are yellow with brown spots or have brown skin; unripe ones will be green. Firm bananas can be substituted for ripe plantains.*

♦ *Hot jalapeño pepper jelly is found in the specialty products section of most supermarkets; if it is unavailable, use any hot pepper jelly.*

1	**cup long-grain white rice**
1	**tablespoon canola oil**
1	**pound ripe plantains or firm bananas**
3	**tablespoons hot jalapeño pepper jelly**
⅓	**cup orange juice**
1½	**tablespoons brown sugar**
½	**teaspoon ground allspice**
	Salt and freshly ground black pepper to taste

Place rice in a strainer and rinse under cold water. Place in a large pot with 3 to 4 quarts of water and bring to a boil. Boil about 10 minutes, or until rice is cooked through but still firm. Drain, rinse under warm water, place in a serving bowl and toss with oil. Meanwhile, peel plantains and cut into small cubes. Melt jelly in a large nonstick skillet. When melted, add orange juice. Add plantains and cook 5 minutes. Add brown sugar and allspice. Toss plantain mixture with rice. Season with salt and pepper as needed.

Sautéed Chicken With Tomatoes

Egg Noodles With Chives

Shopping List

4 chicken breasts (7 ounces each)
4 large tomatoes or 1 can
(28 ounces)
1 small bunch fresh parsley
1 small bunch fresh chives or
scallions
½ pint light cream
2-ounce piece Parmesan cheese
¾ pound broad egg noodles

Staples

onion
butter or margarine
sugar
dry red wine
chicken stock
salt
black peppercorns

Helpful Hints

♦ *For 4 ounces meat per person,
you will need 7 ounces chicken
breast with skin and bones. The
skin is removed before serving.*

♦ *If you don't have ripe tomatoes
on hand, use good-quality canned
whole tomatoes.*

♦ *Cold kills the flavor of tomatoes,
hampers ripening and turns them
mushy. Buy vine-ripened
tomatoes when available and store
them at room temperature.*

♦ *Place tomatoes in a paper bag to
speed the ripening process.*

THIS IS A TRADITIONAL French dish that I keep in my repertoire because I love its sweet tomato sauce. It will go with any type of meat and can be made with either fresh or canned tomatoes. Serve over a bed of egg noodles seasoned with fresh chives. The tomatoes and onions in the sauce provide the vegetables for this meal; another vegetable is not needed. *See photograph, page 101.*

Serves 4.

THIS MEAL CONTAINS A TOTAL OF 783 CALORIES PER SERVING WITH 27 PERCENT OF CALORIES FROM FAT.

⧗ Countdown

♦ *Start onions for tomato sauce.*
♦ *Sauté chicken in a second pan.*
♦ *While chicken cooks, put water for noodles on to boil.*
♦ *Complete chicken sauce.*
♦ *While sauce and chicken are cooking, make noodles.*

SAUTÉED CHICKEN WITH TOMATOES

THE SECRET to this popular French bistro dish is the onions, which are sautéed until they become golden and sweet.

¼	cup defatted chicken stock
1	medium onion, sliced
2	teaspoons butter or margarine
4	7-ounce chicken breasts
	Salt and freshly ground black pepper to taste
⅔	cup dry red wine
4	large ripe tomatoes, diced, or 2 cups canned plum tomatoes
2–3	teaspoons sugar
4	tablespoons light cream
¼	cup chopped fresh parsley for garnish

Heat chicken stock in a nonstick skillet and add onion. Cook until transparent but not brown, about 10 minutes. While onion is cooking, melt butter in a second nonstick skillet and brown chicken breasts on both sides. Reduce heat to medium, salt and pepper chicken, cover and let cook gently for 15 to 20 minutes, or until cooked through.

When onion is golden, add wine and let cook until wine nearly evaporates. Add tomatoes, cover and let simmer until tomatoes have cooked to a sauce, about

10 minutes. Add a little salt and pepper and taste for seasoning, adding more if necessary. Add 2 teaspoons sugar. If the sauce looks a bit watery, remove the lid and cook to reduce; taste and add more sugar if necessary. Remove from the heat and add cream.

Remove skin from chicken and place on warm individual plates. Spoon sauce over chicken and garnish with chopped parsley.

EGG NOODLES WITH CHIVES

FLAT EGG NOODLES are the perfect shape to capture the tomato sauce.

- ¾ pound broad egg noodles
- 2 tablespoons butter or margarine
- ½ cup chopped fresh chives or scallions
- ½ cup freshly grated Parmesan cheese
  Salt to taste

Bring a large pot with 3 to 4 quarts of water to a boil. Add noodles and stir. Bring water back to a boil and cook for 7 minutes, or until noodles are cooked but firm. Drain and toss with butter. Add chives and cheese. Taste for salt and add some if necessary. Serve with chicken.

Honey-Mustard Turkey

Sliced Baby Red Potatoes

Spinach & Asparagus Salad

Shopping List

1¼ pounds turkey breast
    tenderloin
3 red bell peppers
½ pound fresh asparagus
½ pound fresh spinach
1 pound small red potatoes
1 French baguette

Staples

lemon
garlic
honey
Dijon mustard
orange juice
olive oil
canola oil
2 cans chicken stock
    (14½ ounces each)
salt
black peppercorns

I REMEMBER ONE HOLIDAY my family spent on the south coast of England with three children in tow, my in-laws and lots of wind and rain. One bright spot of the weekend was the Easter dinner prepared by the hotel. This dinner was inspired by that memory. Turkey tenderloins, which have been marinated, then cooked in some of the marinade, emerge from the pan coated with a light, slightly sweet orange-honey-mustard glaze. Fresh spinach paired with steamed asparagus in a crisp, delicate salad and sautéed potatoes accompany it. If pressed for time, shorten the salad preparation by omitting the asparagus and using store-bought croutons and bottled low-fat dressing.

    Serves 4.

THIS MEAL CONTAINS A TOTAL OF 656 CALORIES PER SERVING WITH 19 PERCENT OF CALORIES FROM FAT.

⧗ Countdown

- *Make marinade and marinate turkey.*
- *While turkey marinates, cook potatoes.*
- *Prepare salad.*
- *Sauté turkey.*

HONEY-MUSTARD TURKEY

THE THICK CUT of the tenderloin is just right for this preparation, cooking quickly and staying juicy.

1¼	pounds turkey breast tenderloin
½	cup fresh orange juice
¼	cup honey
4	teaspoons Dijon mustard
2	teaspoons canola oil
	Salt and freshly ground black pepper to taste
3	medium-size red bell peppers, cut in thick 2-inch-long slices

Poke several holes in turkey tenderloin at varying intervals. Mix orange juice, honey and mustard together. Place turkey in a plastic bag or glass bowl. Pour marinade over turkey and let stand for 20 minutes.

    Remove turkey from marinade, reserving liquid. Pat dry with a paper towel.

Heat oil in a nonstick skillet and brown turkey over high heat for about 1 minute on each side. Salt and pepper each side. Add red pepper strips and sauté about 30 seconds. Reduce heat and add marinade. Simmer, uncovered, for another 4 minutes. Remove turkey and peppers to a serving plate and spoon sauce over top.

SLICED BABY RED POTATOES

THIN-SKINNED red potatoes, tender and flavorful, are simmered in a little chicken stock. Just wash the skins. They don't need to be peeled.

1   **pound small red potatoes**
2   **cups defatted chicken stock**
1   **tablespoon olive oil**
     Salt and freshly ground black pepper to taste

Helpful Hint

♦ *Slice the potatoes in a food processor to save time.*

Wash potatoes and thinly slice. Place in a saucepan with chicken stock. Cover and simmer for 10 minutes, or until potatoes are soft. Drain. Add olive oil and gently toss potatoes. Add salt and pepper to taste.

SPINACH & ASPARAGUS SALAD

FRESH SPINACH, lightly steamed asparagus and garlic croutons combine in a simple vinaigrette.

½   **pound fresh asparagus**
4   **cups fresh spinach leaves**
1   **large clove garlic, halved**
8   **slices French baguette**
DRESSING
1   **tablespoon fresh lemon juice**
1   **teaspoon Dijon mustard**
2   **tablespoons defatted chicken stock**
2   **teaspoons canola oil**
     Salt and freshly ground black pepper to taste

Helpful Hints

♦ *To save time, cook asparagus in a microwave oven on high for 3 minutes.*

♦ *Buy prewashed spinach leaves if they are available.*

Cut off the woody ends of asparagus. Cut into 2-inch pieces. Bring a small saucepan of water to a boil. Add asparagus and simmer 5 minutes. Drain and refresh under cold water. Or cook in a microwave. Wash spinach leaves and tear into bite-size pieces. Generously rub both sides of sliced bread with cut side of garlic clove. Toast bread until just golden brown. Cut into small squares.

For dressing: Whisk lemon juice and mustard together in a salad bowl. Add chicken stock and mix well. Add oil, salt and pepper. Whisk dressing until smooth. Add spinach, asparagus and bread cubes. Toss well.

Country Turkey Pot Pie

Shopping List

1¼ pounds uncooked turkey breast or 1 pound cooked turkey
4 stalks celery
2 medium carrots
½ pound mushrooms
1 small bunch fresh cilantro or dill
½ pound Yukon Gold or red potatoes
1 can or jar whole pimientos (4 ounces)
1 package plain biscuit dough (9 ounces)

Staples

onion
butter or margarine
flour
1 can chicken stock (14½ ounces)
salt
black peppercorns

Helpful Hints

♦ Use turkey breasts, tenderloin, steaks or any leftover cooked turkey. If using cooked turkey, add it to the sauce just before pouring it into the pie.

♦ Use prepared biscuit dough found in the refrigerator case in most supermarkets. It takes only 15 minutes to cook, while pie pastry takes 20 to 25 minutes.

♦ Use red potatoes if Yukon Gold are unavailable.

♦ Slice vegetables in the food processor using the thin slicing blade.

THIS TURKEY PIE is an entire meal in itself, containing meat, vegetables and starch. It's one of those recipes that remind me of the suppers we had before TV dinners and frozen foods spoiled the idea of chicken or turkey pie.

Serves 4.

THIS MEAL CONTAINS A TOTAL OF 448 CALORIES PER SERVING WITH 20 PERCENT OF CALORIES FROM FAT.

⧗ Countdown

♦ Preheat oven to 400 degrees F for baking pie.
♦ Start potatoes for the turkey pie and let them boil while you prepare the other ingredients.

COUNTRY TURKEY POT PIE

WHEN I HAVE leftover turkey, I make this savory country pie, which uses convenient store-bought biscuit dough for the topping instead of pastry.

½   pound Yukon Gold or red potatoes
2   teaspoons butter or margarine
½   medium onion, sliced
1¼   pounds uncooked turkey breast or about 4 cups cooked turkey, cut into chunks
4   stalks celery, sliced (about 1½ cups)
2   medium carrots, thinly sliced (about 1 cup)
½   pound mushrooms, quartered (about 2 cups)
¼   cup flour
1½   cups defatted chicken stock
¼   cup chopped fresh cilantro or dill
¼   cup drained, coarsely chopped pimientos
    Salt and freshly ground black pepper to taste
1   9-ounce package plain biscuit dough

Preheat oven to 400 degrees F.

Wash potatoes and cut into 1-inch chunks. Place in a pot of cold water, cover and bring to a boil. Boil 15 minutes. Melt butter in a large nonstick skillet and sauté onion for 5 minutes. Add uncooked turkey, celery and carrots. Cook 4 more minutes. Add mushrooms and sauté 2 minutes. Sprinkle flour over vegetables and mix in. Stir in stock.

Simmer to thicken, stirring, about 1 minute. Remove from heat. Mix in cilantro and pimientos. If using cooked turkey, add at this time. Add salt and pepper to taste. Taste for seasoning, adding more if needed. Spoon into a deep pie dish or soufflé dish measuring 7½ inches in diameter.

Open cylinder of biscuit dough and slice premade biscuits in half horizontally so they will be half as thick. Place them as close together as possible over the top of the pie. Bake for 15 minutes. The biscuits will rise and turn golden brown. Serve immediately, giving each person a couple of biscuits along with the pie filling.

Chicken With Parsley-Garlic Sauce

Smothered Potatoes

THIS SOUTH AMERICAN way of serving meat is full of punch. Chimichurri, a spicy parsley sauce, is spooned over grilled boneless chicken breasts and served with potatoes smothered in onions, tomatoes and cheese.

Serves 4.

THIS MEAL CONTAINS A TOTAL OF 648 CALORIES PER SERVING WITH 31 PERCENT OF CALORIES FROM FAT.

⧗ Countdown

- ◆ *Make sauce and marinate chicken.*
- ◆ *Light grill or preheat broiler for chicken.*
- ◆ *If using grill for chicken, preheat broiler for potatoes.*
- ◆ *While chicken marinates, wash and boil potatoes.*
- ◆ *Cook onions for potatoes.*
- ◆ *Grill or broil chicken.*
- ◆ *Finish potatoes and broil them.*

CHICKEN WITH PARSLEY-GARLIC SAUCE

THE STORY GOES that the gauchos, cowboys on the Pampas, developed a delicious steak sauce, called chimichurri, which they kept in old wine bottles with holes pierced in the corks so they could shake it over their meat. The popularity of this sauce spread throughout South America, and now chimichurri sauce is an integral part of many Latin menus. It can be used as a dipping sauce or as a condiment. Half the sauce in this recipe is used for marinating; the other half is served on the side.

1½	cups chopped fresh parsley
½	medium red bell pepper, cut into quarters (about 1 cup)
6	cloves garlic, crushed through a press
½	cup defatted chicken stock
¼	cup canola oil
3	tablespoons apple-cider vinegar
4	5-ounce boneless, skinless chicken breast halves
	Salt and freshly ground black pepper to taste

Chop parsley in a food processor or by hand. Add red pepper and garlic and

Shopping List

4 boneless, skinless chicken breast halves (about 5 ounces each)
1 red bell pepper
1¼ pounds ripe tomatoes or 1 can (28 ounces)
1 large bunch fresh parsley
2 red onions
2 pounds red potatoes
2 ounces white cheese (Queso Blanco or Monterey Jack)

Staples

garlic
Tabasco or other hot pepper sauce
apple-cider vinegar
canola oil
chicken stock
salt
black peppercorns

Helpful Hints

◆ *Make sauce in a food processor to save time.*

◆ *Use flat-leaf parsley if you can find it. It has a sweeter flavor.*

◆ *Serve this sauce over chicken, beef or pork. It keeps several days in the refrigerator.*

◆ *Preheat a gas grill for 10 minutes, or start a charcoal fire 30 minutes ahead or preheat your broiler so that the chicken sears when placed under it.*

mix well in the food processor or, if making by hand, dice red pepper and mix together with parsley and garlic. Add chicken stock, oil and vinegar. Blend thoroughly. Remove fat from chicken and flatten breast halves by smacking them with the palm of your hand until they are about ½ inch thick. Place chicken in a bowl or plastic bag and spoon half the sauce over it, making sure that both sides are covered. Let stand about 20 minutes.

Meanwhile, light a grill or heat the broiler. When the fire is ready, place chicken on the grill or under the broiler. The fire should be hot enough to sear the meat. Grill or broil chicken for about 3 to 4 minutes on each side. Salt and pepper each side. Serve one breast per person with the remaining sauce for dipping.

SMOTHERED POTATOES

Use Queso Blanco, a white soft cheese that melts well, for this easy side dish. Monterey Jack cheese makes a good substitute. The topping should smother the potatoes with flavor.

2	pounds small red potatoes
½	cup defatted chicken stock
3	cups thinly sliced red onions
3	cups diced tomatoes or one 28-ounce can, drained and chopped
	Several dashes Tabasco or other hot pepper sauce
1	tablespoon canola oil
	Salt and freshly ground black pepper to taste
½	cup grated white cheese (Queso Blanco or Monterey Jack)

Wash potatoes, cut into 2-inch cubes and place in a pot with cold water to cover. Cover with a lid, bring to a boil and cook 20 minutes, or until potatoes are soft through. Meanwhile, heat chicken stock in a nonstick skillet and add onions. Cook onions about 10 minutes, until transparent but not brown, adding more stock if necessary. Add tomatoes and Tabasco. Cook until the tomatoes are soft, about 5 minutes. Add oil, salt and pepper to taste. Drain potatoes and transfer to an ovenproof dish or pan and spoon sauce over them. Sprinkle with cheese. Place under a hot broiler for 3 minutes to brown the cheese slightly.

Sweet & Sour Chinese Chicken

Fluffy White Rice

Stir-Fried or Microwaved Snow Peas

Shopping List

4 chicken breasts, with skin and
bones (7 ounces each)
1 fresh pineapple
1 large red bell pepper
1 pound snow peas

Staples

2 cans chicken stock
(14½ ounces each)
garlic
long-grain white rice
brown sugar
cornstarch
low-sodium soy sauce
white-wine vinegar
canola oil
salt
black peppercorns

Helpful Hints

♦ *Buy pineapple that is already*
peeled in the supermarket.

♦ *The sauce can also be used for*
beef, duck or pork.

♦ *This recipe freezes well,*
providing a dish for emergencies.

INSTEAD OF SENDING OUT for Chinese food the next time you covet the exotic, try this easy sweet-and-sour sauce. Made separately, it takes only about 10 minutes to cook. The extra is passed at the table for the rice, and a side dish of stir-fried snow peas with garlic is served alongside.

Serves 4.

THIS MEAL CONTAINS A TOTAL OF 739 CALORIES PER SERVING WITH 21 PERCENT OF CALORIES FROM FAT.

⧗ Countdown

♦ *Preheat broiler.*
♦ *Broil chicken.*
♦ *While chicken cooks, put water for rice on to boil and prepare sauce for chicken.*
♦ *While sauce simmers, cook rice.*
♦ *Prepare snow peas. They should be stir-fried or microwaved just before serving.*
♦ *Finish sauce.*

SWEET & SOUR CHINESE CHICKEN

ALTHOUGH THIS SAUCE requires little attention, it turns out dark, rich and properly balanced between sweet and tangy.

4	**7-ounce chicken breasts**
½	**tablespoon canola oil**
½	**fresh pineapple**
2¼	**cups defatted chicken stock,** *divided*
6	**tablespoons brown sugar**
¼	**cup white-wine vinegar**
2½	**tablespoons low-sodium soy sauce**
4	**teaspoons cornstarch**
1	**large red bell pepper, sliced (about 1 cup)**

Preheat broiler. Brush chicken with oil and place under hot broiler, turning once during the cooking time. It will take about 20 to 25 minutes to cook through.

Make sauce: Cut pineapple in half and remove core. Cut flesh into cubes. Save half pineapple cubes for garnish and place remainder in a saucepan with 2 cups chicken stock and brown sugar. Bring to a boil and reduce to a simmer. Simmer gently for 15 to 20 minutes, or until pineapple is soft. Add wine vinegar and soy sauce. Strain into a clean pan. Simmer for 5 minutes. Mix cornstarch with remaining ¼ cup chicken stock and pour into sauce. Bring sauce to a simmer and cook until thick. Cut red pepper slices in half if very long and add, together with reserved pineapple, to sauce and warm. The pineapple and peppers will still be crunchy.

To serve: Remove skin from chicken breasts. Spoon some sauce with pineapple and red pepper over cooked chicken and bring remaining sauce to the table to serve as needed.

FLUFFY WHITE RICE

I LIKE TO BOIL RICE like pasta, in a pot large enough to let the grains roll freely in the boiling water. This method gives fluffy rice every time.

> **1**   **cup long-grain white rice**
> **2**   **tablespoons canola oil**
>   **Salt and freshly ground black pepper to taste**

Place rice in a strainer and run cold water through to wash it. Bring a large pot with 3 to 4 quarts of water to a boil. Add rice and boil, uncovered, about 10 minutes. Test a grain. Rice should be cooked through, but not soft. Drain into a colander in the sink. Run hot water through rice and stir with a fork. Mix in oil and salt and pepper to taste.

STIR-FRIED OR MICROWAVED SNOW PEAS

SNOW PEAS are available fresh in most supermarkets and take only a few minutes to stir-fry. Snow peas also cook very well in the microwave and retain their crispness and color.

> **1**   **pound fresh snow peas**
> **1**   **tablespoon canola oil**
> **4**   **cloves garlic, crushed through a press**
>   **Salt and freshly ground black pepper to taste**

Trim snow peas and remove strings. Rinse and drain well. Heat oil in a wok or skillet. When oil is very hot, add garlic and snow peas and toss for 1 to 2 minutes. Salt and pepper to taste and serve immediately.

To microwave snow peas: Place peas in a bowl with just the moisture left on them from washing. Cook on high for 1½ minutes. This version omits oil and garlic. Add salt and pepper to taste.

Orange Chicken With Wild Mushrooms

Pureed Potatoes

Shopping List

4 chicken breasts (7 ounces each)
½ pound button mushrooms
½ pound oyster mushrooms
2 pounds Yukon Gold potatoes or
*   red potatoes*
1 small bunch fresh parsley
½ pint light cream

Staples

garlic
honey
orange juice
butter or margarine
skim milk
salt
black peppercorns

A DAY SPENT HUNTING wild mushrooms in the woods with master chef and cookbook author Jacques Pépin resulted in my making this dish. The orange-juice-honey marinade helps tenderize the chicken, leaving the meat with a faintly orange flavor—just the right contrast to the rich-tasting wild mushrooms, whose flavor is intensified by the addition of garlic. The potatoes, made with the buttery-tasting Yukon Gold variety, complete this simple French meal.

   Serves 4.

THIS MEAL CONTAINS A TOTAL OF 624 CALORIES PER SERVING WITH 23 PERCENT OF CALORIES FROM FAT.

⧖ Countdown

♦ *Preheat broiler.*
♦ *Marinate chicken.*
♦ *Put potatoes on to cook.*
♦ *Broil chicken.*
♦ *Prepare mushrooms for chicken.*
♦ *Finish potatoes.*

ORANGE CHICKEN WITH WILD MUSHROOMS

MANY VARIETIES of wild mushrooms have been cultivated and are available in most supermarkets. I use them to add a rich flavor to dishes. Fan-shaped oyster mushrooms, the most readily found, are a beige or cream color and have a delicate flavor when cooked. Portobello, porcini or any other type of wild mushrooms can be used. If you can't find fresh wild mushrooms, use dried ones and mix them with the button mushrooms.

Helpful Hints

♦ *If you have difficulty finding small chicken breasts, buy a large one and ask the meat department to cut it in half.*

♦ *I remove the skin to reduce fat, but I prefer to leave the bone in. It helps keep the chicken moist.*

♦ *Try not to let the mushrooms get too wet while washing them. They will become soggy.*

4	**7-ounce chicken breasts**
⅓	**cup orange juice concentrate**
2	**tablespoons honey**
½	**pound button mushrooms, quartered (about 2 cups)**
½	**pound oyster mushrooms, quartered (about 2 cups)**
1	**tablespoon butter or margarine**
4	**medium cloves garlic, crushed through a press**
¼	**cup chopped fresh parsley**
2	**tablespoons light cream**

Salt and freshly ground black pepper to taste

Preheat broiler. Remove skin and fat from chicken breasts. Mix orange juice concentrate and honey together. Poke several holes in chicken with the tip of a knife. Marinate chicken in orange juice mixture for 20 minutes.

Place on a foil-lined baking tray. Broil for 15 minutes, basting with marinade every 5 minutes. Chicken is done when a meat thermometer reads 160 degrees F.

Rinse, dry and slice mushrooms. Melt butter in a nonstick skillet. Add garlic and then mushrooms. Sauté 10 minutes. Add parsley and cream. Sauté another minute. Add salt and freshly ground black pepper to taste. Serve over chicken.

PUREED POTATOES

ONCE A SPECIALTY ITEM that can now be found in most supermarkets, Yukon Gold potatoes have a creamy texture and buttery flavor. They are particularly good pureed and need very little butter.

2   **pounds Yukon Gold potatoes or red potatoes (about 4 medium)**
2   **tablespoons butter or margarine**
3   **tablespoons skim milk**
     Salt and freshly ground black pepper to taste

Scrub potatoes and cut into 2-inch pieces. Place in a pot and cover with cold water. Cover with a lid and boil for 15 minutes, or until potatoes are soft. Pass through a potato ricer, food mill or place in a food processor. If using the food processor, do not process until completely smooth or the potatoes will be gluey. Transfer to a serving bowl and mix in butter and milk. Add salt and pepper to taste.

Chicken Pizzaioli

Sautéed Potatoes

Fennel Salad

BLACK OLIVES AND TOMATOES combine in this Italian sauce, which goes well with sautéed boneless chicken breasts. If pressed for time, omit the salad and serve celery sticks with the meal.

Serves 4.

THIS MEAL CONTAINS A TOTAL OF 569 CALORIES PER SERVING WITH 28 PERCENT OF CALORIES FROM FAT.

⧗ Countdown
- ♦ *Start potatoes.*
- ♦ *Make sauce for chicken.*
- ♦ *Prepare salad.*
- ♦ *Sauté chicken.*

SAUTÉED POTATOES

RED POTATOES have thin skins and don't need to be peeled. Cutting them into small chunks shortens the cooking time. In a nonstick pan, the potatoes brown without absorbing much oil.

- **2 pounds red potatoes (about 4 medium)**
- **2 tablespoons olive oil**
- **2 tablespoons chopped fresh rosemary or 1 tablespoon dried**
  Salt and freshly ground black pepper to taste

Wash potatoes and cut into 1-inch cubes. Heat oil in a nonstick skillet large enough to hold potatoes in one layer. Raise heat and sauté potatoes, turning frequently, until they are golden brown outside, about 10 minutes. Lower heat and sauté until they are soft inside, about 20 to 25 minutes. Sprinkle with rosemary, salt and pepper to taste.

CHICKEN PIZZAIOLI

PIZZAIOLI SAUCE is a typical Neapolitan dish. This tomato sauce was originally used to disguise poor-quality meat, and the chicken had to be simmered a long time until it was tender. In this recipe, however, the boneless, skinless chicken breasts cook in no time flat.

Shopping List

4 boneless, skinless chicken breast halves (about 5 ounces each)
1 large bulb fennel with leaves or 8 stalks celery
1 small bunch fresh oregano or dried
1 small bunch fresh rosemary or dried
2 pounds red potatoes
10 pitted black olives

Staples

lemon
garlic
sugar
1 can whole tomatoes (14½ ounces)
Dijon mustard
olive oil
chicken stock
salt
black peppercorns

Helpful Hints

♦ *Buy pitted olives.*

♦ *Crush garlic for sauce and chicken at one time and divide, alloting two-thirds for sauce, one-third for chicken.*

SAUCE

1   14½-ounce can whole tomatoes
4   medium cloves garlic, crushed through a press
10 large pitted black olives, quartered
2   tablespoons chopped fresh oregano or ½ tablespoon dried
1   teaspoon sugar
    Freshly ground black pepper to taste

CHICKEN

2   teaspoons olive oil
2   medium cloves garlic, crushed through a press
4   5-ounce boneless, skinless chicken breast halves
    Salt and freshly ground black pepper to taste

For sauce: Simmer tomatoes with juice and garlic in a medium-size saucepan for 10 minutes, breaking up whole tomatoes with a spoon. Add olives and oregano and continue cooking for 5 minutes. Add sugar and pepper and taste for seasoning. Add more, if necessary. Cover and keep warm while chicken is cooking.

For chicken: Heat oil in a nonstick skillet and add garlic. Sauté for ½ minute. Raise heat and brown chicken on both sides. This should take about 1 minute. Salt and pepper both sides. Lower heat and cook 5 minutes. Remove from pan and spoon sauce over chicken.

FENNEL SALAD

FENNEL IS a white bulbous vegetable with a slight anise flavor and a texture similar to celery. It is available year-round. Celery may be used as a substitute. Add a little tarragon to the salad if celery is used.

1   large bulb fennel, sliced (about 4 cups) or celery
2   tablespoons defatted chicken stock
1   tablespoon fresh lemon juice
1   teaspoon Dijon mustard
1   tablespoon olive oil
    Salt and freshly ground black pepper to taste
1   tablespoon chopped fennel leaves

Cut top off fennel. Wash and slice bulb. Mix chicken stock, lemon juice and mustard together in a salad bowl. Add oil and salt and pepper to taste. Toss fennel slices in dressing. Sprinkle with fennel leaves.

Helpful Hint

♦ *Mix dressing in bottom of salad bowl and add fennel slices to save washing an extra mixing bowl.*

Chicken Fajitas

Black Bean "Guacamole"

Shopping List

1¼ pounds boneless, skinless chicken breasts
4 limes
1 small red bell pepper
1 small yellow bell pepper
1 small green bell pepper
3 ripe medium tomatoes
1 bunch fresh cilantro
8 flour tortillas, 8 inches in diameter
1 container nonfat sour cream (8 ounces)
1 can black beans (15 ounces)

Staples

onions (3)
garlic
ground cumin
ground cayenne
orange juice
Tabasco or other hot pepper sauce
canola oil
salt
black peppercorns

Helpful Hints

♦ *Red, yellow and green peppers make this a colorful dish, but you can use just one or any combination of peppers.*

♦ *Flour tortillas can be found in the refrigerated dairy case or the freezer section of most supermarkets.*

♦ *Slice onions in a food processor fitted with a thick slicing blade and peppers in a food processor fitted with a thin slicing blade. Do not clean bowl. Save for "guacamole."*

HERE ARE SOME hot flavors for a family fiesta. Fajitas, tortilla-wrapped chicken and peppers, are an entire meal. Part of the fun is that everyone fills his or her own tortillas. The black bean "guacamole" can be spooned into the fajitas, used as a dip for tortilla chips or eaten as a side dish with a fork.

Serves 4.

THIS MEAL CONTAINS A TOTAL OF 586 CALORIES PER SERVING WITH 21 PERCENT OF CALORIES FROM FAT.

⧗ Countdown

♦ *Preheat oven to 350 degrees F for tortillas.*
♦ *Marinate chicken.*
♦ *Heat tortillas and set aside, wrapped in foil.*
♦ *Make Black Bean "Guacamole" in food processor.*
♦ *Sauté vegetables and chicken.*

CHICKEN FAJITAS

IN TRADITIONAL VERSIONS of this recipe, the meat is marinated overnight and then grilled. Using a warm marinade and cutting the chicken into thin strips shortens the time needed.

MARINADE

¼	cup fresh lime juice
1	tablespoon canola oil
2	teaspoons ground cumin
¼	teaspoon ground cayenne
1¼	pounds boneless, skinless chicken breasts
8	flour tortillas, 8 inches in diameter
1	tablespoon canola oil
2	medium onions, thinly sliced
½	red bell pepper, thinly sliced
½	yellow bell pepper, thinly sliced
½	green bell pepper, thinly sliced
4	medium cloves garlic, crushed through a press
3	ripe medium tomatoes, chopped
½	cup chopped fresh cilantro
	Several drops Tabasco or other hot pepper sauce
1	cup nonfat sour cream

Preheat oven to 350 degrees F.

For marinade: Mix lime juice, oil, ground cumin and cayenne together. Heat for 1 minute in a microwave on high or to boiling on a burner. Remove. Cut chicken into thin strips, about ¼ inch wide. Place in warm lime marinade for 15 minutes, stirring to make sure chicken is completely covered.

Tightly wrap tortillas in foil and place in the preheated oven for 15 minutes. Remove and leave wrapped in foil.

Heat 1 tablespoon oil in a nonstick skillet. Add onions and sauté until transparent, about 10 minutes. Add peppers and garlic and cook another minute. Raise heat and add chicken and any marinade left in bowl. Sauté for 3 minutes, or until chicken is no longer pink inside. Toss chicken and vegetables another minute and keep warm.

To serve: Toss tomatoes with cilantro and Tabasco. Place on a serving dish. Spoon sour cream in mound on the same serving dish. Spoon chicken and vegetables onto a separate warm serving dish, and place wrapped tortillas on a third dish. Each person can fill a tortilla with some or all of the ingredients.

BLACK BEAN "GUACAMOLE"

THIS IS A different twist to the usual guacamole made with avocado. It's easy to make in a food processor, goes perfectly with the fajitas and is low in fat.

¼   **small onion (about 2 tablespoons chopped)**
1   **15-ounce can black beans, drained and rinsed**
2   **tablespoons fresh lime juice**
2   **tablespoons orange juice**
2   **medium cloves garlic, crushed through a press**
     Salt and freshly ground black pepper to taste

Chop onion in a food processor. Add beans, lime juice, orange juice and garlic. Pulse processor until beans are chopped, but not pureed. Taste for seasoning and add salt and pepper as needed. Place in bowl and serve with fajitas.

Island Papaya Chicken

Rice & Peas

I LIKE TO MAKE this tropical dinner either on a cold winter's evening to bring some sunny food into our home or on a hot day when the spices of the Caribbean have a cooling effect. Hot peppers, tropical fruits, nutmeg and ginger create an exciting blend of flavors in the chicken, capturing the essence of Jamaican food quickly and easily. Rice & Peas is the native name for rice and beans. It is also known on the island as Coat of Arms.

Serves 4.

THIS MEAL CONTAINS A TOTAL OF 823 CALORIES PER SERVING WITH 22 PERCENT OF CALORIES FROM FAT.

⧖ Countdown
♦ *Start Rice & Peas.*
♦ *While rice cooks, prepare chicken.*

RICE & PEAS

THIS RECIPE was given to me by the mother of a Jamaican friend who told me, "If you haven't eaten rice and peas on Sunday, you haven't eaten." Scotch bonnet pepper, very much a part of Jamaican cooking, is considered the hottest pepper in the world. If you can't find Scotch bonnets, use any type of chili pepper available.

4	teaspoons canola oil
4	ounces lean ham, diced (1 cup)
¼	medium onion, chopped
2	medium cloves garlic, crushed through a press
1	cup long-grain white rice
1	cup coconut milk
1	cup water
½	cup canned red kidney beans, drained and rinsed
2	teaspoons chopped fresh thyme or ½ teaspoon dried
1	sliver Scotch bonnet pepper or 1 jalapeño pepper, chopped
	Salt and freshly ground black pepper to taste

Heat oil in a large nonstick skillet. Sauté ham, onion and garlic several minutes. Rinse rice and add to the pan. Sauté 1 minute. Add coconut milk, water, beans, thyme and Scotch bonnet pepper. Bring to a simmer, cover and let cook 10 minutes. Stir and cover again and cook about 10 more minutes, or until the rice is cooked through. Taste for seasoning, adding salt and pepper, if needed.

Shopping List

4 boneless, skinless chicken breast
    halves (5 ounces each)
¼ pound lean ham
2 limes
2 ripe papayas
2-inch piece fresh ginger
1 Scotch bonnet or 1 jalapeño pepper
1 small bunch fresh thyme or dried
1 bunch fresh cilantro
1 jar orange marmalade
1 can coconut milk (8 ounces)
1 can red kidney beans (19 ounces)

Staples

garlic
onion
ground nutmeg
ground cayenne
long-grain white rice
canola oil
salt
black peppercorns

Helpful Hints

♦ *Coconut milk is the liquid pressed from the meat of the mature coconut after soaking it in boiling milk or water. It is not the liquid found inside fresh coconuts. Canned unsweetened coconut milk can be found in some supermarkets.*

♦ *You can make a workable substitute for coconut milk by pouring 1 cup boiling water over 2 tablespoons sweetened coconut flakes. Steep 5 minutes, strain and use the liquid.*

♦ *Scotch bonnets should be handled carefully. I use rubber gloves when washing and chopping them. Keep your fingers away from your eyes, or the chilies' oils will burn them.*

ISLAND PAPAYA CHICKEN

PAPAYAS, also known as pawpaws, are abundant throughout the Caribbean. Available all year, they come in a variety of shapes and colors. Their flesh ranges from pale yellow to golden orange, and they have a sweet, fresh flavor similar to that of a melon. When green, the papaya may be boiled or cut in half and baked like a squash. Ripe ones can be pureed for dressings, served in fruit salads or poached for desserts. Since they remain firm when cooked, they're great with meat or poultry.

Helpful Hint

♦ *A quick way to chop ginger is to peel, cut into chunks and press through a garlic press with large holes.*

4	5-ounce boneless, skinless chicken breast halves
2	medium papayas
½	cup orange marmalade
½	cup fresh lime juice
1	teaspoon chopped fresh ginger
1	teaspoon ground nutmeg
	Pinch ground cayenne
2	tablespoons canola oil
½	cup chopped fresh cilantro

Remove fat from chicken and cut into 1-inch cubes. Peel papayas with a vegetable peeler or paring knife and cut in half. Remove seeds and cut into 1-inch cubes, or about the same size as chicken. Place marmalade, lime juice, ginger, nutmeg and cayenne in a saucepan and heat until marmalade is melted and all ingredients are well blended. Heat oil in a nonstick skillet and brown chicken cubes. Add papaya cubes and toss several minutes. Add marmalade sauce and sauté until chicken is cooked through, about 3 to 4 minutes. Spoon onto a serving dish and sprinkle with cilantro.

Ginger Minted Chicken

Orange Carrots

Lemon Barley

Shopping List

*4 boneless, skinless chicken breast
    halves (5 ounces each)*
6 carrots
1 bunch fresh mint
1 bunch fresh sage or dried
1 bunch fresh thyme or dried
1-inch piece fresh ginger
1 box quick-cooking pearl barley

Staples

lemon
onions (2)
garlic
ground cayenne
ground coriander
brown sugar
butter or margarine
nonfat plain yogurt
orange juice
canola oil
salt
black peppercorns

Helpful Hints

♦ *Chopped onion is used in both
the chicken marinade and barley.
Chop the total amount together
and divide as needed.*

♦ *A quick way to chop ginger is to
peel, cut into chunks and press
through a garlic press with large
holes. Press over food or bowl to
catch the juices.*

IF YOU'RE IN THE MOOD for something different, try this blend of Middle Eastern flavors. However exotic this meal may sound, it's actually a simple one. Boneless chicken is marinated in yogurt, spices, mint and fresh ginger, broiled and served on a bed of barley, and accompanied by carrots glazed with orange juice.

Serves 4.

THIS MEAL CONTAINS A TOTAL OF 541 CALORIES PER SERVING WITH 12 PERCENT OF CALORIES FROM FAT.

⧖ Countdown

♦ *Marinate chicken.*
♦ *Preheat broiler.*
♦ *Put water for barley on to boil.*
♦ *While chicken marinates, boil carrots and barley separately.*
♦ *Broil chicken.*
♦ *Finish carrots. Finish barley.*

GINGER MINTED CHICKEN

YOGURT, which probably originated in the Middle East, is an ideal base for marinade since its lactic acid tenderizes the meat. Poking holes in the meat hastens the marinating process.

1	cup nonfat plain yogurt
½	cup coarsely chopped fresh mint
½	medium onion, chopped (about 1 cup)
1	1-inch piece fresh ginger, peeled and chopped (about 1 tablespoon)
4	medium cloves garlic, crushed through a press
2	teaspoons ground coriander
	Pinch ground cayenne
4	5-ounce boneless, skinless chicken breast halves
4	sprigs fresh mint for garnish

Mix yogurt, mint, onion, ginger, garlic, coriander and cayenne together. Remove fat from chicken. With a skewer or knife, poke several holes at varying intervals in chicken. Add to yogurt mixture and marinate 20 minutes, turning once during this time.

Preheat broiler. Line a baking tray with foil. Broil chicken on top rack 5 minutes per side. Serve on a bed of Lemon Barley with sprigs of fresh mint as a garnish.

ORANGE CARROTS

I LIKE GLAZED CARROTS, but they take a long time to cook. In this recipe, you can either boil the carrots or cook them in a microwave and then pour this quick sauce over them.

6	carrots, sliced, or 3 cups sliced baby carrots
1	cup water
¼	cup orange juice
½	tablespoon brown sugar

Combine carrots and water in a saucepan. Cover and bring to a boil. Cook 10 minutes. Drain. Mix orange juice and sugar together. Heat to melt sugar. This may be done in a microwave oven (1 minute on high) or saucepan. Pour over drained carrots.

LEMON BARLEY

QUICK-COOKING barley is easy to make and adds a crunchy texture to the meal.

3	cups water
1	cup uncooked quick-cooking pearl barley
1	teaspoon canola oil
1	medium onion, chopped (about 2 cups)
1	tablespoon chopped fresh sage or 1 teaspoon dried
1	tablespoon chopped fresh thyme or 1 teaspoon dried
	Grated rind from 1 lemon (about 1 teaspoon)
2	tablespoons fresh lemon juice
2	teaspoons butter or margarine
	Salt and freshly ground black pepper to taste

Bring water to a boil and stir in barley. When water returns to a boil, reduce the heat, cover and simmer 10 minutes. Drain. Heat oil in a nonstick skillet and sauté onion until transparent and golden, 10 minutes. Add barley, herbs, lemon rind, juice, butter and salt and pepper to taste, and toss together.

Helpful Hints

♦ *To save time, buy peeled baby carrots and slice in food processor.*

♦ *If microwaving carrots, cook them 8 minutes on high.*

Helpful Hints

♦ *Look for quick-cooking pearl barley, which cooks in half the time of regular barley. Quaker is one of the nationally known brands.*

♦ *Regular barley can also be used; it cooks in about 30 minutes.*

Game Hens in Red Wine

Hot Buttered Noodles

Endive & Watercress Salad

Shopping List

*2 Rock Cornish game hens
    (1¼ pounds each)
1 pound mushrooms
¾ pound Belgian endive
2 carrots
1 small bunch fresh parsley
1 bunch watercress
½ pound linguine*

Staples

*lemon
onion
garlic
Dijon mustard
honey
nonfat plain yogurt
butter or margarine
red wine (Beaujolais or
    Burgundy)
chicken stock
salt
black peppercorns*

Helpful Hints

♦ *Rock Cornish game hens are found in supermarkets, either fresh or frozen.*

♦ *If you have another red wine already opened or more readily available to you, use it instead of the Beaujolais.*

♦ *When ready, the hens can be kept warm in the pan off the heat while the noodles are cooking.*

EACH NOVEMBER the race is on! The romantic idea of rushing Beaujolais to the market when it is young has become a French tradition. Splash a little into this sauce for Cornish game hens, pour yourself a glass and enjoy an easy French dinner. It sounds special enough to warrant hours of preparation, but it can be made in about 45 minutes. Serve the game hens over noodles to soak up the sauce. If you are pressed for time, use your favorite bottled low-fat salad dressing instead of the one given here. *See photograph, page 104.*

Serves 4.

THIS MEAL CONTAINS A TOTAL OF 644 CALORIES PER SERVING WITH 28 PERCENT OF CALORIES FROM FAT.

Countdown

♦ *Put water for noodles on to boil.*
♦ *Prepare hens.*
♦ *While hens are cooking, make salad.*
♦ *While finishing sauce for hens, cook noodles.*

GAME HENS IN RED WINE

INSTEAD OF being roasted whole, the hens are split and cooked in a covered skillet, cutting the preparation time in half.

2	1¼-pound Rock Cornish game hens
1	teaspoon butter or margarine
½	medium onion, diced (about 1 cup)
2	carrots, diced (about 1 cup)
2	medium cloves garlic, crushed through a press
⅔	cup red wine (Beaujolais or Burgundy)
⅔	cup defatted chicken stock
1	pound mushrooms, quartered (about 4 cups whole mushrooms)
	Salt and freshly ground black pepper to taste

Remove fat from cavity of hens and split hens in half. Melt butter in a nonstick skillet just large enough to hold hen halves in one layer. Brown hen halves on both sides, about 6 to 8 minutes. Remove to a plate and add diced onion, carrots and garlic to the pan. Sauté until vegetables start to shrivel, about

5 minutes. Return hen halves to the pan, skin-side down, lower the heat and cover. Cook until pieces are cooked through, about 15 minutes. Remove to a dish and cover with foil to keep warm. Pour off any remaining fat, increase heat to high and deglaze the pan with red wine, scraping browned bits from the bottom of the pan while wine simmers for about 2 minutes. Add chicken stock and mushrooms. Simmer 2 more minutes. Return chicken and any vegetables to the pan and cook to warm through. Serve hen, sauce and vegetables over noodles.

ENDIVE & WATERCRESS SALAD

ENDIVE IS A LOT FASTER to prepare than romaine or iceberg lettuce, because it is so easy to wash. Belgian endive will turn brown if left to soak in water. Wipe it with a damp paper towel or lightly rinse it under water. You don't have to wash each leaf or spin dry.

¾	pound Belgian endive, sliced
1	bunch watercress, washed, stems removed

DRESSING
2	tablespoons fresh lemon juice
2	tablespoons Dijon mustard
2	teaspoons honey
¼	cup nonfat plain yogurt
	Salt and freshly ground black pepper to taste

Helpful Hint

♦ *The quickest way to wash watercress is to place it head first into a bowl of water. Leave for a minute, then lift it out of the bowl. Shake dry and remove stems up to where the leaves start.*

Lightly rinse and dry endive and slice. Wash and dry watercress. Cut off top leaves and discard stems. Place endive and watercress leaves in a salad bowl.

For dressing: In a small bowl, whisk lemon juice, mustard and honey together. Whisk in yogurt. Add salt and pepper to taste. Toss with greens.

HOT BUTTERED NOODLES

USE THIN PASTA such as linguine or fettuccine, with a little butter added to keep it from sticking. Angel-hair pasta is too delicate for this dish, however.

½	pound linguine or fettuccine
2	tablespoons butter or margarine
¼	cup chopped fresh parsley
	Salt and freshly ground black pepper to taste

Bring a large pot with 3 to 4 quarts of water to a boil. Add linguine. Boil about 10 minutes, or until tender but firm. Place butter and parsley in a mixing bowl. Drain pasta and add to the bowl. Butter will melt in hot pasta. Toss until pasta is well coated with butter and parsley. Add salt and pepper to taste. Serve on individual plates with hen, sauce and vegetables spooned over top.

Lemon Peppered Chicken

Rosemary Cannellini Beans

Steamed Carrots & Zucchini Sticks

See photograph, page 169.

I MAKE THIS DISH quite often when we have people over for a barbecue. It's a light alternative to tomato-based barbecue sauce. For the sake of speed, I use boneless breasts of chicken. Canned cannellini beans cooked with garlic and rosemary, and crunchy carrot and zucchini sticks are colorful additions to this spicy Italian meal. *See photograph, page 169.*

Serves 4.

THIS MEAL CONTAINS A TOTAL OF 579 CALORIES PER SERVING WITH 24 PERCENT OF CALORIES FROM FAT.

⧗ Countdown

♦ *Light grill or preheat broiler.*
♦ *Marinate chicken.*
♦ *While chicken is marinating, cut and steam carrots and zucchini and make cannellini beans.*
♦ *Grill chicken.*

LEMON PEPPERED CHICKEN

THE CHICKEN takes on a spicy, citrus flavor that is both hot and refreshing.

4	5-ounce boneless, skinless chicken breast halves
⅓	cup fresh lemon juice
¼	cup olive oil
2	tablespoons cracked black peppercorns
	Vegetable-oil cooking spray

Remove fat from chicken. Poke several holes at varying intervals in chicken and place in a small bowl just large enough to hold chicken or in a plastic bag. Mix lemon juice, olive oil and pepper together. Pour over chicken and let marinate 20 minutes. Remove from marinade.

If using grill, sear chicken breasts 1 minute on each side and then move off the direct heat and continue to cook for 4 to 5 minutes longer, or broil for 3 to 4 minutes on each side.

Shopping List

4 boneless, skinless chicken breast halves (5 ounces each)
½ pound carrots
½ pound zucchini
2 lemons
1 small bunch fresh parsley
1 small bunch fresh rosemary or dried
2 cans cannellini or Great Northern beans (19 ounces each)

Staples

garlic
olive oil
butter or margarine
vegetable-oil cooking spray
chicken stock
salt
black peppercorns

Helpful Hints

♦ *Preheat a gas grill for 10 minutes, or start a charcoal fire 30 minutes ahead, or preheat broiler 10 minutes before needed.*

♦ *To keep chicken from burning on the barbecue, spray the grates with vegetable-oil cooking spray, sear the breasts about 1 minute on each side and then move them to an area of the grill that is not directly over the heat to finish cooking.*

STEAMED CARROTS & ZUCCHINI STICKS

I FREQUENTLY SERVE THIS DISH for dinner parties because it is so easy and looks pretty. You can cut the vegetables in a food processor and place in the steamer ahead of time, then steam for 10 minutes before serving.

- 4   medium carrots, cut into julienne sticks
- 2   medium zucchini, cut into julienne sticks
- 2   tablespoons butter or margarine
- 2   tablespoons chopped fresh parsley
     Salt and freshly ground black pepper to taste

Place carrots in the bottom of a steaming basket and place zucchini on top. Place basket over 1 inch salted water. Cover and steam for 10 to 12 minutes, until tender, but not too soft. Place in a serving bowl and add salt and pepper to taste. Melt butter and parsley in a saucepan or microwave oven and pour over vegetables.

ROSEMARY CANNELLINI BEANS

LOTS OF GARLIC and fresh rosemary flavor these large white kidney beans. This dish only needs to be warmed through and can be made on top of the stove or in a microwave.

- 2   19-ounce cans cannellini beans
- ⅓   cup defatted chicken stock
- 4   medium cloves garlic, crushed through a press
- 1   tablespoons chopped fresh rosemary or ½ tablespoon dried
     Salt and freshly ground black pepper to taste

Drain but do not rinse cannellini beans. Place in a saucepan with chicken stock, garlic and rosemary. Cook about 5 minutes, or until beans are warmed through. Drain. Add salt and pepper to taste.

Helpful Hint

♦ *Cut carrots and zucchini in a food processor fitted with a julienne blade. If you do not have a special blade, simply slice them using a thick slicing blade or by hand with a knife.*

Helpful Hints

♦ *If using a microwave, cook on high for 3 to 4 minutes.*

♦ *Great Northern beans may be substituted for the cannellini.*

Pecan-Crusted Chicken

Roasted Yam or Sweet Potato Slices

Lettuce & Tomatoes With Creamy Dressing

Shopping List

*4 boneless, skinless chicken breast
   halves (5 ounces each)
1 small head Romaine lettuce
2 large ripe tomatoes
2 pounds yams or sweet potatoes
2 ounces pecans*

Staples

*ground cayenne
honey mustard
butter or margarine
skim milk
eggs (3)
nonfat plain yogurt
cornmeal
sherry-wine vinegar
vegetable-oil cooking spray
salt
black peppercorns*

Helpful Hint

*♦ The chicken needs to be baked
and the yams broiled. This can all
be done in one oven by baking the
chicken first, removing it to a
warm plate and turning the oven
to broil.*

THESE RECIPES OFFER a modern twist to some old-time Southern favorites. Pecans form a crunchy coating for boneless chicken breasts that are served with roasted yam or sweet potato slices. If pressed for time, use a bottled low-fat creamy dressing for the salad.

   Serves 4.

THIS MEAL CONTAINS A TOTAL OF 748 CALORIES PER SERVING WITH 29 PERCENT OF CALORIES FROM FAT.

⧗ Countdown

♦ *Start yams boiling.*
♦ *Preheat oven to 400 degrees F for chicken.*
♦ *While yams boil, marinate chicken in milk and make salad.*
♦ *Prepare chicken and keep warm.*
♦ *Broil potatoes.*

ROASTED YAM OR SWEET POTATO SLICES

THE YAMS or sweet potatoes are first parboiled, then crisped under the broiler.

   **2   pounds yams or sweet potatoes
   2   tablespoons butter or margarine
        Vegetable-oil cooking spray
        Salt and freshly ground black pepper to taste**

   Peel potatoes, leave whole and place in a small pot with cold water to cover. Cover with a lid and bring to a boil. Cook for 15 minutes. Melt butter; this can be done in a microwave. Remove potatoes and cut into very thin slices, about ¼ inch thick. The potatoes will still be firm in the center.
   Line two baking trays with foil and place roasting racks over them. Spray the racks with vegetable-oil cooking spray and arrange slices in one layer. Brush or spoon melted butter over each slice. Sprinkle with salt and pepper. Place under a hot broiler for 4 minutes. Remove and turn the slices. Brush with butter and sprinkle with salt and pepper. Return to the broiler for another 3 minutes. Surface will be crisp and center soft and flavorful. Remove to individual plates. Makes about 40 slices.

PECAN-CRUSTED CHICKEN

BAKING RATHER THAN deep-frying chicken is a healthful technique that produces crisply coated moist meat without the fuss or fat of frying.

- 1 cup skim milk
- 1½ teaspoons ground cayenne
- 4 5-ounce boneless, skinless chicken breast halves
- 1 cup cornmeal
- ½ teaspoon salt
- 1 teaspoon freshly ground black pepper
- 3 egg whites, lightly beaten
- ½ cup chopped pecans
- 1 tablespoon butter or margarine

Preheat oven to 400 degrees F. Mix milk and cayenne pepper together. Remove fat from chicken and pound until about 1 inch thick. This can be done with a meat mallet or the bottom of a sturdy skillet. Marinate chicken breasts in the milk for 10 minutes.

Mix cornmeal with salt and pepper. Remove chicken from milk and roll in cornmeal, making sure to coat chicken completely. Dip chicken into egg whites and roll in pecans. Melt butter in a nonstick skillet. When it is hot, brown chicken breasts. Turn and brown other sides. When chicken is golden on both sides, about 3 minutes, remove to a baking tray and place in oven for 4 minutes to finish the cooking. Chicken will be crisp on the outside and juicy on the inside. Place on a warm plate and cover with foil to keep warm while the yams are broiling.

LETTUCE & TOMATOES WITH CREAMY DRESSING

TO ROUND OUT this Southern-style quick dinner, arrange a bed of lettuce and some sliced tomatoes on each plate and spoon a little dressing on top.

- ½ small head romaine lettuce
- 2 large ripe tomatoes

DRESSING
- ½ cup nonfat plain yogurt
- 4 teaspoons honey mustard
- 4 teaspoons sherry-wine vinegar

Helpful Hint

♦ *Honey mustard is commonly available in supermarkets.*

Wash and dry lettuce and tear into bite-size pieces. Wash and slice tomatoes. Arrange on individual plates.

For dressing: Whisk yogurt and mustard together. Add sherry-wine vinegar and blend together. Taste. Add more mustard, if needed. Spoon over lettuce and tomatoes.

Curried Chicken

Diced Tomatoes & Onions

Basmati Rice

Shopping List

*1¼ pounds boneless, skinless
    chicken breasts
4 shallots or ¼ small onion
4 ripe medium tomatoes
2 jalapeño chili peppers
1 small bunch fresh cilantro
2 Granny Smith apples
1 small package slivered almonds
½ pint heavy cream
1 bag white basmati rice
    (14 ounces)*

Staples

*onion
raisins
ground cinnamon
curry powder
ground cardamom
sugar
flour
butter or margarine
white vinegar
canola oil
1 can chicken stock (14½ ounces)
salt
black peppercorns*

Helpful Hint

*♦ You can buy imported basmati
rice in some supermarkets.
Domestic Texmati rice is more
readily available. Use whichever
one is easiest for you to find.*

WHEN I FEEL LIKE a touch of the exotic, I turn to Indian food. Although some people think this cuisine is time-consuming, these dishes can be prepared swiftly. If pressed for time, omit the diced tomatoes and onions and serve sliced tomatoes instead. *See photograph, page 175.*

    Serves 4.

THIS MEAL CONTAINS A TOTAL OF 761 CALORIES PER SERVING WITH 28 PERCENT OF CALORIES FROM FAT.

⧖ Countdown

♦ *Start rice.*
♦ *While rice is boiling, make chicken.*
♦ *Finish rice.*
♦ *Prepare tomatoes.*

BASMATI RICE

INDIAN BASMATI RICE makes a perfect side dish for your curry. It has a distinct flavor and smells something like popcorn while cooking.

    1   **cup white basmati rice**
    2   **tablespoons canola oil**
    ½   **cup raisins**
    ¼   **cup slivered almonds**
        Salt and freshly ground black pepper to taste

    Place rice in a strainer and run cold water through to wash it. Fill a large saucepan with 3 to 4 quarts of water, bring to a boil and slowly pour in rice. Boil rapidly, uncovered, for about 10 minutes. Test a grain. The rice should be cooked through, but not soft. Drain into a colander. Place in a serving bowl and toss in oil and add raisins, almonds and salt and pepper. Taste for seasoning and add more salt and pepper, as necessary.

CURRIED CHICKEN

CURRY IS A MIXTURE of infinite variability. The curry powder sold in supermarkets is a combination of about 15 herbs, spices and seeds. Although good cooks often prefer to make their own curry mixture using the freshest ingredients, this short-cut combination of ground cardamom and curry powder gives the right effect, while saving a great deal of effort.

1¼	pounds boneless, skinless chicken breasts
2	tablespoons butter or margarine
2	tart apples such as Granny Smith, peeled, cored and cut into small cubes
4	shallots, chopped
4	teaspoons curry powder
2	teaspoons ground cinnamon
2	teaspoons ground cardamom
4	teaspoons flour
1	14½-ounce can defatted chicken stock
2	tablespoons heavy cream
	Salt and freshly ground black pepper to taste

Trim fat from chicken breasts and cut into 2-inch cubes. Melt butter in a nonstick skillet just large enough to hold chicken pieces. When butter is sizzling, brown chicken on all sides. Remove to a warm plate and cover with foil. Lower the heat and add apple cubes. Toss gently in the pan for several minutes, without breaking them up. Remove to the plate with browned chicken. Add chopped shallots to the pan and sauté 1 minute, or until they start to shrivel. Add curry powder, cinnamon and cardamom. Cook for several seconds to release the flavor from the spices. Add flour and cook, stirring, so the spices do not burn, for ½ minute. Slowly pour in stock, stirring constantly. Let sauce simmer for 3 minutes. Return chicken, apples and any juices from meat to the pan. Add cream and salt and pepper to taste. Mix well. Let simmer very gently for 5 minutes, or until chicken is cooked through. Serve on rice.

DICED TOMATOES & ONIONS

CALLED KACHOMBER, this dish is served with curry dishes in many Indian restaurants. The delicate blend of salt, sugar and vinegar is the secret to its taste.

4	ripe medium tomatoes, seeded and diced (about 4 cups)
½	medium onion, diced (about 1 cup)
½	cup chopped fresh cilantro
2	medium jalapeño peppers, seeded and chopped, or to taste
¼	cup white vinegar
2	teaspoons sugar
1	teaspoon salt

In a bowl, mix tomatoes with onions and add cilantro and jalapeño peppers. In a small bowl, mix vinegar, sugar and salt together. Taste and add more salt or sugar as needed. Pour over salad and toss.

Helpful Hints

♦ *Make sure your curry powder is fresh. It lasts only about 6 months on the shelf, and the fresh spice will make a big difference.*

♦ *Ground cardamom can be found in the spice section of most supermarkets.*

♦ *If you don't have shallots, use ¼ small onion.*

Helpful Hint

♦ *To seed tomatoes, cut in half and squeeze out seeds.*

Devil's Chicken

Sautéed Garlic Potatoes

Watercress & Endive Salad

Shopping List

*4 boneless, skinless chicken breast
halves (6 ounces each)
1 bunch watercress
¾ pound Belgian endive
2 pounds red potatoes
1 small jar coarse-grain mustard
½ pint heavy cream*

Staples

*lemon
garlic
butter or margarine
flour
Dijon mustard
canola oil
dry vermouth
chicken stock
salt
black peppercorns*

ONE OF OUR FAVORITE DINNERS served at a local bistro when we lived in Paris was sautéed chicken and garlic-flavored red potatoes. A salad of watercress and Belgian endive can be added, with bottled low-fat dressing if you need an extra shortcut.

> *Serves 4.*

THIS MEAL CONTAINS A TOTAL OF 657 CALORIES PER SERVING WITH 24 PERCENT OF CALORIES FROM FAT.

⧖ Countdown

- *Start potatoes.*
- *While potatoes cook, make chicken.*
- *Make salad.*

SAUTÉED GARLIC POTATOES

SAUTÉED POTATOES are a nice alternative to French fries. Cutting them into small pieces helps them to cook faster. Red potatoes are firm, moist and sauté well.

2	pounds red potatoes
2	tablespoons butter or margarine
6	large cloves garlic, unpeeled
	Salt and freshly ground black pepper to taste

Wash potatoes and cut into small (about 1-inch) chunks. Heat butter in a nonstick skillet large enough to hold potatoes in one layer. Add garlic and sauté for about 1 minute. Add potatoes and sauté until they are golden on all sides, about 15 minutes. Sprinkle with a little salt and cover. Reduce heat and cook gently for about 10 minutes, or until soft, tossing or stirring potatoes from time to time. Remove garlic and season with a little more salt and pepper to taste.

DEVIL'S CHICKEN

Two TYPES of strong, flavorful mustards give the sauce its character.

1	tablespoon butter or margarine
¼	cup flour
	Salt and freshly ground black pepper
4	6-ounce boneless, skinless chicken breast halves
⅓	cup dry vermouth
2	tablespoons Dijon mustard
2	tablespoons coarse-grain mustard
⅓	cup water
2	tablespoons heavy cream

Melt butter in a large nonstick skillet. Season flour with salt and pepper and dredge chicken in flour, shaking off any excess. Brown chicken on both sides. Add vermouth to pan. Cook 1 minute. In a small bowl, blend mustards into water and add to pan. Bring liquid to a simmer, scraping up browned bits in the pan. Cover and simmer for 5 minutes. Remove meat to individual dishes and cover to keep warm. Add cream, salt and pepper to pan to taste. Mix well. If you like a stronger mustard flavor, add more. Spoon sauce over chicken and serve with potatoes.

WATERCRESS & ENDIVE SALAD

WATERCRESS MIXED with Belgian endive dressed with a low-fat vinaigrette complete this French menu.

1	bunch watercress
¾	pound Belgian endive
½	tablespoon fresh lemon juice
½	teaspoon Dijon mustard
1	tablespoon defatted chicken stock
1	teaspoon canola oil
	Salt and freshly ground black pepper to taste

Helpful Hint

♦ *A quick way to wash watercress is to place it head first into a bowl of water. Leave for a minute, then lift it out of the bowl. Shake dry and remove stems up to where the leaves start.*

Wash watercress well and remove about 1 inch from thick stem ends. Wipe endive with a damp paper towel. Slice a ½-inch piece from the flat bottom and discard. Cut endive in diagonal rounds and place in a bowl with watercress. In a small bowl, whisk lemon juice and mustard together. Whisk in chicken stock and oil. Add salt and pepper to taste. Toss with salad.

Stacked Quesadillas

Southwestern Layered Salad

Shopping List

1 pound smoked turkey
1 medium green bell pepper
2 medium red bell peppers
2 large yellow tomatoes or red tomatoes
3 red tomatoes
2 red onions
1 head iceberg lettuce
3 jalapeño peppers
1 bunch fresh cilantro
¼ pound fresh goat cheese
1 package Monterey Jack cheese (2 ounces)
8 flour tortillas, 8 inches in diameter
1 can corn or 1 package frozen (11-ounce can or 10-ounce package)
1 can black beans (15 ounces)

Staples

lemon
garlic
butter or margarine
olive oil
vegetable-oil cooking spray
chicken stock
salt

Helpful Hints

♦ *Ripe red tomatoes can be substituted for yellow tomatoes.*

♦ *Chop vegetables in food processor to save time.*

WHEN I INVITE FRIENDS over for a casual Sunday night supper, I often serve this variation on a traditional quesadilla. It's really a hot sandwich, Tex-Mex style. Taking the place of bread, tortillas are covered with smoked turkey, salsa and creamy-textured fresh goat cheese, and broiled with Monterey Jack cheese on top. The salad, a layered arrangement of tomatoes, corn, canned black beans and lettuce, completes the meal colorfully. Serve with beer.

Serves 4.

THIS MEAL CONTAINS A TOTAL OF 707 CALORIES PER SERVING WITH 27 PERCENT OF CALORIES FROM FAT.

⧗ Countdown

♦ *Preheat oven to 350 degrees F.*
♦ *Make quesadillas.*
♦ *While quesadillas bake, prepare salad.*

STACKED QUESADILLAS

THESE SANDWICHES may also be cut into pieces and served as snacks.

½	**cup defatted chicken stock**
1	**pound smoked turkey, cut in ¼-inch pieces**
2	**medium red bell peppers, seeded and chopped (about 2 cups)**

SALSA

2	**yellow tomatoes, diced (about 2 cups)**
2	**tablespoons chopped red onion**
2	**medium jalapeño peppers, seeded and chopped**
1	**cup chopped fresh cilantro**
	Vegetable-oil cooking spray
8	**flour tortillas, 8 inches in diameter**
1	**tablespoon butter or margarine**
¼	**pound fresh goat cheese**
½	**cup shredded Monterey Jack cheese**
	Salt and freshly ground black pepper to taste

Preheat oven to 350 degrees F. Heat chicken stock in a nonstick skillet and add turkey and peppers. Sauté 2 minutes, or until liquid has evaporated, and set aside.

For salsa: Combine tomatoes, onion, peppers and cilantro. Toss gently.

Season with salt and pepper. Taste and add more if necessary.

To assemble and serve: Spray two baking trays with vegetable-oil cooking spray and place 2 tortillas on each baking sheet. Spread all 4 tortillas with butter. Spoon turkey mixture onto tortillas. Cut goat cheese into pieces and evenly sprinkle over tortillas. Spread salsa over cheese. Cover with remaining 4 tortillas. Top each quesadilla with Monterey Jack cheese. Bake 10 minutes, or until the cheese is melted and the filling is hot. Place under a broiler for 2 minutes to brown the top lightly.

Makes 4 quesadillas.

LAYERED SOUTHWESTERN SALAD

BEANS ARE A CLASSIC INGREDIENT of Southwestern cooking and make a healthful salad. Black beans, black-eyed peas, pinto beans or red beans are often used.

Helpful Hint

♦ *If using frozen corn, cook for 1 minute in the microwave or blanch in boiling water before using.*

3	ripe tomatoes, *divided*
½	medium red onion, chopped
1	medium jalapeño pepper, seeded and chopped
	Salt and freshly ground black pepper to taste
1	15-ounce can black beans, drained and rinsed
4	cups washed, shredded iceberg lettuce
1	medium green bell pepper, chopped
1	cup canned or frozen, thawed corn kernels

DRESSING
¼	cup defatted chicken stock
2	tablespoons fresh lemon juice
4	teaspoons olive oil
4	medium cloves garlic, crushed through a press
	Salt and freshly ground black pepper to taste

Finely chop 2 tomatoes. This can be done in a food processor. Add onion, jalapeño pepper, salt and pepper. Taste for seasoning and add more if necessary. Mix together with black beans. Layer lettuce, then green pepper, then half the black bean mixture in a bowl. Spoon corn over top. Slice remaining tomato and arrange slices around top and spoon remaining black bean mixture onto tomatoes.

For dressing: In a small bowl, whisk together chicken stock, lemon juice and olive oil and add garlic. Add salt and pepper to taste. Pour half the dressing over salad and serve the rest on the side.

Sesame Chicken

Curried Rice

Melon & Cucumber Salad

FROM THEIR COLONIAL PAST, the English learned to enjoy Indian and Chinese cooking, and gradually the exciting flavors crept into their own cooking. In many English pubs, you find mango chutney served beside cheese, pickles and bread, and curry powder appears in many English dishes. This dinner is a blend of Chinese, Indian and English flavors. If pressed for time, serve sliced tomatoes on the side in place of the salad.

    Serves 4.

THIS MEAL CONTAINS A TOTAL OF 833 CALORIES PER SERVING WITH 18 PERCENT OF CALORIES FROM FAT.

⧗ Countdown

♦ *Preheat oven to 350 degrees F for chicken.*
♦ *Marinate chicken.*
♦ *While chicken marinates, prepare rice.*
♦ *Make salad.*
♦ *Complete chicken.*

SESAME CHICKEN

MY HUSBAND loves to make Chinese food, and Chinese five-spice powder is one of his favorite ingredients. Actually, this aromatic blend consists of many more than five spices, including cinnamon, fennel, licorice root, anise, ginger, chili pepper, allspice and cloves. It is found in the spice section of most supermarkets.

1¼	**pounds boneless, skinless chicken breasts**
2	**tablespoons low-sodium soy sauce**
2	**tablespoons maple syrup**
2	**tablespoons dry sherry**
1	**teaspoon peeled, chopped fresh ginger or ¼ teaspoon ground**
1	**teaspoon Chinese five-spice powder**
¼	**cup sesame seeds**
¼	**cup all-purpose flour**
	Salt and freshly ground black pepper to taste
1	**teaspoon peanut oil**
	Several red lettuce leaves, washed and dried

Preheat oven to 350 degrees F. Cut chicken into pieces about 1 by 2 inches. Mix soy sauce, maple syrup, sherry, ginger and five-spice powder together. Place chicken in a bowl or plastic bag and marinate 20 minutes, turning once during that time.

Place sesame seeds on a baking tray and toast in oven for 10 minutes, or until slightly brown. Drain chicken, reserving 2 tablespoons marinade. Dredge chicken in flour seasoned with a little salt and pepper. Shake off any excess. Heat oil in a nonstick skillet. Add chicken to pan and brown on both sides, about 1 minute per side. Spoon 2 tablespoons marinade over chicken. Reduce heat and sauté another minute, or until chicken is cooked through. Remove from heat and roll chicken in sesame seeds. Line a serving plate with leaves and spoon chicken on top.

CURRIED RICE

I LIKE TO BOIL RICE like pasta, in a pot large enough to let the grains roll freely in the boiling water. This method gives fluffy rice every time.

1	cup long-grain white rice
½	cup nonfat mayonnaise
½	cup dried cranberries or raisins
½	cup mango chutney plus more to taste
2	tablespoons sliced almonds
4	teaspoons curry powder
¼	cup fresh lemon juice
	Salt and freshly ground black pepper to taste

Helpful Hint

♦ *Instead of using yogurt, you can thin the mayonnaise with 1 to 2 tablespoons warm water, if you prefer.*

Place rice in a strainer and run cold water through to rinse it. Bring a large pot with 3 to 4 quarts of water to a boil. Add rice and boil, uncovered, about 10 minutes. Test a grain. Rice should be cooked through but not soft. Drain into a colander in the sink. Run hot water through rice and stir with a fork. Mix mayonnaise, cranberries, chutney, almonds and curry together in a serving bowl. Add lemon juice to thin. Taste and add more chutney, if needed. Add rice and mix with a fork. Add salt and pepper to taste.

MELON & CUCUMBER SALAD

USE A MELON in the summer or pears in the winter. The sweet fruit gives this salad a delicious taste and texture.

1	ripe tomato, cut into 1-inch wedges
½	cantaloupe or other melon, seeded and cubed (about 2 cups)
1	cucumber, peeled, seeded and cubed (about 1½ cups)
1	tablespoon fresh lemon juice
1	tablespoon Dijon mustard
2	tablespoons defatted chicken stock

Helpful Hint

♦ *Any type of melon can be used. Be sure that it is ripe.*

2   teaspoons canola oil
    Salt and freshly ground black pepper to taste
2   tablespoons chopped fresh mint

Combine tomato, melon and cucumber. Whisk lemon juice and mustard together. Whisk in chicken stock, then oil. Add salt and pepper to taste. Toss tomato, melon and cucumber with dressing. Sprinkle mint on top.

Turkey Enchiladas

Esquites (Fried Corn)

A DELIGHTFUL MEXICAN TEACHER in my London cooking school introduced me to this meal. The fresh goat cheese filling gives these enchiladas a tangy, creamy taste, while the tomato sauce has just a hint of peppery spice. The accompanying fried corn has a little more fire.

    Serves 4.

THIS MEAL CONTAINS A TOTAL OF 795 CALORIES PER SERVING WITH 26 PERCENT OF CALORIES FROM FAT.

⧗ Countdown

♦ *Start tomato sauce for enchiladas.*
♦ *Preheat oven to 250 degrees F for enchiladas.*
♦ *Make enchiladas.*
♦ *While enchiladas warm in the oven, make Esquites.*

TURKEY ENCHILADAS

THE FRENCH have their crepes, the Russians their blinis and the Mexicans their tortillas. Corn or flour tortillas are used to make enchiladas, which are usually filled with meat, chopped onions and grated cheese.

TOMATO SAUCE

2	28-ounce cans tomato sauce
½	medium onion, coarsely chopped (about 1 cup)
4	large jalapeño peppers
½	cup chopped fresh cilantro or flat-leaf parsley
1	teaspoon sugar
	Salt and freshly ground black pepper to taste

FILLING

¾	pound cooked turkey breast
2	teaspoons ground cumin
½	pound fresh goat cheese
¼	cup chopped fresh cilantro or flat-leaf parsley
8	flour tortillas, 8 inches in diameter
½	cup grated Cheddar or Jarlsburg cheese
½	medium onion, coarsely chopped (about 1 cup)

Preheat oven to 250 degrees F.

For tomato sauce: Place tomatoes, onion and jalapeño peppers in a large

Shopping List

¾ pound low-fat, low-sodium cooked turkey
2 medium-size green bell peppers
6 jalapeño peppers
1 bunch fresh cilantro
1 small bunch fresh parsley
1 package fresh goat cheese (8 ounces)
2-ounce piece Cheddar or Jarlsburg cheese
8 flour tortillas, 8 inches in diameter
2 cans corn or 4 packages frozen corn (17-ounce cans, 10-ounce packages)

Staples

onions (2)
ground cumin
canola oil
sugar
2 cans tomato sauce (28 ounces each)
salt
black peppercorns

Helpful Hints

♦ *You will need 3½ cups chopped onion for these recipes. Chop the onions all at once and divide as directed. This can be done easily in the food processor.*

♦ *Fresh goat cheese is sold in specialty food shops and many supermarkets. A soft Bel Paese cheese can be substituted.*

♦ *The chili peppers are used whole in the sauce, giving it just a hint of spicy flavor. If you like your sauce hot, cut open the peppers, remove the seeds, slice the peppers and add to the sauce.*

saucepan and bring to a boil. Reduce heat and simmer, uncovered, 10 minutes. Add the cilantro, sugar, salt and pepper to taste. Cover to keep warm and set aside.

For filling: Remove skin from turkey and dice. Sprinkle with ground cumin. Mix with goat cheese and cilantro. Divide the filling into 8 portions. To fill enchiladas, dip the tortillas into the tomato sauce. Make sure they are completely covered in sauce. Remove to a plate and spoon one portion of the filling into the center of each tortilla. Roll up and place in an ovenproof dish. Spoon some of the sauce over the top of the enchiladas, cover with foil and place in the oven to keep warm.

To serve: Remove from the oven and place 2 enchiladas on each plate. Remove the chili peppers from the sauce and spoon the warm sauce over the enchiladas. Sprinkle the cheese and onions on top and serve with Esquites.

ESQUITES (FRIED CORN)

CORN IS AN IMPORTANT PART of Mexican cooking. This dish takes only minutes to make when using frozen or canned corn.

½   tablespoon canola oil
1   small onion, chopped (about 1½ cups)
2   medium jalapeño peppers, seeded and chopped
2   medium green bell peppers, sliced (about 2 cups)
4   cups canned or frozen corn
½   cup chopped fresh parsley
    Freshly ground black pepper to taste

Heat oil in a nonstick skillet and add onion. Sauté about 5 minutes. Raise the heat and add chili peppers and green peppers. Cook on high for 1 minute. Add corn and parsley and continue to pan-fry for 3 minutes, or until the corn is warmed through. Stir constantly. Add pepper to taste and serve.

Chicken Scaloppine

Pasta Pagliacci

CREATED BY Elizabeth Gardner Adams of Gardner's Markets to celebrate the music of Verdi for Greater Miami Opera's 50th anniversary season, this dinner is easy, delicious and sings with the flavors of Italy. The delicate pink pasta sauce combines the sweetness of sun-dried tomatoes with the bite of peperoncini.

If pressed for time, use flavored bread crumbs instead of the plain ones and omit the oregano and cheese in the chicken dish.

Serves 4.

THIS MEAL CONTAINS A TOTAL OF 684 CALORIES PER SERVING WITH 18 PERCENT OF CALORIES FROM FAT.

⌛ Countdown

- *Put a pot of water for pasta on to boil.*
- *Boil chicken stock and soak sun-dried tomatoes for pasta.*
- *Make chicken.*
- *While chicken simmers, make pasta. (Chicken will need to be removed from heat before pasta dish is completed.)*

PASTA PAGLIACCI

PEPERONCINI ARE hot Tuscan peppers and can be found pickled in the condiment section of most supermarkets. They're great on sandwiches or with pasta.

1½	cups dry-pack sun-dried tomatoes
2¼	cups boiling defatted chicken stock, *divided*
½	medium onion, chopped (about 6 tablespoons)
2	medium cloves garlic, crushed through a press
1	tablespoon olive oil
1	medium green bell pepper, diced (about 1 cup)
1	medium yellow bell pepper, diced (about 1 cup)
3	tablespoons tomato paste
12	peperoncini
1	tablespoon fresh thyme or 1 teaspoon dried
1	cup chopped fresh basil or fresh opal basil
1	tablespoon balsamic vinegar
½	pound fettuccine

Place a large pot with 3 to 4 quarts of water on to boil. Cut sun-dried tomatoes in half and soak in 2 cups hot chicken stock for 5 minutes. Heat

Shopping List

4 boneless, skinless chicken breast halves (5 ounces each)
3 ounces dry-pack sun-dried tomatoes (not in oil)
1 medium green bell pepper
1 medium yellow bell pepper
1 small bunch fresh thyme or dried
1 bunch fresh basil or opal basil
1 jar peperoncini (12 ounces)
½-ounce piece Parmesan cheese
½ pound fettuccine

Staples

onion
garlic
eggs (2)
oregano
plain bread crumbs
tomato paste
olive oil
balsamic vinegar
dry white wine
1 can chicken stock (14½ ounces)
salt
black peppercorns

Helpful Hints

- *Substitute green or red bell pepper for the yellow pepper if necessary.*

- *The deep purple leaves of opal basil, when you can find them, add color and texture to this dish.*

remaining ¼ cup chicken stock in a nonstick skillet. Add onion and sauté until golden, about 10 minutes. Add garlic and cook another minute. Add oil, peppers and sun-dried tomatoes, reserving soaking liquid. Sauté 3 minutes. Add tomato paste, peperoncini, thyme, basil and balsamic vinegar. Remove from heat and add water from sun-dried tomatoes. Mix well and taste for seasoning.

Boil pasta about 10 minutes, or until tender but firm. Drain. Toss in sauce. Add salt and pepper to taste.

CHICKEN SCALLOPPINE

THE COATING on this chicken helps to keep it juicy. Try not to overcook the chicken or it will become dry.

4	5-ounce boneless, skinless chicken breast halves
½	cup plain bread crumbs
2	tablespoons freshly grated Parmesan cheese
1	teaspoon dried oregano
2	egg whites
1	tablespoon olive oil
½	cup dry white wine
	Salt and freshly ground black pepper to taste

Remove fat from chicken breasts and flatten by slapping them with the palm of your hand. Mix bread crumbs, cheese and oregano together. Add a little salt and pepper to taste. Beat egg white until foamy and dip chicken in it. Coat chicken with bread crumbs and dip again in egg whites. Coat with bread crumbs a second time. Heat oil in a nonstick skillet and brown chicken on both sides, about 3 minutes. Reduce heat, add wine and cover. Cook 5 more minutes. There will be no wine left in the pan. Serve chicken with pasta.

Key West Shrimp (PAGE 116)

Herbed Grilled Veal (PAGE 230)

Penne Pasta Primavera (PAGE 40)

Vietnamese Stir-Fried Beef & Bok Choy (PAGE 184)

Sautéed Chicken With Tomatoes (PAGE 58)

Italian Fish Soup (PAGE 34)

Vietnamese Sweet & Sour Fish (PAGE 140)

Game Hens in Red Wine (PAGE 78)

CHAPTER 3

Fish & Seafood Dinners

Fish & Seafood Dinners

◆

Bowtie Pasta With Artichoke Hearts

Skewered Shrimp

Shopping List

1 pound jumbo shrimp (about 20)
5 ripe medium tomatoes
2 lemons
1 small bunch fresh chervil or
  flat-leaf parsley
1 can artichoke hearts (17 ounces)
¼ pound lean ham
2-ounce piece Parmesan cheese
1 pound farfalle (bowtie) pasta

Staples

onions (2)
garlic
olive oil
chicken stock
salt
black peppercorns

Helpful Hints

♦ *Chervil is sometimes called French parsley. It looks a little like parsley, but its leaves are more delicate and fernlike. It has a slight anise flavor similar to that of fennel. Flat-leaf parsley can be substituted.*

♦ *You can substitute frozen or jarred (but not marinated) artichokes if you can't find canned.*

"MAKE SURE you have a lot of pasta tonight," was the common cry in my house when my sons were involved in sports. Made with bowtie pasta and artichoke hearts, this is nearly a meal in itself, with the shrimp served as a colorful side dish.

   Serves 4.

THIS MEAL CONTAINS A TOTAL OF 567 CALORIES PER SERVING WITH 25 PERCENT OF CALORIES FROM FAT.

⧗ Countdown

♦ *Make sauce for pasta.*
♦ *Marinate shrimp.*
♦ *Put water for pasta on to boil.*
♦ *Preheat broiler.*
♦ *Make pasta.*
♦ *Skewer and broil shrimp.*

BOWTIE PASTA WITH ARTICHOKE HEARTS

FARFALLE means butterflies in Italian, and this pasta looks something like little bows or butterflies. Their shape is perfect because they are large enough to hold the vegetable ingredients of the sauce without becoming overwhelmed.

SAUCE

¼	cup defatted chicken stock
2	medium onions, thinly sliced (2 cups)
1	17-ounce can artichoke hearts
¼	cup fresh lemon juice
2	medium cloves garlic, crushed through a press
	Salt and freshly ground black pepper to taste
4	ounces lean ham, diced (about 1 cup)
5	ripe medium tomatoes, diced (about 4 cups)

PASTA

1	pound farfalle (bowtie) pasta
2	tablespoons olive oil
¼	cup chopped fresh chervil or flat-leaf parsley
½	cup freshly grated Parmesan cheese

For sauce: Heat chicken stock in a large nonstick skillet. Sauté onions over medium heat for 5 minutes. Drain artichokes and cut in half and add to onions with lemon juice and garlic. Season with salt and pepper and cook for 5 more minutes. Add ham and tomatoes. Increase heat and cook for 20 minutes.

For pasta: Meanwhile, put a large pot with 3 to 4 quarts of water on to boil. When it is boiling, add pasta and cook for about 10 minutes, until tender but firm. Drain and place in a large serving bowl or pasta dish. Toss with olive oil. Stir in artichoke sauce. Add chervil and Parmesan and toss again. Add salt and pepper to taste.

SKEWERED SHRIMP

MARINATED and briefly broiled, these come out nicely juicy, with just a hint of garlic.

20	jumbo shrimp
⅓	cup olive oil
2	medium cloves garlic, crushed through a press

Shell, devein and rinse shrimp. Mix olive oil and garlic together in a small bowl or plastic bag. Marinate shrimp in oil for 20 minutes. Preheat the broiler. Place 5 shrimp on each skewer and broil for 3 to 5 minutes, depending on the size. Shrimp are done when they are pink and no longer translucent.

Helpful Hints

♦ *To devein shrimp, remove shell and slit shrimp down the back. Remove black vein, rinse and drain.*

♦ *Be careful not to overcook shrimp or they will become rubbery.*

♦ *Many markets will shell shrimp for you; I find the small extra charge is worth the time saved.*

Pernod Shrimp

Tarragon Rice

Shopping List

*1¾ pounds jumbo shrimp
(about 20 per pound)
4 shallots
1 bulb fennel or 4 stalks celery
1 small bunch fresh tarragon or
dried
2 ounces Pernod or Ricard
½ pint heavy cream
1 French baguette*

Staples

*butter or margarine
long-grain white rice
dry white wine
canola oil
salt
black peppercorns*

I LEARNED TO ENJOY anise-flavored liqueur in Paris, where it was a popular apéritif at our local brasserie. It also provides an excellent flavoring for shellfish. With some fluffy rice and French bread to soak up the sauce, you can achieve a thoroughly Gallic taste with very little effort.

Serves 4.

THIS MEAL CONTAINS A TOTAL OF 789 CALORIES PER SERVING WITH 20 PERCENT OF CALORIES FROM FAT.

⌛ Countdown

- ◆ *Start cooking rice.*
- ◆ *While rice is cooking, make shrimp.*
- ◆ *Finish rice.*

TARRAGON RICE

THE TARRAGON ADDS a delicate anise flavor to the rice. It can be omitted if you don't have any on hand. I prefer to cook rice in a lot of boiling water so that it rolls in the water. It's easy to make and fluffy each time.

- **1 cup long-grain white rice**
- **2 tablespoons canola oil**
- **1 teaspoon chopped fresh tarragon leaves or ½ teaspoon dried**
  Salt and freshly ground black pepper to taste

Place rice in a strainer and wash under cold water. Bring a large pot with 3 to 4 quarts of water to a boil. Add rice and boil, uncovered, for about 10 minutes. Test a few grains to see if they are cooked. They should be cooked through but still firm. Drain into a colander and rinse with warm water. Place back in the pot, stir in oil with a fork and add tarragon, salt and pepper.

PERNOD SHRIMP

FENNEL, a white bulbous vegetable with a slight anise flavor and a texture similar to celery, is sautéed with shrimp and shallots. The shallots cook to a paste and, combined with the cream and the Pernod, yield a smooth, rich sauce for the rice.

2	tablespoons butter or margarine
4	medium shallots, peeled and coarsely chopped
1	medium bulb fennel, diced, or 4 stalks celery (about 3 cups)
1¾	pounds jumbo shrimp, shelled and deveined
¼	cup Pernod or Ricard
½	cup dry white wine
2	tablespoons heavy cream
	Salt and freshly ground black pepper to taste
1	French baguette

Melt butter in a large nonstick skillet; add shallots and fennel. Sauté 5 minutes. Add shrimp and sauté another minute, tossing them in the pan. Pour in Pernod and flambé. Do this carefully: As soon as Pernod is hot, tip the pan and, averting your face, let the liqueur catch the gas flame. If using an electric stove, ignite with a match, averting your face. Be sure to have a cover nearby as a safety measure.

Add wine and let shrimp simmer for 3 minutes. Remove shrimp with a slotted spoon. Raise the heat and reduce juices in the pan by half. Add cream and cook on low heat 1 minute. Return shrimp to the pan to warm through. Add salt and pepper to taste. Serve on a bed of Tarragon Rice. Slice baguette and serve in bread basket with shrimp and rice.

Helpful Hints

♦ *Be careful not to overcook shrimp or they will become rubbery.*

♦ *Pernod and Ricard are anise-flavored liqueurs. Liqueurs are often available in miniature bottles.*

♦ *If fennel is difficult to find, celery is a good substitute.*

♦ *Onion can be used instead of shallots.*

♦ *Chop shallots in a food processor.*

♦ *Slice fennel in a food processor, then cut slices into smaller pieces with a knife.*

♦ *To devein shrimp, remove shells and slit shrimp down the back. Remove black vein, rinse and drain.*

Hot & Spicy Stir-Fried Shrimp

Stir-Fried Noodles

Pickled Carrot Salad

Shopping List

1½ pounds large shrimp
8 carrots
4 shallots
10 jalapeño peppers
1 small head lettuce
1-inch piece fresh ginger
4 stalks lemon grass or 2 lemons
1 ounce unsalted, roasted peanuts
½ pound fresh Chinese egg noodles

Staples

onion
garlic
ketchup
brown sugar
sugar
white vinegar
peanut oil
chicken stock
salt

Helpful Hint

♦ *Slice carrots in a food processor fitted with a thin slicing blade.*

WHENEVER I'm in the mood for Thai food, I love making this dish. With subtle peanut overtones and a garlic bite, the shrimp is full of hot, spicy flavors. The noodles are stir-fried in the same pan. The crunchy carrots in the salad soak up the sugar and vinegar of their marinade, and their coolness acts as a refreshing foil to the fire of the shrimp. *See photograph, page 174.*

Serves 4.

THIS MEAL CONTAINS A TOTAL OF 636 CALORIES PER SERVING WITH 15 PERCENT OF CALORIES FROM FAT.

⧗ Countdown

♦ *Marinate carrots.*
♦ *Put water for noodles on to boil.*
♦ *Chop vegetables for shrimp.*
♦ *Boil noodles and set aside while you make shrimp.*
♦ *Make shrimp in wok; do not wash wok.*
♦ *Stir-fry noodles in wok.*
♦ *Drain carrots.*

PICKLED CARROT SALAD

I USE THIS as a refreshing side dish for many Asian-style meals.

8	medium carrots, thinly sliced
4	tablespoons chopped onion
1	cup water
6	tablespoons sugar
2	whole jalapeño peppers
¾	cup white vinegar
1	teaspoon salt
4	lettuce leaves, washed, for garnish

Place carrots and onion in a bowl. Mix water and sugar together. Add whole peppers. Heat in a saucepan or in a microwave oven to dissolve sugar. Do not let water boil; sugar will start to crystallize if you do. Add vinegar and salt. Stir well. Pour over carrots and onions and let steep about 30 minutes. To serve, drain, remove peppers and spoon carrots onto a bed of lettuce.

HOT & SPICY STIR-FRIED SHRIMP

THIS DISH is typical of the simple specialties prepared on portable braziers throughout the street markets of Southeast Asia. Despite the fact that it contains eight jalapeños, the dish is not particularly hot. If you are in the mood for an eight-alarm meal, don't seed the jalapeños, or for a less raging blaze, seed half of them. Make sure everything is ready before you start to stir-fry. I place each ingredient on a dish in the order it goes into the wok. Then I don't need to look at the recipe.

2	teaspoons peanut oil
4	medium shallots, chopped
4	medium cloves garlic, chopped
4	teaspoons chopped fresh ginger
4	stalks lemon grass, sliced, or grated rind from 2 lemons
8	medium jalapeño peppers, seeded and chopped
1½	pounds large shrimp, shelled and deveined
⅓	cup defatted chicken stock or water
1	tablespoon ketchup
2	teaspoons brown sugar
2	tablespoons chopped unsalted, roasted peanuts

Heat oil in a wok or skillet. Add shallots and cook 1 minute. Add garlic and ginger. Cook another minute. Add lemon grass, peppers and shrimp. Add chicken stock, ketchup and sugar. Stir-fry 2 to 3 minutes. Toss with peanuts and remove from wok. Stir-fry noodles in same wok and serve shrimp over noodles.

STIR-FRIED NOODLES

THESE FRESH Chinese noodles pick up the flavors of the shrimp and sauce.

½	pound fresh Chinese egg noodles
1	tablespoon peanut oil
2	tablespoons defatted chicken stock

Bring a large pot with 3 to 4 quarts of water to a boil. Add noodles and cook for 3 minutes. Drain thoroughly and set aside. As soon as shrimp are removed from the wok, add oil, then noodles and stir-fry in the remaining sauce for 3 to 4 minutes. Add chicken stock to moisten. Spoon onto individual plates and serve the shrimp on top.

Helpful Hints

♦ *All the chopping for this dish can be done in the food processor. There is no need to clean the bowl after each ingredient is chopped.*

♦ *Lemon grass is available in the produce section of some supermarkets. It looks something like a scallion, but the stalks are a pale green color, hard and dry. I always buy some whenever I see it, because it freezes well and its delicate lemony flavor adds special aromatic overtones to Asian dishes. It is also sold dried. Substitute grated lemon rind if you can't find lemon grass.*

♦ *To save time chopping ginger, I peel the skin, cut it into small pieces and place it in a garlic press with large holes.*

♦ *To devein shrimp, remove shells and slit shrimp down the back. Remove black vein, rinse and drain.*

Helpful Hint

♦ *Fresh Chinese egg noodles are found refrigerated in the produce section of most supermarkets. Dried Chinese noodles may be substituted. In that case, boil the noodles according to the package instructions.*

Grilled Dilled Seafood Kabobs

Fluffy Rice

Shopping List

¾ pound swordfish
12 large shrimp
12 sea scallops
1 lime
1 red bell pepper
1 green bell pepper
1 small bunch fresh dill

Staples

garlic
long-grain white rice
butter or margarine
olive oil
salt
black peppercorns
4 skewers (12 inches each)

Helpful Hints

♦ *Preheat a gas grill for 10 minutes, or start a charcoal fire 30 minutes ahead or preheat broiler 10 minutes before needed.*

♦ *Buy shelled shrimp, if possible.*

♦ *To devein shrimp, remove shells and slit shrimp down back. Remove black vein, rinse and drain.*

♦ *Be careful not to overcook seafood, or it will become rubbery.*

SHORTLY AFTER THE DEVASTATION of Hurricane Andrew, I received a call from one of my readers whose kitchen had been flooded: "My collection of your recipes was destroyed. Could you replace some of them, especially the grilled seafood?" I, too, would be at a loss without this favorite. Grilled or broiled, it brings out all the natural flavors of the fish.

Serves 4.

THIS MEAL CONTAINS A TOTAL OF 546 CALORIES PER SERVING WITH 25 PERCENT OF CALORIES FROM FAT.

⧗ Countdown

♦ *Marinate fish and peppers.*
♦ *Preheat grill or broiler.*
♦ *While fish marinates, prepare rice.*
♦ *Cook kabobs.*

GRILLED DILLED SEAFOOD KABOBS

MARINATING FISH not only adds to the flavor, but helps ensure that all the ingredients cook evenly. The kabobs will cook best if you start with a hot grill or broiler, and they take only about 5 minutes. The pieces will be crisp outside and moist and tender inside.

MARINADE

¼	cup olive oil
1	tablespoon fresh lime juice
1	tablespoon chopped fresh dill or 2 teaspoons dried
2	medium cloves garlic, crushed through a press
1	teaspoon freshly ground black pepper
½	teaspoon salt

KABOBS

¾	pound swordfish
12	large shrimp
12	sea scallops
1	red bell pepper
1	green bell pepper

For marinade: Thoroughly mix ingredients together in a bowl large enough to hold seafood in a single layer.

For kabobs: Remove swordfish from bone and cut off skin. Cut fish into

2-inch cubes (12 cubes). Shell shrimp and devein. Rinse scallops. Cut peppers in half and remove stems and seeds. Cut into quarters or sixths depending on size. You will need pieces large enough to fit on the skewer. Place fish, shrimp, scallops and vegetables in marinade and leave for 20 minutes, turning every 5 minutes or so.

To finish: Alternate swordfish, peppers, shrimp and scallops on four 12-inch skewers. Grill for 2½ minutes per side. Do not overcook fish. Serve immediately.

FLUFFY RICE

I LIKE TO BOIL RICE in a large pot of water so that it rolls in the water.

1 **cup long-grain white rice**
2 **tablespoons butter or margarine**
   Salt and freshly ground black pepper to taste

Place rice in a strainer and wash under cold water. Place in a large pot with 3 to 4 quarts water and add rice. Bring water to a boil and gently boil rice, uncovered, for about 10 minutes. Test a few grains to see if they are cooked through but still firm. Strain into a colander and rinse with warm water. With a fork, stir in butter and add salt and pepper.

Key West Shrimp

Tropical Coleslaw

Cuban Bread

Shopping List

1¾ pounds large shrimp
4 Key limes or 2 regular limes or
*   bottled Key lime juice*
2 pink grapefruit
½ head cabbage
2 carrots
1 medium red onion
Old Bay or other seafood seasoning
Cuban, sourdough, French or
*   Italian bread (enough for at*
*   least 8 slices)*

Staples

garlic
sugar
Dijon mustard
nonfat mayonnaise
butter or margarine
2 cans or bottles beer
*   (12 ounces each)*
white vinegar
salt
black peppercorns

I LIKE TO SERVE this dinner informally as they do in Key West, leaving the shrimp in their shells and spreading newspapers on the table. Complete this meal with crusty, warm Cuban bread and ice-cold beer. Friends tell me they love this meal for festive entertaining. If pressed for time, serve a tossed green salad instead of coleslaw. *See photograph, page 97.*

Serves 4.

THIS MEAL CONTAINS A TOTAL OF 710 CALORIES PER SERVING WITH 11 PERCENT OF CALORIES FROM FAT.

⧗ Countdown

♦ *Make coleslaw.*
♦ *Preheat oven to 350 degrees F for bread.*
♦ *Make shrimp.*
♦ *While shrimp steams, warm bread and make Key Lime Mustard.*

TROPICAL COLESLAW

THIS COLESLAW takes only minutes to make if I slice everything in my food processor. Just a bit of cabbage goes a long way; you don't need a whole head. Most supermarkets sell cabbage cut in half or will cut one for you, if you ask.

½	head medium cabbage, thinly sliced (about 4 cups)
2	medium carrots, thinly sliced (about 1 cup)
½	medium red onion, thinly sliced (about 1 cup)
2	medium-size pink grapefruit, cut into segments
½	cup nonfat mayonnaise
½	cup white vinegar
1	rounded tablespoon Dijon mustard
2	tablespoons sugar
	Salt and freshly ground black pepper to taste

Slice cabbage, carrots and onion in a food processor or by hand. Cut grapefruit sections from fruit. Add to cabbage mixture. Toss. Mix mayonnaise, vinegar, mustard, sugar, salt and pepper together. Taste, adding more sugar or mustard as needed. Toss dressing with vegetables.

KEY WEST SHRIMP

OLD BAY SEASONING, which is available in the spice section of any supermarket, gives a pickling-spice zing to these shrimp, while the beer imparts subtle sweetness.

- 1¾   pounds large shrimp
- 2   cans or bottles beer (24 ounces in all)
- 2   tablespoons Old Bay Seasoning or any fish- or crab-boil seasoning

Rinse shrimp and drain. Pour beer into a stainless-steel pan and add seasoning. Bring beer to a boil and add shrimp. As soon as beer returns to a boil, remove shrimp with a slotted spoon. Serve immediately with Key Lime Mustard.

KEY LIME MUSTARD

KEY LIMES have a special acid taste and a highly pronounced citrus flavor that cuts the mayonnaise. Bottled Key lime juice or regular lime juice may be substituted.

- ¾   cup nonfat mayonnaise
- 4   tablespoons Dijon mustard
- ¼   cup Key lime juice or regular lime juice
        Salt and freshly ground black pepper to taste

Mix mayonnaise, mustard and lime juice together and taste. Add salt and pepper if needed. Serve with Key West Shrimp.

CUBAN BREAD

USE SOURDOUGH, French or Italian bread if you don't have Cuban.

- 1   loaf Cuban bread
- 2   tablespoons butter or margarine
- 2   teaspoons minced garlic

Preheat oven to 350 degrees F. Melt butter and garlic together. This can be done in a microwave oven. Brush on top of bread. Warm in oven for 5 minutes.

Mango Shrimp

Black Bean & Rice Salad

Corn & Pimiento Salad

Shopping List

1¼ pounds large shrimp
1½ pounds ripe mangoes
   (1 large or 2 small)
   or ripe peaches or pineapple
1 medium jalapeño pepper
1 small head red leaf lettuce
1 medium red bell pepper
1 bunch fresh mint
1 bunch fresh cilantro
1 small jar pickled cocktail onions
3 cans or 3 packages frozen corn
   (11-ounce cans or 10-ounce
   packages)
1 small jar or can whole pimientos
   in water
1 can black beans (15 ounces)

Staples

long-grain white rice
onion
lemon
sugar
nonfat mayonnaise
nonfat plain yogurt
honey mustard
horseradish
Dijon mustard
sherry-wine vinegar
canola oil
chicken stock
salt
black peppercorns

I LIKE TO MAKE this collection of colorful salads for supper when it's too hot to heat up the kitchen. They are also great for a light brunch on Sundays. Taken together, they present a dazzling array of colors, textures and flavors: orange and pink shrimp salad with sweet mangoes and the sting of jalapeño and horseradish; red and yellow corn salad, bound with a honey-mustard creamy vinaigrette; and white rice and black bean salad, lightly seasoned with fresh cilantro.

If pressed for time, omit one of the salads.

Serves 4.

THIS MEAL CONTAINS A TOTAL OF 561 CALORIES PER SERVING WITH 5 PERCENT OF CALORIES FROM FAT.

⧗ Countdown

♦ *Start rice for salad.*
♦ *Make shrimp.*
♦ *Complete rice salad.*
♦ *Make corn salad.*

BLACK BEAN & RICE SALAD

IN EVERY Cuban restaurant, black beans and rice are staples. In a salad, the combination is irresistible.

½	cup uncooked long-grain white rice
1½	cups canned black beans, drained and rinsed
½	cup coarsely chopped fresh cilantro
¼	medium onion, coarsely chopped (about ¼ cup)
	Salt and freshly ground black pepper to taste
1	tablespoon fresh lemon juice
1	teaspoon Dijon mustard
2	tablespoons defatted chicken stock
2	teaspoons canola oil

Place rice in a strainer and wash under cold water. Fill a large pot with 3 to 4 quarts cold water and add rice. Bring to a boil and cook gently for about 10 minutes. Test a few grains to see if they are cooked through but still firm. Strain into a colander and rinse with warm water. Place rice and beans in a bowl and add cilantro and onion. Season with salt and pepper. Whisk lemon juice and mustard together in a small bowl. Whisk in chicken stock. Blend in oil. Pour over salad and toss. Taste and add more salt and pepper, if necessary.

MANGO SHRIMP

LUSCIOUS, low in calories and second only to the banana in worldwide popularity, mangoes are now available in most supermarkets throughout the United States. Their flavor has been described as a cross between a peach and pineapple. If you can't find any mangoes, use one of those fruits instead.

1½	pounds ripe mangoes, 1 large or 2 small (2 cups cubes)
1¼	pounds large shrimp

DRESSING

½	cup nonfat mayonnaise
1	tablespoon horseradish
1	tablespoon Dijon mustard
2	teaspoons fresh lemon juice
1	teaspoon sugar
1	medium jalapeño pepper, seeded and chopped
	Freshly ground black pepper to taste

GARNISH

8–10	red lettuce leaves
1	medium red bell pepper, diced
¼	cup coarsely chopped fresh mint leaves

Peel mangoes and cut into cubes. Shell and devein shrimp. Bring a pot with 1 to 2 quarts of water to a boil and add shrimp. When bubbles start to appear around edges and water begins to turn cloudy, remove from heat and let sit 1 minute. Remove shrimp and cut into same-size pieces as mango. Place in serving bowl with mango.

For dressing: Mix all ingredients together. Taste for seasoning and add more lime juice or pepper, if necessary. Spoon just enough dressing over mango and shrimp to bind it together.

Wash and dry lettuce leaves and arrange on a serving platter. Spoon salad onto lettuce. Sprinkle pepper over salad with chopped mint. Refrigerate if you are not serving within ½ hour; serve at room temperature.

Helpful Hints

♦ *Shrimp, crab or lobster can be used for this salad.*

♦ *Buy shelled shrimp or ask the fish department to shell them for you. Or buy good-quality cooked shrimp. To devein shrimp, remove shells and slit shrimp down the back. Remove black vein, rinse and drain.*

♦ *Substitute ripe peaches or pineapple for mangoes, if necessary.*

♦ *To cut a mango into cubes quickly: Slice off each side of the mango as close to the seed as possible. Take the mango half in your hand, skin side down. Score the fruit in a cross-hatch pattern through to the skin. Bend the skin backwards so that the cubes pop up. Slice the cubes away from the skin. Score and slice any fruit left on the pit.*

CORN & PIMIENTO SALAD

YELLOW CORN and red pimientos contrast in this couldn't-be-simpler salad. I like to keep some canned corn and a jar of pimientos on hand so that I can make it quickly.

¼ cup nonfat plain yogurt
½ tablespoon honey mustard
2 teaspoons sherry-wine vinegar
3 cups drained canned corn or frozen, thawed
⅓ cup diced pimiento
3 pickled cocktail onions, chopped (about 1 tablespoon)
   Salt and freshly ground black pepper to taste

Mix yogurt, honey mustard and sherry-wine vinegar together in a serving bowl. Add corn, pimiento and onions. Toss together. Add salt and pepper to taste.

Garlic Shrimp

Saffron Rice

Sautéed Escarole

THIS LIGHT, garlicky preparation for shrimp typifies *tapas,* the dishes served in taverns all across Spain, where friends meet for a leisurely afternoon or evening snack. We love it for dinner, with lots of bread, baked rice with saffron, and greens sautéed with pine nuts, raisins and garlic.

Serves 4.

THIS MEAL CONTAINS A TOTAL OF 561 CALORIES PER SERVING WITH 27 PERCENT OF CALORIES FROM FAT.

Countdown

♦ *Preheat oven to 350 degrees F for rice.*
♦ *Make rice.*
♦ *Make escarole.*
♦ *Make shrimp and serve sizzling hot as soon as it is ready.*

SAFFRON RICE

SHORT-GRAIN RICE gives this dish a creamy taste, but long-grain rice can be substituted.

2	tablespoons butter or margarine
2	tablespoons chopped onion
1	cup Valencia-style rice or long-grain rice
2	cups defatted chicken stock
¼	cup chopped fresh parsley
2	sprigs fresh thyme or 1 teaspoon dried
8	threads saffron
	Salt and freshly ground black pepper to taste

Preheat oven to 350 degrees F. In an ovenproof casserole dish, melt butter over a burner. Add onion and gently sauté until transparent, about 5 minutes. Add rice and stir to coat with butter. Add chicken stock, parsley, thyme and saffron. Add a little salt and pepper to taste. Bring to a boil, cover and place in the oven for 15 minutes. Remove from oven and let sit, covered, for 10 minutes before serving. Taste for seasoning, adding more salt and pepper, if necessary.

Shopping List

1½ pounds shelled medium shrimp
1 small head escarole or spinach
1 small bunch fresh parsley
1 small bunch fresh thyme or dried
8 threads saffron or turmeric
3 ounces raisins
1 ounce pine nuts
1 ounce lean ham, optional
*6 ounces short-grain rice
  (Valencia-style)*

Staples

lemon
onion
garlic
butter or margarine
bay leaf
Tabasco or other hot pepper sauce
olive oil
chicken stock
salt
black peppercorns

Helpful Hints

♦ *Turmeric can be substituted for saffron. Although the flavor will be different, the dish will still be very good.*

♦ *Arborio, the short-grain rice from Italy, can be substituted for Spanish short-grain (Valencia-style) rice.*

SAUTÉED ESCAROLE

Helpful Hints

♦ *Garlic is used in the shrimp recipe as well. Crush all the garlic together at one time and divide.*

♦ *Substitute spinach if you can't find escarole.*

♦ *Slice escarole in a food processor fitted with a thick slicing blade.*

THE FLAVORS OF GARLIC, pine nuts, raisins and saffron are apt complements for the slightly bitter greens, which become succulently tender when sautéed. Escarole, sometimes called batavia, has curly, broad leaves, with a lighter colored, almost white, heart.

1	cup defatted chicken stock
1	tablespoon fresh lemon juice
1	small head escarole, sliced (about 4 cups)
¼	cup raisins
2	tablespoons pine nuts
2	medium cloves garlic, crushed through a press
	Salt and freshly ground black pepper to taste

Heat chicken stock and lemon juice in a nonstick skillet and add escarole. Cover and poach 2 minutes. Remove from pan with slotted spoon. Place in a serving bowl. Add raisins, pine nuts and garlic to pan. Sauté, uncovered, until stock reduces to just a few drops. Return escarole to pan and sauté to blend ingredients, about 1 minute. Add salt and pepper to taste.

GARLIC SHRIMP

Helpful Hints

♦ *Buy preshelled shrimp. Many markets sell shrimp that is already shelled or will shell it for you for a small charge. I find that the slightly higher cost is worth the time saved.*

♦ *To devein, remove shells and slit shrimp down the back. Remove black vein, rinse and drain.*

♦ *Be careful not to overcook shrimp or they will become rubbery.*

THIS RECIPE was inspired by a conversation with Penelope Casas, author of *The Foods and Wines of Spain*.

1½	pounds shelled medium shrimp, deveined
2	tablespoons olive oil
4	medium cloves garlic, crushed through a press
1	bay leaf
1	ounce lean ham, chopped (about ¼ cup), *optional*
	Several drops Tabasco or other hot pepper sauce
	Salt and freshly ground black pepper to taste

Dry shrimp after deveining. Heat oil in a nonstick skillet. Sauté garlic and bay leaf together over medium heat until garlic starts to turn golden, not brown. Add shrimp and ham, tossing in the pan for about 1 to 2 minutes. Add Tabasco to taste and sprinkle with a little salt and pepper. Remove bay leaf. Serve immediately in the same pan while it is sizzling.

Scallops in Light Wine Sauce

Rice With Mushrooms

According to Greek mythology, Aphrodite, the goddess of love and beauty, rose from the sea riding on a scallop shell. When looking for a Valentine's dinner one year, I combined Greek mythology and the romance of French cuisine in this elegant meal. Scallops poached in a wine sauce enriched with cream are accompanied by rice flavored with porcini mushrooms.

Serves 4.

THIS MEAL CONTAINS A TOTAL OF 613 CALORIES PER SERVING WITH 26 PERCENT OF CALORIES FROM FAT.

⧖ Countdown

- ♦ *Put water for dried mushrooms on to boil and soak mushrooms.*
- ♦ *Prepare vegetables for scallops.*
- ♦ *While vegetables sauté, make rice.*
- ♦ *Complete scallops.*

SCALLOPS IN LIGHT WINE SAUCE

SCALLOPS NEED very little cooking. Prolonged heating will shrink and toughen them. In this recipe, the scallops are gently poached in a light wine sauce that keeps them juicy and tender.

1	tablespoon butter or margarine
1	medium onion, thinly sliced (about 1 cup)
2	medium leeks, green tops removed, thinly sliced (about 2 cups)
2	medium stalks celery, thinly sliced (about 1 cup)
2	large carrots, thinly sliced on the diagonal (about 2 cups)
½	teaspoon sugar
2	bay leaves
1½	cups dry white wine
1½	cups clam juice
½	cup heavy cream
1	pound fresh scallops
½	pound snow peas, trimmed
	Salt and freshly ground black pepper to taste

Melt butter in a large nonstick skillet. Sauté onion, leeks and celery for 10 minutes, covered. Add 2 tablespoons water if onion begins to stick.

Add carrots, sugar and bay leaves and sauté, uncovered, another 5 minutes. Add white wine and clam juice and reduce by half, about 5 minutes. Add cream

Shopping List

1 pound fresh scallops
2 leeks
2 stalks celery
2 large carrots
½ pound snow peas
1 ounce dried porcini or other dried
*   wild mushrooms*
2 bottles clam juice (8 ounces each)
½ pint heavy cream
1 package white basmati rice or
*   other long-grain white*
*   (14 ounces)*

Staples

onion
bay leaves
butter or margarine
sugar
dry white wine
salt
black peppercorns

Helpful Hints

♦ *Slice onion, leeks and celery in a food processor fitted with a thin slicing blade.*

♦ *Buy large carrots, peel and slice on a diagonal so they are about the same size and shape as the snow peas.*

♦ *Be careful to remove all sand from the folds of the leek stalks. To do this, cut them in half lengthwise and in half again and rinse them well under running water.*

and simmer on low heat for 1 minute. Add scallops and snow peas and continue to simmer about 2 minutes. Do not overcook; scallops will be a milky color when done. Add salt and pepper to taste. Remove bay leaves before serving.

RICE WITH MUSHROOMS

PORCINI mushrooms (also called cèpes) have a wonderful pungent flavor. They are available dried, and I always keep some on hand. Only a few are needed. If you cannot find them, use another dried mushroom or sauté button mushrooms and add them to the rice.

Helpful Hint

♦ *Basmati rice is a fragrant Indian rice that can be found in most supermarkets. Long-grain white rice may be substituted.*

1 ounce dried porcini mushrooms (about 1 cup)
1 cup boiling water
1 cup white basmati rice or other long-grain white
1 tablespoon butter or margarine
  Salt and freshly ground black pepper to taste

Soak dried mushrooms in 1 cup boiling water for 15 minutes.

Place rice in a strainer and rinse under cold water. Check for any small stones while rinsing. Fill a medium-size pot three-quarters full with cold water and add rice. Bring water to a boil and boil rice, uncovered, for about 10 minutes, or until rice is cooked through but still firm. Drain. Place in a serving bowl and mix in butter. Drain mushrooms and cut into small pieces, if necessary. Stir into rice. Add salt and pepper to taste.

Mussels in White Wine

Potatoes Vinaigrette

THIS DISH BRINGS BACK memories of dinners in Normandy. It is really three different dishes for the effort of two. First, mussels are steamed in an aromatic broth of wine, chopped carrots and celery and served; then the broth is quickly reduced by boiling and served as a separate course, along with potato salad and bread. If pressed for time, omit the potatoes or use a store-bought vinaigrette dressing for them. The mussels are quite filling on their own.

Serves 4.

THIS MEAL CONTAINS A TOTAL OF 887 CALORIES PER SERVING WITH 22 PERCENT OF CALORIES FROM FAT.

⧗ Countdown

- *Preheat oven to 350 degrees F for bread.*
- *Sauté vegetables for mussels while you clean shells.*
- *Put potatoes on to boil.*
- *While potatoes cook, warm bread and finish mussels.*
- *Finish potatoes.*

MUSSELS IN WHITE WINE

THIS DISH is a meal in itself. Serve the mussels in a large soup bowl. Let the broth reduce while you eat the mussels and then serve it with the vegetables in the same bowls. Be sure to have plenty of fresh French bread to soak up every last drop.

2	tablespoons butter or margarine
1	medium red onion, thinly sliced (about 1 cup)
2	medium carrots, thinly sliced (about 1 cup)
2	medium stalks celery, thinly sliced (about 1 cup)
1	cup dry white wine
	Freshly ground black pepper to taste
3	pounds mussels
¼	cup chopped fresh parsley
1	French baguette

Preheat oven to 350 degrees F for bread. Melt butter in a large saucepan. Sauté onion, carrots and celery until they start to shrivel, but not brown, about 10 minutes. Add white wine and some freshly ground pepper. Add mussels and cover tightly. Bring liquid to a boil. Let boil about 3 minutes. Wine will boil up over mussels and they will open. As soon as they are open, remove from heat. Do

Shopping List

3 pounds mussels
2 carrots
3 stalks celery
2 medium red onions
1 small bunch fresh parsley
1 small head romaine lettuce
2 large ripe tomatoes
1½ pounds small red potatoes
8 pitted black olives
1 French baguette

Staples

butter or margarine
Dijon mustard
red-wine vinegar
dry white wine
canola oil
chicken stock
salt
black peppercorns

Helpful Hints

- *To clean mussels: Carefully scrub with a vegetable brush under cold water. Scrape off the beard or thin hairs along the shell. The mussels should be clean, but don't worry about barnacles. If any mussels are open, tap them gently. Discard any that do not close.*

- *Slice onion, carrots and celery in a food processor fitted with a thin slicing blade.*

not overcook, or mussels will become rubbery.

To finish and serve: With a slotted spoon, lift mussels from the pan and place in 4 large soup bowls, discarding any mussels that have not opened. Sprinkle with parsley and serve. Warm bread 5 minutes, or until crusty. Slice warm bread and place in a bread basket and serve. Meanwhile, bring mussel-cooking liquid to a boil and reduce rapidly by half. Serve broth with vegetables in separate bowls. Leave about ¼ inch of broth in the pan to avoid including any sand from mussels.

POTATOES VINAIGRETTE

THIS WARM French potato salad is a light combination of potatoes, tomatoes and black olives served over lettuce.

1½	pounds small red potatoes
1	small head romaine lettuce
8	pitted black olives
2	large tomatoes

VINAIGRETTE

2	tablespoons red-wine vinegar
1½	tablespoons Dijon mustard
⅓	cup defatted chicken stock
2	tablespoons canola oil
3	tablespoons chopped red onion
	Salt and freshly ground black pepper to taste

Scrub potatoes and place in a saucepan with enough cold water to cover. Cover and bring to a boil and cook for 20 minutes.

To microwave potatoes: Pierce them and place in 2 inches of water in a microwave-safe bowl. Microwave on high for 10 minutes. Check to see if they are done. If they are still hard in the center, microwave for 2 more minutes on high.

Meanwhile, wash and dry lettuce and tear into small pieces. Rinse olives and cut in half or quarters if they are large. Cut tomatoes in eighths.

For vinaigrette: In a medium bowl, mix vinegar and mustard together and whisk in chicken stock and oil. Add onion and salt and pepper to taste.

When potatoes are cooked, drain and dice into ½-inch cubes. Toss cubes in vinaigrette while they are still warm. Add olives and tomatoes and toss again. Spoon over lettuce.

Barbecued Balsamic Swordfish

Hot Arugula (or Watercress) Pasta

WHEN SWORDFISH IS FRESH, it only needs this simple way of cooking. Briefly marinated in a slightly sweet vinegar with cilantro and garlic, it is then quickly grilled or broiled. With the fish, I like to serve pasta and greens. The pungent, slightly bitter, slightly sweet flavor of arugula suits pasta especially well, but watercress tastes good too.

    Serves 4.

THIS MEAL CONTAINS A TOTAL OF 523 CALORIES PER SERVING WITH 26 PERCENT OF CALORIES FROM FAT.

⧗ Countdown

♦ *Place a pot of water on to boil for pasta.*
♦ *Marinate swordfish.*
♦ *While swordfish marinates, cook pasta and prepare arugula.*
♦ *Cook swordfish and finish pasta.*

BARBECUED BALSAMIC SWORDFISH

BALSAMIC VINEGAR is red-wine vinegar that has been aged in wooden barrels. It adds a rich flavor to this marinade. Time the cooking carefully. There's nothing worse than overdone swordfish; it loses its flavor and tastes like cardboard.

4	5-ounce swordfish steaks or 1 large steak, cut in quarters
¼	cup balsamic vinegar
3	tablespoons olive oil
½	cup fresh cilantro, including stems, coarsely chopped
2	medium cloves garlic, crushed through a press
	Salt and freshly ground black pepper to taste

Rinse swordfish and poke several holes at varying intervals on both sides to aid in absorbing marinade. Make marinade by mixing remaining ingredients together. Place swordfish in a small bowl or plastic bag and pour marinade over fish. Marinate for 20 minutes.

When grill is hot, drain swordfish. Place swordfish on the grates for 1 minute. Lift and make a quarter turn, leaving swordfish on same side. This will help prevent fish from sticking and will make a cross-hatch pattern. Cook for 2 more minutes. Turn over, baste fish with marinade and repeat cooking process. Alternatively, broil under broiler for 3 minutes on each side, basting fish when you turn it.

Shopping List

4 swordfish steaks (5 ounces each)
1 small bunch fresh cilantro
½ pound fettuccine
1 pound arugula or watercress
2 jalapeño peppers
2-ounce piece Parmesan cheese

Staples

garlic
balsamic vinegar
olive oil
salt
black peppercorns

Helpful Hints

♦ *Preheat a gas grill or broiler for 10 minutes or start a charcoal fire 30 minutes ahead.*

♦ *If using a grill, make sure the grates are clean and spray with vegetable-oil cooking spray so the fish will not stick.*

♦ *Garlic is used in both recipes. Crush all garlic together and divide.*

♦ *As cilantro is used only in the marinade, chop stems and leaves together; there is no need to waste time separating the leaves.*

HOT ARUGULA
(OR WATERCRESS) PASTA

Helpful Hint

♦ *Buy good-quality Parmesan and ask the market to grate it for you or cut into small pieces and chop in a food processor. It freezes well, so keep some on hand.*

ARUGULA HAS BECOME a popular addition to cold salad, and my Italian friends also like to serve it cooked in pasta.

½ **pound fettuccine**
1 **pound arugula or watercress**
2 **tablespoons olive oil**
4 **medium cloves garlic, crushed through a press**
2 **jalapeño peppers, seeded and chopped**
    Salt and freshly ground black pepper to taste
½ **cup freshly grated Parmesan cheese**

Bring a large pot of 3 to 4 quarts of water to a boil and add pasta. Cook for about 10 minutes. Drain. Meanwhile, discard thick stem ends of arugula; wash and dry leaves. Heat olive oil in a large nonstick skillet and add arugula, garlic and jalapeño peppers. Sauté for several minutes. Add drained pasta to the pan and toss. Add salt and pepper to taste and toss again. Pass Parmesan cheese at the table.

Poached Salmon With Parsley Sauce

Fresh Asparagus

Dilled Baby Red Potatoes

EVEN THOUGH we can now get these foods throughout most of the year, for me, spring dinner still means poached salmon, fresh asparagus and tiny new potatoes. If you are in a hurry, omit the asparagus or use a bottled low-fat dressing for it. *See photograph, page 170.*

Serves 4.

THIS MEAL CONTAINS A TOTAL OF 561 CALORIES PER SERVING WITH 32 PERCENT OF CALORIES FROM FAT.

⧗ Countdown
- *Make court bouillon for salmon.*
- *Start cooking potatoes.*
- *Cook asparagus and make vinaigrette.*
- *Prepare salmon and make sauce.*
- *Finish potatoes.*

POACHED SALMON

THIS IS A FAIL-SAFE method of cooking salmon: It remains moist, juicy and flavorful. The trick to poaching any fish is to slightly undercook it. It will continue to cook in its own heat for a few minutes after you have removed it from the poaching liquid. To test for doneness, insert a knife into the meat and pull the flesh away; it should be opaque, not clear.

COURT BOUILLON

5	cups water
2½	cups dry white wine
4	carrots, peeled and sliced
1	medium onion, sliced
½	lemon, sliced
12	black peppercorns
2	parsley sprigs
1–2	bay leaves
1¼	pounds salmon fillets or four 5-ounce fillets

Shopping List

1¼ pounds salmon fillets or 4 pieces
   (5 ounces each)
4 carrots
1 pound asparagus
2 pounds small red potatoes
1 small bunch fresh parsley
1 small bunch fresh dill or dried
2 lemons

Staples

onion
bay leaves
Dijon mustard
butter or margarine
nonfat mayonnaise
canola oil
dry white wine
chicken stock
salt
black peppercorns

Helpful Hints

- *If salmon is bought in 1 piece, cut it into 4 equal portions. It will be easier to poach this way.*

- *When poaching salmon, the liquid should tremble, not boil.*

For court bouillon: Place all ingredients in a skillet large enough to hold salmon. Bring to a simmer and let cook gently for 20 minutes.

Just before serving, slip salmon into liquid and let simmer gently for approximately 4 minutes, or until fish is opaque.

To serve: Carefully remove fillets from liquid with a spatula and place on individual dishes. Serve with Parsley Sauce.

PARSLEY SAUCE

LEMON JUICE and fresh parsley make this sauce refreshing and light.

- ¾ cup nonfat mayonnaise
- ½ cup chopped fresh parsley
- 3 tablespoons fresh lemon juice
  Salt and freshly ground black pepper to taste

Mix mayonnaise, parsley and lemon juice together. Add salt and pepper to taste. Serve with salmon.

DILLED BABY RED POTATOES

SMALL RED POTATOES have thin skins and don't need peeling. Cut any big ones in half so they cook in the same amount of time.

- 2 pounds small red potatoes
- 2 tablespoons butter or margarine
- 3 tablespoons defatted chicken stock
- ¼ cup chopped fresh dill or 2 tablespoons dried
  Salt and freshly ground black pepper to taste

Carefully wash potatoes. Place in a pot and add water to cover potatoes. Cover pot and bring to a boil. Boil gently for 20 to 25 minutes, or until cooked through. Heat butter and chicken stock in a saucepan or microwave and add dill.

Toss potatoes in dill butter to coat them. Add salt and freshly ground black pepper to taste.

FRESH ASPARAGUS

THE GREEKS AND ROMANS considered asparagus precious, and to protect it they built high walls around their gardens. Today, this exotic member of the lily family fits with the emphasis on light, healthy foods. This dish may be served as a first course or as a salad.

1	pound asparagus (6–8 spears per person)

VINAIGRETTE

2	tablespoons defatted chicken stock
1	tablespoon fresh lemon juice
2	teaspoons canola oil
1	teaspoon Dijon mustard
	Salt and freshly ground black pepper to taste

Snap off stems of asparagus at the point where they break easily. If stems feel tough, peel them. Thin spears do not need peeling.

To steam: Stand spears upright in an asparagus steamer or tall pot in about 4 inches of water. Cover and bring water to a boil. Steam for about 5 to 8 minutes, or until stems are tender.

To boil: Bring water to a boil in a pot that will fit spears lying on their sides. Add asparagus. Simmer gently for about 5 minutes, or until tender.

To microwave: Place asparagus in a microwavable dish that will fit spears lying on their sides. Add ¼ cup water. Cover tightly with plastic wrap and microwave on high for 2 to 3 minutes, turning once during cooking. Test for tenderness. Remember that microwaved foods continue to cook after the power is turned off. Let asparagus stand for a minute before testing.

For vinaigrette: Whisk vinaigrette ingredients together and add salt and pepper to taste.

Serve asparagus with some of the sauce poured over tips. Pass the remainder of the sauce at the table.

Helpful Hints

♦ *Look for firm, straight asparagus spears with closed, compact tips.*

♦ *Asparagus should have a rich green color and be of uniform size to ensure even cooking.*

♦ *Asparagus is easy to cook by any of three cooking methods: steaming, boiling or microwaving.*

Herbed Mahimahi

Brown Rice

Quick Stir-Fried Vegetables

Shopping List

*1¼ pounds mahimahi fillets or
  cod, haddock, bass or grouper
½ pound broccoli florets
2 carrots
½ pound snow peas
½ pound mushrooms
1 small bunch fresh basil or parsley
2-inch piece fresh ginger
1 small jar pine nuts*

Staples

*brown rice
onion
garlic
butter or margarine
nonfat plain yogurt
olive oil
peanut oil
low-sodium soy sauce
salt
black peppercorns*

WHEN I FIRST STARTED my cooking school in the late '70s, I noticed that none of my students cooked fish at home, mostly because they didn't know how. Fish is the original fast food, however, and this recipe for broiled mahimahi can be used as a model for cooking any type of white fish in minutes.

　　Serves 4.

THIS MEAL CONTAINS A TOTAL OF 566 CALORIES PER SERVING WITH 34 PERCENT OF CALORIES FROM FAT.

⧗ Countdown

◆ *Preheat broiler for fish.*
◆ *Start cooking rice.*
◆ *While rice is cooking, stir-fry vegetables.*
◆ *Broil fish.*

BROWN RICE

YOGURT GIVES THE RICE a tangy flavor, eliminating the need for butter or oil to moisten it.

> 1　**cup brown rice**
> 2　**cups water**
> 　　**Salt and freshly ground black pepper to taste**
> ½　**cup nonfat plain yogurt**

　　Place rice in a strainer and wash under cold running water. Pour 2 cups water into a saucepan and add rice. Cover and bring water to a boil. Remove cover, reduce heat to a simmer and simmer gently for 30 minutes. Test to see if rice is cooked. It should be cooked through, but not soft. If not, cook another 5 minutes. All water should be absorbed. Spoon into serving bowl and add salt and pepper to taste. Spoon yogurt over rice.

QUICK STIR-FRIED VEGETABLES

THESE STIR-FRIED VEGETABLES add a crunchy texture to the meal. You can use any combination. Slice them in the food processor to save time.

- ½ pound broccoli florets, halved if large
- 2 medium carrots, sliced (about 1 cup)
- ½ pound mushrooms, sliced (about 2 cups)
- ½ pound snow peas, trimmed
- 1 tablespoon peanut oil
- 2 medium cloves garlic, crushed through a press
- ½ medium onion, sliced (about 1 cup)
- 1 2-inch piece fresh ginger, chopped
- ½ cup low-sodium soy sauce

Wash and prepare vegetables. Place all ingredients on a plate or chopping board in the order they will be cooked. Heat oil in a wok or skillet and add garlic, onion and ginger. Toss 1 minute. Add broccoli and carrots and toss 2 more minutes. Add mushrooms and snow peas and cook 1 minute. Add soy sauce and cook 30 seconds. Spoon into a bowl and serve immediately with rice and fish.

Helpful Hints

♦ *Buy precut broccoli florets at the market to save time.*

♦ *Place all ingredients on a plate in the order they go into the wok. This saves looking at the recipe while you're stir-frying.*

♦ *A quick way to chop ginger is to peel it, cut it into chunks and press it through a garlic press with large holes.*

HERBED MAHIMAHI

MAHIMAHI IS a sweet, firm-fleshed white fish. Any firm white fish, such as cod, haddock, bass or grouper, may be used.

- 1¼ pounds mahimahi fillets
- 1 teaspoon olive oil
- 4 tablespoons butter or margarine
- 2 tablespoons pine nuts
- 3 tablespoons chopped fresh basil or parsley
- Salt and freshly ground black pepper to taste

Preheat broiler for 10 minutes. Place fish on a broiler pan and brush with olive oil. Broil for 8 minutes. To check for doneness, stick the point of a knife into the flesh. If it is opaque, it is ready. Broil 2 more minutes, if necessary.

While fish is cooking, melt butter with pine nuts. This can be done in a microwave oven on high for 1 minute. Remove fish to a serving plate and pour butter mixture over it. Sprinkle with chopped basil. Add salt and pepper to taste.

Tuscan Tuna & Bean Salad

Zucchini & Tomato Salad

Shopping List

1 medium red onion
1 head red leaf lettuce
1½ pounds zucchini
4 medium tomatoes
1 bunch fresh parsley
1 small bunch fresh oregano or
dried
Italian bread sticks or Italian or
French bread
1 can (12½ ounces) solid white
tuna, packed in water, or
2 cans (6⅛ ounces each)
2 cans cannellini, navy or Great
Northern beans (19 ounces
each)

Staples

red-wine vinegar
olive oil
salt
black peppercorns

Helpful Hints

♦ *Use a good-quality, solid white*
tuna packed in water.

♦ *Be sure your dried herbs are*
relatively new. If they have been
sitting in your spice rack for 6
months or more, it's time to buy
new bottles.

I LIKE TO SERVE this meal when we have other families over for lunch or dinner. It's a tasty alternative to tuna salad and appeals to all age groups. For an accompanying salad, lightly cooked zucchini is tossed with fresh tomatoes and vinaigrette.

Serves 4.

THIS MEAL CONTAINS A TOTAL OF 825 CALORIES PER SERVING WITH 26 PERCENT OF CALORIES FROM FAT.

⧗ Countdown

♦ *Preheat oven to 350 degrees F if serving bread.*
♦ *Put water for zucchini on to boil.*
♦ *Make tuna salad.*
♦ *Warm bread.*
♦ *Make zucchini salad.*

TUSCAN TUNA & BEAN SALAD

TUNA AND CANNELLINI BEANS are Italian staples and combine in a delicious salad for warm evenings. Some crusty bread and cool Frascati or Pinot Grigio wine are all I need to feel transported to Tuscany.

2	19-ounce cans small white beans: cannellini, navy or Great Northern
½	medium red onion, diced (about 1 cup)
1	12½-ounce can or two 6⅛-ounce cans water-packed solid white tuna
1	cup chopped fresh parsley, *divided*
¼	cup olive oil
1	tablespoon red-wine vinegar
	Salt and freshly ground black pepper to taste
1	head red leaf lettuce
	Italian bread sticks or 8 slices Italian or French bread

Preheat oven to 350 degrees F, if serving bread. Drain and rinse beans. Place in a serving bowl and add onion. Drain tuna and break into large flakes. Add to beans. Add ½ cup parsley, oil, vinegar and a little pepper and gently toss. Taste. Add salt, more vinegar or pepper if needed. Warm bread in oven for about 5 minutes.

Wash and dry lettuce leaves. Arrange on a serving platter and spoon salad over leaves. Sprinkle with remaining parsley. Fill a bread basket with bread sticks or warm bread.

ZUCCHINI & TOMATO SALAD

I LOVE TO SEE fresh tomatoes and zucchini in the markets when they're in season, and what better way to serve them than in a cool, refreshing salad.

1½	**pounds zucchini**
4	**ripe medium tomatoes, cubed (about 3 cups)**
2	**tablespoons olive oil**
3	**tablespoons chopped fresh oregano or 1 tablespoon dried**
3	**tablespoons chopped fresh parsley**
	Salt and freshly ground black pepper to taste

Wash and trim zucchini and cut into julienne strips about ¼ inch thick and 2 inches long. Place zucchini in a pot of boiling salted water. As soon as water returns to boil, drain and refresh zucchini under cold water to stop cooking and set color. Toss zucchini and tomatoes in oil and sprinkle with oregano and parsley. If using dried oregano, chop it with fresh parsley. Add salt and pepper to taste and toss again.

Helpful Hints

♦ *If you do not have a julienne blade for your food processor, slice the zucchini with a thick slicing blade or by hand with a knife.*

♦ *Add a little salt to the water after it starts to boil. Salted water takes longer to boil.*

♦ *If you can't find fresh oregano, chop some fresh parsley with dried oregano. The juices from the parsley will help release the flavor of the dried herb.*

Honey-Glazed Mahimahi

Parsley Potatoes

Sautéed August Vegetables

Shopping List

*1½ pounds mahimahi fillets or
  cod, haddock, bass or grouper*
2 red bell peppers
2 green bell peppers
1½ pounds zucchini
1 medium red onion
2 large tomatoes
1 pound baby red potatoes
1 bunch fresh parsley
1-inch piece fresh ginger
*1 small loaf coarse-grained
  country bread*

Staples

lemon
garlic
honey
sherry-wine vinegar
butter or margarine
olive oil
salt
black peppercorns

IN LATE AUGUST, when there's an abundance of zucchini, tomatoes and peppers in the farmer's markets and nearly everyone with a backyard garden has an oversupply, this sauté offers a quick and easy way to enjoy the season's abundance. The sautéed fish takes on a gingery flavor with sweet overtones. *See photograph, page 173.*

   Serves 4.

THIS MEAL CONTAINS A TOTAL OF 642 CALORIES PER SERVING WITH 18 PERCENT OF CALORIES FROM FAT.

Countdown
- *Start cooking potatoes.*
- *Marinate fish.*
- *Cook vegetables.*
- *While vegetables cook, make fish.*
- *Finish potatoes.*

PARSLEY POTATOES

IF YOU CAN'T FIND baby red potatoes, use larger ones and cut them into quarters.

   1   **pound baby red potatoes**
   1   **tablespoon butter or margarine**
   1   **cup chopped fresh parsley**
       Salt and freshly ground black pepper to taste

   Wash potatoes. Place in a pot of cold water. Cover and bring to a boil. Boil gently for 20 to 25 minutes, or until cooked through. Melt butter in a saucepan or in the microwave and add parsley. Toss potatoes in parsley butter to coat them. Add salt and freshly ground black pepper to taste.

HONEY-GLAZED MAHIMAHI

ANY FIRM, white fish may be used. The marinade, intensified through boiling, becomes the basis for a light sauce.

- 2 **tablespoons honey**
- 2 **tablespoons sherry-wine vinegar**
- 2 **teaspoons chopped fresh ginger**
- 2 **medium cloves garlic, crushed through a press**
- 1½ **pounds fresh mahimahi fillets**
- 1 **tablespoon olive oil**
  Salt and freshly ground black pepper to taste
- 1 **small loaf coarse-grained country bread**

Mix honey, vinegar, ginger and garlic together in a bowl large enough to hold fish. Rinse fish under cold water and pat dry with a paper towel. Place in honey mixture and let marinate for 20 minutes.

Heat oil in a nonstick skillet large enough to hold fish in one layer. Remove fish from the marinade, reserving it for later use. When oil is hot, add fish. Sauté for about 5 minutes and turn. Salt and pepper the cooked side. Sauté another 5 minutes. The fish is done when it is no longer translucent in the center. Remove fish to a serving dish or to individual plates and cover with foil to keep warm. Pour marinade into the pan, scraping up any browned bits as you do. Raise the heat and reduce sauce until it is thick and syrupy, about 2 to 3 minutes. Pour glaze over mahimahi. Slice bread and serve with fish and vegetables.

SAUTÉED AUGUST VEGETABLES

CHOOSE FIRM, fresh vegetables, which need little cooking to bring out their flavor.

- 1 **tablespoon olive oil,** *divided*
- 2 **medium cloves garlic, crushed through a press**
- 1½ **pounds zucchini, cut into 1-inch pieces**
- 2 **medium red bell peppers, cut into 1-inch pieces**
- 2 **medium green bell peppers, cut into 1-inch pieces**
- 1 **medium red onion, sliced**
- 2 **tomatoes, cut into eighths**
- 1 **tablespoon fresh lemon juice**
  Salt and freshly ground black pepper to taste

Heat ½ tablespoon olive oil in a large nonstick skillet. Add garlic and sauté 1 minute. Add vegetables and sauté over medium-high heat for 20 minutes, stirring occasionally. The vegetables should be soft but still crunchy. In a serving bowl, mix remaining ½ tablespoon olive oil with lemon juice and add salt and pepper. Toss sautéed vegetables in the bowl.

Helpful Hints

♦ *To save time in chopping the ginger, peel the skin, cut the ginger into small pieces and place in a garlic press with large holes. Hold the ginger over the marinade as you press to catch all the juice.*

♦ *You can use cod, haddock, bass or grouper in place of mahimahi.*

♦ *A fish that is 1 inch thick should take about 10 minutes to cook. If your fish is thicker, cook it a little longer, or if thinner, cook it a shorter time.*

Swordfish With Pecan-Parsley Pesto

Tomato-Cilantro Couscous

Shopping List

4 swordfish steaks (5 ounces each)
  or halibut, tuna or flounder
3 limes
1 jalapeño pepper
1¼ pounds spinach
1 ripe tomato
1 bunch flat-leaf parsley
1 small bunch fresh cilantro
1 small package pecans (2 ounces)
1 can tomato juice (6 ounces)
1 package precooked couscous
  (10 ounces)

Staples

garlic
olive oil
chicken stock
salt
black peppercorns

Helpful Hints

♦ *Prewashed spinach is available in some markets.*

♦ *Frozen leaf spinach can be used instead of fresh. This saves the time of washing the spinach, though it isn't quite as flavorful. Buy two 10-ounce boxes.*

♦ *Halibut, tuna or flounder can be used instead of swordfish. Allow 10 minutes cooking time for each inch of thickness.*

IN THIS COLORFUL, tempting dinner, baked swordfish on spinach is paired with one of the fastest pasta dishes: couscous, which has been fluffed with tomato juice, tomatoes and fresh cilantro. I created this meal after a visit to Philadelphia's Rittenhouse Hotel, whose restaurant is known for its light, bistro-style menu.
  Serves 4.
THIS MEAL CONTAINS A TOTAL OF 500 CALORIES PER SERVING WITH 22 PERCENT OF CALORIES FROM FAT.

Countdown

♦ *Preheat oven to 375 degrees F for fish.*
♦ *Make pesto.*
♦ *Make couscous.*
♦ *Make swordfish.*
♦ *Steam spinach.*

SWORDFISH WITH PECAN-PARSLEY PESTO

PESTO SAUCE makes a crunchy topping for the swordfish, which is served on a soft bed of spinach.

PESTO

4	tablespoons fresh lime juice, *divided*
	Grated rind from 2 limes
1	cup chopped flat-leaf parsley
4	medium cloves garlic, crushed through a press
2	tablespoons pecans
2	tablespoons water
1	medium jalapeño pepper, seeded and chopped
4	5-ounce swordfish steaks
	Salt and freshly ground black pepper to taste
1¼	pounds spinach
2	teaspoons olive oil

Preheat oven to 375 degrees F. Set aside 1 teaspoon lime juice for spinach.
For pesto: Combine remaining lime juice, rind, parsley, garlic, pecans, water

and jalapeño in a food processor. Blend to a smooth paste, adding a little additional water if too dry.

Line a baking tray with foil. Season swordfish with salt and pepper. Preheat an iron or nonstick skillet and sear fish on high heat on top of the stove for 30 seconds on each side. Place on baking tray and spread pesto on top. Bake 10 minutes per inch of thickness.

Meanwhile, remove large stems of spinach and wash. Place spinach in a steaming basket over ½ inch boiling water. Steam 5 minutes. Place in a bowl and mix in reserved 1 teaspoon lime juice and olive oil. Add salt and pepper to taste. Divide among 4 plates, place fish on top and serve.

TOMATO-CILANTRO COUSCOUS

Couscous is another form of pasta, which is made by moistening hard durum wheat and rolling it in flour to form tiny pellets. Precooked couscous takes only minutes to cook.

Helpful Hint

♦ *Make sure that the couscous package is marked "precooked"; check the ingredient label.*

¾	cup tomato juice
¾	cup defatted chicken stock
1	cup precooked couscous
1	cup diced ripe tomato
½	cup chopped fresh cilantro
2	teaspoons olive oil
	Salt and freshly ground black pepper to taste

Combine tomato juice and chicken stock in a saucepan. Bring to a boil. Place couscous in a serving bowl. Pour boiling liquid over couscous and stir with a fork. Let stand 6 minutes. Add tomato, cilantro and oil and fluff with a fork to separate grains. Add salt and pepper to taste.

Vietnamese Sweet & Sour Fish

Stir-Fried Noodles & Green Beans

Shopping List

1½ pounds mahimahi fillets or
   flounder, cod or grouper
2 scallions
2 carrots
1 daikon (white radish) or 8
   regular radishes
1 tomato
½ pound fresh green beans
¾ pound fresh Chinese egg noodles
1 bottle fish sauce (optional)

Staples

garlic
onion
sugar
cornstarch
low-sodium soy sauce
white vinegar
peanut oil
salt
black peppercorns

Helpful Hints

♦ *Fish sauce can be found in Asian or other specialty stores.*

♦ *White radish, or daikon, is common in many supermarkets. It looks something like a large, thick, white carrot and can be eaten raw or cooked. Peel it like a carrot. Substitute regular radishes in this recipe if daikon is unavailable. You will need 8 large ones.*

♦ *Keep any unused portion of white radish tightly wrapped in plastic wrap in the refrigerator. It will keep 3 or 4 days this way.*

♦ *Any fish such as flounder, cod or grouper may be used.*

EVER SINCE I was introduced to it, Vietnamese cooking has been one of my favorites. This simple stir-fried fish relies on herbs and sauces for its delicate flavor. *See photograph, page 103.*

   Serves 4.

THIS MEAL CONTAINS A TOTAL OF 518 CALORIES PER SERVING WITH 14 PERCENT OF CALORIES FROM FAT.

⧗ Countdown

♦ *Put water for noodles on to boil.*
♦ *Cut vegetables for fish.*
♦ *Boil noodles and drain.*
♦ *Make fish.*
♦ *Stir-fry noodles.*

VIETNAMESE SWEET & SOUR FISH

NUOC MAM, or fish sauce, is used in Thai and Philippine cooking as well as in Vietnamese. Made from fresh anchovies that are fermented, it is used in these countries in much the same way that we use salt. It adds depth of flavor, but it can be omitted if difficult to obtain.

SAUCE

¼	cup sugar
¼	cup cornstarch
1	cup water
2	tablespoons low-sodium soy sauce
2	tablespoons white vinegar
4	teaspoons fish sauce (*nuoc mam*)

FISH & VEGETABLES

1½	pounds mahimahi fillets
4	teaspoons peanut oil
½	medium onion, thinly sliced (about 1 cup)
2	medium cloves garlic, crushed through a press
2	scallions, thinly sliced
2	medium carrots, peeled and shaved into strips with a peeler (about 1 cup)
1	medium white radish, peeled and shaved into strips with a peeler (about 1 cup)
1	medium tomato, cut into 6 wedges

For sauce: In a small bowl, mix all ingredients together.

For fish and vegetables: Rinse fish and pat dry. Heat oil in a wok or skillet over medium-high heat. Add fish and sauté about 5 minutes, turning once during the cooking. Remove from wok and place on a serving dish. Cover with foil to keep warm. Turn up the heat and add onion. Stir-fry 1 minute. Add garlic and cook a few seconds. Add remaining vegetables. Stir-fry another minute. Stir sauce and add to vegetables. Stir-fry on high heat for 2 minutes. Sauce will thicken and turn shiny. Divide fish in 4 portions and spoon vegetables and sauce over the top, leaving about half the sauce in the wok for stir-frying the noodles.

STIR-FRIED NOODLES & GREEN BEANS

HAVE EVERYTHING READY to stir-fry before you start cooking. As soon as the fish and sauce are removed from the wok, add the noodles. They will pick up any remaining flavors in the pan.

¾   pound fresh Chinese egg noodles
½   pound fresh green beans, cut into 1-inch lengths (about 2 cups)
     Salt and freshly ground black pepper to taste

Bring a pot with 3 to 4 quarts of water to a boil and add noodles and beans. After water returns to a boil, boil for 2 minutes. Drain. As soon as sweet-and-sour sauce has been spooned over fish, add noodles and beans to the wok. Stir-fry for 3 to 4 minutes. Add salt and pepper to taste.

Helpful Hints

♦ *Chinese egg noodles can be found in the refrigerated case in the produce department of most markets.*

♦ *Egg noodles should be well drained before stir-frying. Put a pot of water on to boil first and cook the noodles as soon as the water is ready. Drain while you prepare the fish.*

Rosemary Baked Snapper

Basil Spaghetti

Gratinéed Zucchini

ONE OF MY COLLEAGUES at the *Miami Herald* complained one day that he didn't know what to do with the beautiful whole fish he saw in the markets. I created this dish for him. Sweet rosemary perfumes the fish, while the herbs in the spaghetti and the mild, cheesy flavor of the baked zucchini continue the summery Mediterranean theme.

   Serves 4.

THIS MEAL CONTAINS A TOTAL OF 529 CALORIES PER SERVING WITH 30 PERCENT OF CALORIES FROM FAT.

Countdown

♦ *Preheat oven to 350 degrees F for zucchini and for fish, if you plan to bake it. If grilling fish, light a charcoal grill 30 minutes before needed, or start a gas grill 10 minutes before use.*

♦ *Put water for pasta on to boil.*

♦ *Prepare fish.*

♦ *While fish is cooking, make zucchini and cook pasta.*

♦ *While pasta and zucchini cook, make sauce for fish.*

ROSEMARY BAKED SNAPPER

WIDELY GROWN in the Mediterranean region, rosemary is often used in Italian cooking. When it is fresh and added sparingly, it provides a fragrant flavor for fish and meat. In this recipe, it is stuffed into the cavity of the fish.

1	3-pound red snapper or yellowtail
	Vegetable-oil cooking spray
8	sprigs fresh rosemary or 2 tablespoons dried

SAUCE

½	cup chopped fresh parsley
2	tablespoons olive oil
1	teaspoon minced garlic
2	large ripe tomatoes, quartered, or 2 cups canned whole tomatoes, drained and chopped
2	tablespoons chopped fresh oregano or 2 teaspoons dried
1	teaspoon ground cayenne
1	tablespoon red-wine vinegar

Shopping List

3-pound red snapper, yellowtail, flounder or sole
2 large ripe tomatoes or 1 can (19 ounces)
1½ pounds zucchini
1 small bunch fresh rosemary or dried
1 small bunch fresh parsley
1 small bunch fresh basil
1 small bunch fresh oregano or dried
1-ounce piece Parmesan cheese
½ pound spaghetti

Staples

garlic
ground cayenne
butter or margarine
red-wine vinegar
olive oil
vegetable-oil cooking spray
salt
black peppercorns

Helpful Hints

♦ *When you buy your fish, ask for it cleaned, but with the head and tail left on.*

♦ *Any nonoily fish such as flounder or sole can be used.*

♦ *The sauce is made separately and can be used on any barbecued, broiled or baked fish.*

Salt and freshly ground black pepper to taste

Preheat oven to 350 degrees F or start the barbecue. Make sure fish has been thoroughly cleaned. Rinse inside and outside. Spray skin with vegetable-oil cooking spray and fill the cavity with rosemary. Spray a shallow baking dish, if using the oven. Place fish in the dish and bake for 20 minutes. If using a barbecue, make sure the grates are clean and place fish on the grates. If you have a fish rack, it will be much easier to turn and remove fish. Grill 10 minutes per side. Check to see that fish is cooked through. If it is a thick fish, it may need 5 more minutes.

For sauce: Blend parsley, oil and garlic together in a food processor. Add tomatoes, oregano, cayenne and vinegar and process to puree the mixture. Add salt to taste. If you do not have a food processor, chop all ingredients finely and mix them together. Transfer mixture to a saucepan and heat to warm through. Taste for seasoning. Add salt and pepper as needed.

GRATINÉED ZUCCHINI

THE ZUCCHINI can be baked in the same oven as the fish. Parboiling it shortens the baking time.

1½	**pounds zucchini**
1	**tablespoon butter or margarine**
¼	**cup freshly grated Parmesan cheese**
	Salt and freshly ground black pepper to taste

Preheat oven to 350 degrees F. Carefully wash zucchini and trim ends. Bring a medium-size pot with 1 to 2 quarts of water to a boil and add zucchini. Boil 5 minutes. Drain and let cool several minutes. Meanwhile, butter a shallow ovenproof dish. Cut zucchini into ¼-inch slices. Line the bottom of the dish with one layer of zucchini slices. Sprinkle with a little Parmesan cheese and dot with some butter. Sprinkle with a little salt and pepper. Cover with another layer of zucchini slices and repeat the process again. Continue in this manner until all zucchini is used, making sure the top layer is cheese. Bake zucchini for 15 minutes, or until cheese has melted.

Helpful Hints

♦ *Buy firm, deep green zucchini. Soft or old ones are bitter and will spoil the dish.*

♦ *Good Parmesan is important. If you can't find any, use a good-quality hard cheese such as Cheddar or gruyère.*

BASIL SPAGHETTI

SERVE THE FISH over a bed of spaghetti, tossed with some olive oil, fresh basil, salt and pepper. The sauce from the fish will further flavor the pasta.

½   **pound spaghetti**
2   **tablespoons olive oil**
1   **bunch fresh basil, chopped**
     Salt and freshly ground black pepper to taste

Bring a large pot with 3 to 4 quarts of water to a boil. Add spaghetti. Boil about 10 minutes. It should be just cooked through, but not too soft. Drain. Toss with olive oil and basil. Add salt and pepper to taste. Serve on individual plates. Place fish on top and spoon sauce over.

Fragrant Fish Parcels

Pearl Barley

THIS IS A WONDERFUL and easy way to cook fish. Sealed in the package with wine and a bouquet of vegetables and herbs, it steams in its own juices. These parcels can be served directly at the table or opened in the kitchen, removed from the paper and served on individual plates. I prefer to have each person open his or her own so that the first whiff can be savored as the parcel is opened. *See photograph, page 176.*

Serves 4.

THIS MEAL CONTAINS A TOTAL OF 562 CALORIES PER SERVING WITH 30 PERCENT OF CALORIES FROM FAT.

⧗ Countdown
- *Preheat oven to 450 degrees F for fish.*
- *Put water for barley on to boil.*
- *Make fish.*
- *Finish barley.*

FRAGRANT FISH PARCELS

LOUIS XIV so loved fresh fish that he had it rushed from Boulogne and Dieppe to Versailles by relay teams so he could enjoy it the day after it was caught. Luckily, we don't have to resort to such lengths. This method of cooking fish takes advantage of freshness and lends itself to infinite variations: in the fish, in the vegetables, in the herbs and in the liquids chosen.

2	tablespoons butter or margarine, *divided*
2	medium carrots, cut in julienne slices (about 1 cup)
¼	medium onion, sliced (about ½ cup)
10	medium mushrooms, thinly sliced
4	sprigs fresh basil or cilantro, leaves chopped
4	7-ounce white fish fillets
¼	cup defatted chicken stock
¼	cup dry white wine
	Salt and freshly ground black pepper to taste
	Vegetable-oil cooking spray

Preheat oven to 450 degrees F. Cut 4 circles of aluminum foil or parchment paper about 10 inches in diameter. Place 1 tablespoon butter in a small nonstick skillet and add carrots and onion. Cover and cook gently for 5 minutes. Add mushrooms and cook, covered, for 3 more minutes. Add basil to the pan and

Shopping List

4 fish fillets (7 ounces each): yellowtail, sole, flounder or snapper
2 medium carrots
¼ pound mushrooms
1 small bunch fresh basil, cilantro, tarragon or dill
1 package quick-cooking barley (6 ounces)

Staples

onion
butter or margarine
dry white wine
chicken stock
vegetable-oil cooking spray
salt
black peppercorns
aluminum foil or parchment paper

Helpful Hints

- *Fish parcels need to bake in a very hot oven. Be sure to preheat your oven at least 15 minutes before it is needed.*

- *Any mild, flaky white fish will do: yellowtail, sole, flounder or snapper.*

- *Fresh tarragon or dill can also be used if basil and cilantro are unavailable.*

- *Cut vegetables in a food processor fitted with a julienne blade or if you don't have one, use a thick slicing blade or slice them by hand with a knife.*

cook, covered, another 2 minutes. Spoon vegetables onto the center of each aluminum foil circle. Place 1 fish fillet on top of vegetables. Put a piece of remaining 1 tablespoon butter on each fillet. Add 1 tablespoon stock and 1 tablespoon wine to each parcel. Sprinkle with a little salt and black pepper. Close the parcels and seal the edges. If using foil, bend the edges over and press together. If using parchment paper, fold the edges together and then fold them around the semicircle, overlapping the previous fold as you go. Spray a baking tray with vegetable-oil cooking spray and place the parcels on the tray. Bake 5 minutes. The fish is done when it is no longer translucent. If using a larger fish, cook 3 to 5 minutes longer.

To serve: Place each parcel on an individual plate along with cooked barley and let each person open it at the table. Or, lift fish and vegetables onto each plate and pour the sauce over.

PEARL BARLEY

Helpful Hint

♦ *Look for quick-cooking pearl barley, which cooks in half the time of regular. If you can't find it, use regular barley, which will take about 30 to 35 minutes to cook.*

BARLEY IS USED MOSTLY for stews and soups, but it is very good boiled, seasoned and served as an alternative to rice. Its mild, nutty flavor complements the fish and vegetables beautifully.

3   cups water
1   cup quick-cooking pearl barley
4   tablespoons butter or margarine
    Salt and freshly ground pepper to taste

Put water on to boil. Add barley and bring to a boil. Lower heat, cover and simmer for 10 to 12 minutes, or until soft. Drain. Mix in butter, salt and pepper. Serve with fish.

Grilled Fish With Pineapple Salsa

Poblano Rice

SALSA BRINGS A FRESH, crisp, tangy touch to fish without a lot of fat. No wonder it has become America's favorite condiment, outselling ketchup.

Serves 4.

THIS MEAL CONTAINS A TOTAL OF 571 CALORIES PER SERVING WITH 15 PERCENT OF CALORIES FROM FAT.

⌛ Countdown

- *Preheat a charcoal fire 30 minutes before needed, or a gas grill for 10 minutes, or preheat oven to 450 degrees F for fish.*
- *Marinate fish.*
- *Cook rice.*
- *Make fish and salsa.*

POBLANO RICE

POBLANO PEPPERS are cone-shaped, medium-hot peppers. They are sometimes called ancho peppers. If you have trouble finding them, substitute jalapeño peppers, using half the amount called for.

1	cup long-grain white rice
1	tablespoon olive oil
½	medium red onion, diced (about 1 cup)
¼	cup water
2	medium poblano peppers, seeded and chopped (about ½ cup) or 4 medium jalapeño peppers, seeded and chopped (about ¼ cup)
1	medium red bell pepper, diced (about 1 cup)
½	cup low-fat sour cream
	Salt and freshly ground black pepper to taste
¼	cup freshly grated Parmesan cheese

Rinse rice and place in a pot with 3 to 4 quarts of water. Bring to a boil and cook, uncovered about 10 minutes. Drain. Toss with olive oil. While rice cooks, cook onion in a nonstick saucepan with water until transparent, about 10 minutes. Add all peppers and sauté another 2 to 3 minutes. Toss peppers and sour cream with rice. Add salt and pepper to taste. Sprinkle Parmesan on top.

Shopping List

1¼ pounds white fish or 4 fillets (5 ounces each): yellowtail, red snapper or sole
½ ripe pineapple
1 medium tomato
1 bunch fresh cilantro
1 small red onion
1 jalapeño pepper
2 limes
2 poblano peppers or 4 jalapeño peppers
1 red bell pepper
1 container low-fat sour cream (8 ounces)
1-ounce piece Parmesan cheese

Staples

onion
garlic
ground cumin
long-grain white rice
sugar
low-sodium soy sauce
olive oil
canola oil
salt
black peppercorns

Helpful Hint

- *Onion is used in both salsa and rice recipes. Chop all the onion at one time in a food processor and divide as needed.*

GRILLED FISH
WITH PINEAPPLE SALSA

THIS REFRESHING and bright pineapple salsa gets its distinctive taste from cumin.

MARINADE

2	tablespoons low-sodium soy sauce
1	tablespoon canola oil
1	tablespoon fresh lime juice
½	medium onion, diced (about 1 cup)
2	medium cloves garlic, crushed through a press
4	5-ounce white fish fillets or 1¼ pounds fish, cut into 4 portions
6	sprigs fresh cilantro

SALSA

2	cups fresh pineapple, diced
1	ripe medium tomato, diced
½	cup chopped fresh cilantro
2	tablespoons chopped red onion
1	medium jalapeño pepper, seeded and chopped
½	tablespoon sugar
1	teaspoon ground cumin
	Salt and freshly ground black pepper to taste

Light grill or preheat oven to 450 degrees F.

For marinade: Mix soy sauce, oil, lime juice, onion and garlic together. Place fish in marinade for 15 minutes.

Cut four 10-inch-square pieces of aluminum foil. Remove fish from marinade, saving liquid. Place each portion of fish on a piece of aluminum foil and spoon any remaining marinade over fish. Place a sprig of cilantro on each piece. Bring the edges together, seal each packet and place on the grill or a baking tray in the oven. For a 1-inch fillet, cook 10 minutes, or until opaque. Turn fish packet over once or twice during the cooking. Check fish by opening the foil and sticking the point of a knife into meat. Place a packet on each plate and let the guests open their own or remove fish from the packet and serve on individual plates.

For salsa: Mix all ingredients together. Taste for seasoning and add more sugar, cumin, salt or pepper as needed. Place in a serving dish and serve with fish.

Portuguese Fish

Potato-Garlic Sauté

IF YOU WALK along the beach in Portugal at sunset, you're likely to see fishing boats pulling in with their catch. Fresh fish is an important part of their cuisine. This Portuguese-style meal features baked fish in a spicy red sauce and a stovetop potato dish.

Serves 4.

THIS MEAL CONTAINS A TOTAL OF 560 CALORIES PER SERVING WITH 19 PERCENT OF CALORIES FROM FAT.

⧗ Countdown

♦ *Preheat oven to 375 degrees F for fish.*
♦ *Make fish.*
♦ *Make potatoes.*

PORTUGUESE FISH

THE PORTUGUESE usually cook their fish whole, but to speed up the cooking time, I use fish fillets instead.

SAUCE

2	teaspoons olive oil
1	medium onion, sliced (about 2 cups)
4	medium cloves garlic, crushed through a press (about 2 teaspoons)
1	medium jalapeño pepper, seeded and chopped
4	large ripe tomatoes, cut in sixths
⅓	cup dry red wine
2	bay leaves
	Salt and freshly ground black pepper to taste

FISH

2	teaspoons olive oil
1½	pounds fish fillets
	Salt and freshly ground black pepper to taste

Preheat oven to 375 degrees F.

For sauce: Heat oil in nonstick skillet and add onion. Sauté until transparent, about 5 minutes. Add garlic and jalapeño and sauté another minute. Add tomatoes, wine and bay leaves. Cover and gently simmer for about 10 minutes, stirring occasionally to keep sauce from sticking to the bottom of the pan. Uncover and simmer 5 minutes. Add salt and pepper as necessary.

Shopping List

1½ pounds fish fillets: yellowtail, grouper or flounder
2 jalapeño peppers
4 large ripe tomatoes
2 pounds red potatoes

Staples

onions
garlic
bay leaves
olive oil
cider vinegar
chicken stock
dry red wine
salt
black peppercorns

Helpful Hints

♦ *Use yellowtail, grouper or flounder or any other nonoily white fish.*

♦ *Crushed garlic is used in both recipes. Prepare at one time and divide in half.*

♦ *Slice onion in a food processor to save time.*

For fish: Lightly oil the inside of an ovenproof dish large enough to hold fish in one layer. Place fish in the dish and sprinkle with salt and pepper. Spoon sauce over fish and cover with foil. Place in oven and bake for 20 minutes. Remove bay leaves before serving.

POTATO-GARLIC SAUTÉ

POTATOES FLAVORED with vinegar and garlic are a popular Portuguese dish.

- 2 **pounds red potatoes**
- 2 **cups defatted chicken stock**
- ¼ **cup cider vinegar**
- 4 **medium cloves garlic, crushed through a press**
- 2 **tablespoons olive oil**
  Salt and freshly ground black pepper to taste

Wash and thinly slice potatoes. This can be done in a food processor fitted with a slicing blade. Place in a large skillet with chicken stock. Lower heat slightly and simmer 10 minutes, or until potatoes are soft. Remove cover and add vinegar and garlic. Simmer, uncovered, 5 minutes. Remove potatoes to serving bowl with a slotted spoon, leaving behind liquid. Add oil, salt and pepper and toss to mix thoroughly.

Baked Stuffed Snapper

Glazed Carrots

Lemon-Butter Potatoes

THE SNAPPER IS STUFFED with Parmesan cheese and a mixture of chopped onions and mushrooms, traditionally known as duxelles. Once the fish is in the oven, you can forget about it and go on to make the rest of the meal.

Serves 4.

THIS MEAL CONTAINS A TOTAL OF 580 CALORIES PER SERVING WITH 16 PERCENT OF CALORIES FROM FAT.

⧗ **Countdown**
- *Preheat oven to 400 degrees F for fish.*
- *Prepare fish and make stuffing.*
- *Cook carrots.*
- *Stuff and bake fish.*
- *Cook potatoes.*

BAKED STUFFED SNAPPER

THERE ARE ABOUT 250 species of snapper, 15 of which can be found in the waters of the Atlantic Ocean from North Carolina to the Gulf of Mexico off Florida. I prefer to buy whole fish rather than fillets. You can tell if it is really fresh by seeing that the eyes are bright and clear, the gills still red, and the flesh firm to the touch.

	Vegetable-oil cooking spray
¼	cup defatted chicken stock
1	medium onion, sliced (about 2 cups)
2	medium cloves garlic, crushed through a press
½	pound mushrooms, sliced (about 2 cups)
½	cup freshly grated Parmesan cheese
1	cup chopped fresh parsley
	Salt and freshly ground black pepper to taste
2	2¼-pound whole snappers or 4 6-ounce snapper fillets

Preheat oven to 400 degrees F. Line a baking tray with foil and spray it with vegetable-oil cooking spray. Heat chicken stock in a nonstick skillet and sauté onion gently, without browning, for about 5 minutes. Add garlic and sauté 1 minute. Add mushrooms and sauté 2 more minutes. Mix in cheese and parsley

Shopping List

2 whole snappers (2¼ pounds each)
  or 4 snapper fillets
  (6 ounces each)
½ pound mushrooms
6 carrots or 1 pound baby carrots
2 pounds small red potatoes
1 small bunch fresh parsley
1 small bunch fresh chives or
  scallions
2-ounce piece Parmesan cheese

Staples

lemon
onion
garlic
nutmeg
sugar
butter or margarine
vegetable-oil cooking spray
chicken stock
salt
black peppercorns

Helpful Hints

- *Any nonoily whole fish can be used for this recipe.*

- *Ask your fish market to remove bones from fish while leaving on the head and tail. It will take them only a few minutes to do this and will make stuffing and serving the fish easy.*

- *If you prefer, fillets can be used.*

and add salt and pepper to taste. Rinse fish and pat dry. Salt and pepper the inside of the fish. Spoon mushroom stuffing into fish pocket. Fasten with wooden toothpicks and place fish on the baking tray. If using fillets, place 2 fillets, skin-side down, on the baking tray and spoon stuffing onto them. Place 2 other fillets, skin-side up, over stuffing. Tie together with kitchen string. Place in oven for 25 minutes, or until the fish flesh is no longer translucent and begins to flake.

To serve: If using whole snappers, place on a serving platter and bring them to the table whole. To slice whole fish into 2 center-cut portions, make one slice in the center all the way through and then one slice in front of the head and another in front of the tail. Repeat with the other fish. If using fillets, make one slice through both fillets in the center and serve on individual plates.

GLAZED CARROTS

GLAZING CARROTS brings out their natural sweetness. Peeled baby carrots are now available in the markets. Use these and slice them in a food processor.

> 6 **medium carrots, sliced (about 3 cups) or 1 pound baby carrots**
> 2 **teaspoons sugar**
> 2 **teaspoons butter or margarine**

Place carrots in a medium-size saucepan. Cover with water. Add sugar and butter. Boil until all of the liquid has evaporated and carrots are glazed, about 25 minutes.

LEMON-BUTTER POTATOES

Helpful Hint

♦ *Melt butter in a microwave-safe serving bowl and add the cooked potatoes to the bowl. This will save washing an extra pot.*

SMALL RED POTATOES have thin skins so you only need to wash them lightly with a vegetable brush.

> 2 **pounds small red potatoes**
> 2 **tablespoons butter or margarine**
> 2 **tablespoons fresh lemon juice**
> 2 **tablespoons chopped fresh chives or scallions**
> ¼ **teaspoon ground nutmeg**
>   **Salt and freshly ground black pepper to taste**

Wash potatoes, cut into 1-inch chunks and place in a pot of cold water to cover. Cover and bring to a boil. Boil until tender, about 20 minutes. Melt butter in a stainless-steel or enamel pan or in the microwave on high for 30 seconds. Add lemon juice, chives, nutmeg, salt and pepper. Warm without boiling. When potatoes are done, place in a serving bowl and pour lemon-butter sauce over them.

Salmon With Steamed Vegetables

Dilled Potatoes

SALMON FROM CHILE, the Pacific Northwest or Norway is readily available year-round. Cooking the salmon in foil brings out its flavor, and the tomatillos give this otherwise traditional meal a Southwestern accent.

Serves 4.

THIS MEAL CONTAINS A TOTAL OF 583 CALORIES PER SERVING WITH 31 PERCENT OF CALORIES FROM FAT.

⧖ Countdown
- *Preheat oven to 450 degrees F for salmon.*
- *Make potatoes.*
- *While potatoes are boiling, make fish.*

DILLED POTATOES

I LIKE TO USE red potatoes for boiling. They don't absorb a lot of the water and are low in starch, with a slightly waxy texture. They hold their shape when boiled or sautéed.

2	pounds red potatoes, washed and cut into 1-inch cubes
½	cup chopped fresh dill or 2 tablespoons dried
2	tablespoons butter or margarine
	Salt and freshly ground black pepper to taste

Place potatoes in a saucepan and cover with cold water. Cover the pan and bring the water to a boil. Boil for 20 minutes, or until potatoes are cooked through. Drain and toss with dill and butter. Add salt and pepper to taste.

SALMON WITH STEAMED VEGETABLES

TOMATILLOS, also known as husk tomatoes or Mexican green tomatoes, are the main ingredient for many salsas. The fruit looks like a green cherry tomato with a weblike leaf covering, which should be removed. They lend a tart, lemony flavor that enhances both the poached vegetables and salmon.

	Vegetable-oil cooking spray
1¼	pounds salmon fillet
4	tomatillos, washed and cubed (about 1 cup)
2	small yellow squash, washed and cubed (about 1 cup)
1	cucumber, peeled and cubed (about 1 cup)

Shopping List

1¼ pounds salmon fillet, about 1½ inch thick
2 small yellow squash
1 cucumber
4 tomatillos
2 pounds red potatoes
1 small bunch fresh dill or dried

Staples

onion
Tabasco or other hot pepper sauce
nonfat plain yogurt
butter or margarine
vegetable-oil cooking spray
salt
black peppercorns
aluminum foil

Helpful Hints

- *To save time and preserve flavor and vitamins, leave skins on potatoes, but wash them well.*

- *Cutting potatoes into small chunks helps them cook faster.*

Helpful Hints

- *You can buy either salmon steaks or fillets. If you use salmon steaks, increase the cooking time to account for the thicker slices.*

- *Canned tomatillos can be used for this dish. They are available in supermarkets.*

¼ **medium onion, diced**
1 **teaspoon Tabasco or other hot pepper sauce**
   Salt and freshly ground black pepper to taste
¼ **cup nonfat plain yogurt**

Preheat oven to 450 degrees F. Cut a sheet of aluminum foil about 3 feet long, or large enough to enclose salmon. Spray foil with vegetable-oil cooking spray. Rinse salmon, pat dry and place in the middle of the foil. Cut all vegetables and toss with Tabasco sauce and a little salt and pepper to taste. Spoon vegetables over fish. Bring the sides of the foil together and seal the packet. Spray baking sheet with vegetable-oil cooking spray and place fish packet on top. For a 1½-inch-thick fillet, bake 15 minutes. If you are using a ½-inch fillet, bake 6 minutes. You can check to see if fish is done by opening the packet and sticking a knife into fish. If it is opaque and not translucent, it is ready.

To serve: Open the packet and stir yogurt into vegetables. Spoon vegetables onto individual plates, divide fish into 4 portions and place a piece of fish on each plate.

Chinese Steamed Whole Fish

Stir-Fried Spinach & Noodles

STEAMING FISH helps preserve its delicate flavor and texture, keeping it juicy and moist. The fresh fish readily absorbs the Asian flavors and spices, producing a succulent, mild dish.

Serves 4.

THIS MEAL CONTAINS A TOTAL OF 702 CALORIES PER SERVING WITH 17 PERCENT OF CALORIES FROM FAT.

⏳ Countdown

♦ *Put water for noodles on to boil.*
♦ *Make fish.*
♦ *While fish steams, stir-fry noodles.*

CHINESE STEAMED WHOLE FISH

TO STEAM THE FISH WHOLE, you will need a pot wide enough to hold the plate that supports the fish. Restaurants use a large bamboo steamer. The easiest thing to do at home is to place a vegetable steamer opened as flat as possible in a large pot. A plate can then be balanced on the steamer. Or, you can place a meat rack in a roasting pan that has a cover. If you do not have a pot large enough, cut the fish in half and use a smaller plate.

This recipe calls for making deep slashes on each side of the fish to keep the skin from bursting and to allow the flavors from the vegetables and sauce to penetrate during the quick cooking.

2	pounds whole fish (yellowtail, snapper, sole or other white fish)
8	scallions, trimmed
2	carrots, peeled
½	pound mushrooms, thinly sliced (about 2 cups)
1	2-inch piece fresh ginger, chopped (about 4 teaspoons)
⅓	cup dry sherry
2	teaspoons low-sodium soy sauce
1	teaspoon sesame oil
1	teaspoon sugar

Rinse fish and pat dry. Slash both sides diagonally through to the bone at about 1-inch intervals. Place fish on plate that will fit in a steamer. Cut scallions into thin slivers. Cut carrots into very thin strips. Place scallions, carrots, mushrooms and ginger on top of fish. Mix sherry, soy sauce, sesame oil and sugar together. Pour over fish. Fill steamer with water about 1 inch deep and bring to a

Shopping List

2 pounds whole fish: yellowtail, snapper, sole or other white fish
1 pound fresh spinach
½ pound mushrooms
12 scallions
2 carrots
3-inch piece fresh ginger
¾ pound fresh Chinese egg noodles

Staples

garlic
sugar
low-sodium soy sauce
sesame oil
dry sherry
salt
black peppercorns

Helpful Hints

♦ *It is easier to tell if a fish is fresh when you buy it whole rather than already cut into fillets.*

♦ *If you prefer, ask to have the head removed when you buy the fish. Be sure that all scales have been removed.*

♦ *A quick way to chop ginger is to peel, cut into chunks and press through a garlic press with large holes.*

boil. Place the plate on a steaming rack and cover. Steam vigorously for 15 minutes, replenishing water if necessary.

STIR-FRIED SPINACH & NOODLES

SOME OF THE flavoring ingredients in this dish are similar to those in the fish, but stir-frying gives quite a different taste.

¾ pound fresh Chinese egg noodles
1 pound fresh spinach
4 scallions
⅓ cup dry sherry
¼ cup low-sodium soy sauce
1 teaspoon sugar
1 tablespoon sesame oil
1 1-inch piece fresh ginger, chopped (about 2 teaspoons)
2 medium cloves garlic, crushed through a press
   Salt and freshly ground black pepper to taste

Bring a pot with 3 to 4 quarts of water to a boil. Add noodles and simmer 3 minutes, or until soft but not sticky. Drain. Carefully wash spinach, dry and cut into small pieces, about 3 to 4 inches. Trim root ends of scallions, wash and slice. Mix sherry, soy sauce and sugar together.

Heat sesame oil in a wok or skillet and add scallions, ginger and garlic. Let cook a few seconds and add spinach. Pour sauce over spinach. Add noodles and stir-fry 2 minutes. Add salt and pepper to taste. Toss all ingredients together. Serve with fish.

CHAPTER 4

Beef Dinners

Beef Dinners

◆

Chili Con Carne

Avocado Salad

When I'm having a large crowd over for a casual evening, I like to make a big pot of chili, and to make it more festive, I serve it in a large loaf of hollowed-out bread lined with foil. Whether for 2 or 20, this dish makes a perfect meal.

Serves 4.

This meal contains a total of 887 calories per serving with 17 percent of calories from fat.

⧖ **Countdown**

♦ *Preheat oven to 350 degrees F for bread.*
♦ *Make chili.*
♦ *While chili cooks, make salad.*

CHILI CON CARNE

Some like it hot, some like it mild, but almost everyone likes it. The degree of heat is up to you.

1½	teaspoons olive oil
1	medium onion, diced (about 2 cups)
4	medium cloves garlic, crushed through a press
¾	pound ground round
3	cups canned red kidney beans, drained and rinsed
4	cups canned crushed tomatoes
3	tablespoons chili powder
2	teaspoons ground cumin
	Salt and freshly ground black pepper to taste
1	loaf sourdough bread

Garnish, *optional*

1	cup nonfat sour cream
¼	medium onion, diced (about 1 cup)
1	cup chopped fresh cilantro

Preheat oven to 350 degrees F to warm bread. Heat olive oil in a large nonstick skillet and sauté onion about 5 minutes. Add garlic and sauté 3 to 4 minutes. Add meat and brown. Add kidney beans to meat along with tomatoes, chili powder and cumin. Simmer 20 minutes. Add salt and pepper and taste for seasoning. Add more chili powder or cumin as needed. Warm bread in oven for 5

Shopping List

¾ pound ground round
1 pound ripe avocado
1 head romaine lettuce
1 bunch fresh cilantro, optional
1 container nonfat sour cream
    (8 ounces)
1 loaf sourdough bread

Staples

lemon
onions (2)
garlic
chili powder
ground cumin
1 can crushed tomatoes (32 ounces)
1 can red kidney beans (27 ounces)
canola oil
olive oil
chicken stock
Dijon mustard
salt
black peppercorns

Helpful Hints

♦ *This dish freezes so well that you may wish to double the recipe and freeze half for another quick dinner.*

♦ *I have called for red kidney beans in this recipe, but white cannellini beans work very well and give a softer, lighter texture.*

minutes, or until crusty.

Slice bread and place in bread basket. Serve chili and pass the bowls of sour cream, onion and cilantro to go with it.

AVOCADO SALAD

To HELP AVOCADO RIPEN, remove the small stem from the narrow end and place in a paper bag in a warm spot.

½   **head romaine lettuce**
1   **large ripe avocado, weighing about 1 pound, or 2 small avocados**
DRESSING
2   **tablespoons defatted chicken stock**
1   **tablespoon fresh lemon juice**
1   **tablespoon Dijon mustard**
2   **teaspoons canola oil**
    Salt and freshly ground black pepper to taste

Wash, drain and tear lettuce into bite-size pieces. Peel, halve, pit avocado, and cut into slices. In a medium bowl, thoroughly whisk together chicken stock and lemon juice with mustard. Add oil and whisk again. Add salt and pepper to taste. Toss avocado in dressing. Place lettuce in salad bowl and pour dressing with avocado on top. Toss and serve.

Gyro Sandwiches

Greek Salad

Shopping List

*1¼ pound flank, skirt or lean
    sirloin steak*
3 tomatoes
1 cucumber
1 head iceberg lettuce
1 red onion
1 large green bell pepper
4 radishes
*1 small bunch fresh oregano or
    dried*
1 small bunch fresh dill or dried
2 ounces feta cheese
12 pitted black olives
1 can chick-peas (16 ounces)
*6 plain or whole-wheat pita
    breads*

Staples

lemon
garlic
nonfat plain yogurt
olive oil
Dijon mustard
dry red wine
salt
black peppercorns

Helpful Hints

♦ *To bruise garlic, tap whole cloves
with the flat side of a knife. This
will release some of the juice.*

♦ *Make tzaziki sauce in a food
processor to save time.*

♦ *1½ sandwiches per person is
usually plenty.*

WHILE VISITING Tampa, Florida, I was introduced to a charming Greek enclave of quaint restaurants, each with a tempting display of all types of Greek foods at reasonable prices. This meal was inspired by that visit. Served on their own, gyro sandwiches make a lunch or light supper and, with the salad, a wonderfully casual complete meal. If pressed for time, make a tossed salad with whatever greens you have on hand and serve with a bottled low-fat dressing.

    Serves 4.

THIS MEAL CONTAINS A TOTAL OF 783 CALORIES PER SERVING WITH 29 PERCENT OF CALORIES FROM FAT.

⧖ Countdown

♦ *Preheat oven to 400 degrees F for pita bread.*
♦ *Marinate meat.*
♦ *Make salad.*
♦ *Make tzaziki sauce and finish gyros.*

GYRO SANDWICHES

GYROS ARE pita bread sandwiches filled with meat, lettuce, cucumber, tomatoes and yogurt or tzaziki, a yogurt-cucumber sauce. These sandwiches are usually made with compressed meat—pieces of lamb and beef pressed together—cooked on a vertical spit. For this recipe, I have used strips of marinated beef instead. The tzaziki is also delicious as a vegetable dip.

1¼	**pounds flank, skirt or lean sirloin steak**

MARINADE

1	**cup dry red wine**
4	**teaspoons fresh lemon juice**
8	**medium cloves garlic, bruised**
4	**teaspoons chopped fresh oregano or 2 teaspoons dried**

TZAZIKI SAUCE

½	**cucumber**
1	**cup nonfat plain yogurt**
2	**medium cloves garlic, crushed through a press**
2	**tablespoons chopped red onion**
2	**teaspoons chopped fresh dill or 1 teaspoon dried**
1	**teaspoon fresh lemon juice**
	Salt and freshly ground black pepper to taste

            6   plain or whole-wheat pita breads
            2   teaspoons olive oil
GARNISH
            1   medium tomato, diced
            1   cup peeled, diced cucumbers
            2   cups shredded iceberg lettuce

Preheat oven to 400 degrees F. Remove fat from meat and cut into thin strips, cutting against the grain if you are using flank steak.

For marinade: Mix all ingredients together. Place meat in a plastic bag or nonaluminum bowl and pour in marinade. Let marinate 20 minutes, turning once.

Make tzaziki sauce: Peel, seed and chop cucumber. Drain. Mix with yogurt, garlic, red onion, dill, lemon juice and salt and pepper to taste.

Warm pita breads in oven for about 5 minutes and cut in half. Carefully open bread and place on a serving plate.

Heat olive oil in a nonstick skillet and sauté meat about 1 minute for rare or 3 minutes for medium. Add salt and pepper to taste, place on a small serving plate and cover to keep warm.

To serve: Place tomato, cucumbers, lettuce and tzaziki sauce in separate bowls. Serve fillings, meat and bread at the table so that people can help themselves; or if you prefer, fill pita breads in the kitchen and serve them on individual plates.

GREEK SALAD

GREEK SALADS are almost a meal in themselves, accented with olives, chick-peas and feta cheese.

           12   leaves iceberg lettuce
            2   tomatoes, cut in eighths
            1   large green bell pepper, seeded and sliced
            8   slices red onion
            4   radishes, sliced
            1   cup canned chick-peas, drained
           12   pitted black olives
            ½   cup feta cheese
DRESSING
            2   tablespoons fresh lemon juice
            2   teaspoons Dijon mustard
            4   teaspoons olive oil
                Salt and freshly ground black pepper to taste

Wash, dry and tear lettuce into bite-size pieces. Toss with tomatoes, green pepper, onion, radishes, chick-peas and olives. Crumble feta cheese on top.

For dressing: Whisk lemon juice and mustard together until smooth. Whisk in olive oil. Add salt and pepper to taste. Pour over salad and toss.

Helpful Hint

♦ *Feta cheese is a sheep's milk cheese that is essential for a Greek salad. It can be found in the dairy case or deli of the supermarket.*

Picadillo (Sloppy Joe)

Fluffy Rice

Tomato & Onion Salad

Shopping List

1 pound ground round
1 small red onion
2 green bell peppers
4 ripe medium tomatoes
1 small bunch fresh cilantro
15 pitted green olives
1 small jar capers

Staples

onions (2)
garlic
nonfat plain yogurt
honey mustard
long-grain white rice
raisins
Worcestershire sauce
1 can tomato sauce (15 ounces)
sherry-wine vinegar
white vinegar
olive oil
chicken stock
salt
black peppercorns

Helpful Hint

♦ *Picadillo freezes well. If you have time, make extra and freeze for another quick meal.*

THE STORY GOES that Sloppy Joe's Restaurant in Key West took this traditional Cuban dish and served it over two halves of Cuban bread, calling it a Sloppy Joe. I found out just how enticing this version of Key West's famous dish was when I made it on television. Before I was even off the set, the crew descended on me, forks in hand. If pressed for time, use a bottled low-fat dressing for the salad.
    Serves 4.

THIS MEAL CONTAINS A TOTAL OF 624 CALORIES PER SERVING WITH 17 PERCENT OF CALORIES FROM FAT.

⧗ Countdown

♦ *Put water for rice on to boil.*
♦ *Make Picadillo.*
♦ *Cook rice.*
♦ *Make salad and dressing.*

PICADILLO

THERE ARE PROBABLY as many picadillo variations as there are people who make it, but olives and capers are always part of the recipe.
    I usually serve my picadillo with rice or potatoes. To serve it Sloppy Joe-style, cut oblong rolls in half and scoop out the insides. Toast lightly, spoon the warm picadillo mixture on top and serve.

½	cup defatted chicken stock
2	medium onions, chopped (about 2 cups)
4	medium cloves garlic, crushed through a press
2	green bell peppers, diced (about 2 cups)
1	pound ground round
1	15-ounce can tomato sauce
15	pitted green olives, chopped
2	tablespoons capers, drained
½	cup raisins
2	tablespoons Worcestershire sauce
2	tablespoons white vinegar
	Salt and freshly ground black pepper to taste

Heat chicken stock in a nonstick skillet and add onions. Cook until onions are golden, being careful not to burn them, about 10 minutes. Add garlic and green peppers and cook 5 minutes. Add beef and break up into small pieces as it browns. Add tomato sauce and mix well. Add remaining ingredients and cook on low heat, stirring occasionally, until meat is cooked through and flavors are blended, about 15 minutes. Taste for seasoning. Add salt and pepper to taste and more vinegar and Worcestershire sauce, if necessary.

FLUFFY RICE

I LIKE TO COOK my rice almost like pasta in a large pot of water so it can move around freely. It's a simple process, and the rice turns out light and fluffy.

- 1 cup long-grain white rice
- 2 tablespoons olive oil
  Salt and freshly ground black pepper to taste

Place rice in a strainer and wash under cold water. Fill a large pot with 3 to 4 quarts water and add rice. Bring water to a boil and gently boil rice, uncovered, for about 10 minutes. Test a few grains to see if they are cooked through but still firm. Strain into a colander and rinse with warm water. With a fork, stir in oil and add salt and pepper.

TOMATO AND ONION SALAD

YOU CAN GARNISH this simple salad with basil, parsley, cilantro or any herbs that look fresh.

- 4 ripe medium tomatoes
- ¼ cup nonfat plain yogurt
- 2 teaspoons honey mustard
- 2 teaspoons sherry-wine vinegar
- ¼ cup diced red onion
  Salt and freshly ground black pepper to taste
- 2 tablespoons chopped fresh cilantro or other fresh herbs

Slice tomatoes and arrange on a serving plate. Whisk yogurt and mustard together and whisk in vinegar. Add onion. Salt and pepper tomatoes and spoon sauce over them. Sprinkle with cilantro.

Steak au Poivre

Leeks Vinaigrette

Roasted Garlic Potatoes

Shopping List

4 steaks: tenderloin, rib eye or
New York strip (5 ounces each)
2 pounds red potatoes
1½ pounds leeks
½ pint heavy cream

Staples

lemon
garlic
butter or margarine
Dijon mustard
canola oil
Cognac or brandy (3 ounces)
chicken stock
vegetable-oil cooking spray
salt
black peppercorns

Helpful Hints

♦ *Melt butter with garlic in the microwave to save time.*

♦ *Make sure the oven is hot when the potatoes are started.*

WHENEVER MY FAMILY wants a special dinner, steak is usually at the top of the list. In fact, one Valentine's Day, I conducted my own informal survey and found that steak was mentioned most often by men and women alike as their favorite romantic meal. This is a French dinner for any special occasion: a birthday, Valentine's Day or just a quiet evening at home.

If pressed for time, use a low-fat bottled vinaigrette for the leeks.

Serves 4.

THIS MEAL CONTAINS A TOTAL OF 677 CALORIES PER SERVING WITH 32 PERCENT OF CALORIES FROM FAT.

⧗ Countdown

♦ *Preheat oven to 450 degrees F for potatoes.*
♦ *Cook potatoes.*
♦ *Make leeks.*
♦ *Cook steak.*

ROASTED GARLIC POTATOES

THESE POTATOES can cook on their own in the oven while you prepare the rest of the dinner.

> Vegetable-oil cooking spray
> 2 pounds red potatoes
> 1 tablespoon butter or margarine
> 2 medium cloves garlic, crushed through a press
> Salt and freshly ground black pepper to taste

Preheat oven to 450 degrees F. Cover a baking tray large enough to hold potatoes in one layer with foil. Spray with vegetable-oil cooking spray. Wash potatoes and cut into ½- to 1-inch cubes. Melt butter and garlic together. Place potatoes on baking tray and toss in butter mixture. Place in oven for 15 minutes. Turn potatoes and roast another 10 minutes. Add salt and pepper to taste.

LEEKS VINAIGRETTE

THIS IS A typically French way of serving leeks. They become very tender and pick up the delicate mustard flavor of the vinaigrette.

- 1½ pounds leeks
- 1 tablespoon fresh lemon juice
- 2 teaspoons Dijon mustard
- 2 tablespoons defatted chicken stock
- 2 teaspoons canola oil
  Salt and freshly ground black pepper to taste

Trim ragged green ends of leeks and roots. Slice leeks in half lengthwise and in half again. Wash carefully under cold running water. Place them on their sides in a lasagna pan large enough to hold them and add ¼ inch water. Microwave on high, uncovered, for 10 minutes, or until leeks are tender. Or, boil leeks in a skillet large enough to fit them lying on their sides and covered with water.

While leeks are cooking, make vinaigrette. Whisk lemon juice and mustard together until smooth. Add stock and oil. Add salt and pepper to taste. When leeks are cooked, carefully lift them out of water and drain them on a rack in the sink. Place them on an oval dish and spoon vinaigrette over the top.

Helpful Hint

♦ *Leeks cook perfectly in a microwave. I use a lasagna dish, which is large enough to hold the leeks lying on their sides. They can be served in the same dish. Alternatively, you can cook the leeks in a skillet for 10 minutes and transfer them to a serving dish.*

STEAK AU POIVRE

I USED TO MARVEL at how easy many traditional French dishes are to cook. This is one of the simplest. I love cracked pepper with a delicious piece of beef and a contrasting cool, creamy sauce.

- 4 5-ounce steaks (tenderloin, rib eye, New York strip)
- 2 tablespoons cracked black pepper
- 1 tablespoon butter
- ⅓ cup Cognac or brandy
- 2 tablespoons heavy cream

Remove fat from steak. Cover steak with cracked pepper and press it into meat with the palm of your hand. Melt butter in a nonstick skillet. Raise the heat and brown steaks on each side. Lower the heat and cook until done, about 1½ minutes on each side, depending on thickness. For well done, cook about 3 minutes on each side. Remove steak to a warm serving dish and cover with foil to keep warm.

Pour off fat and add Cognac to the pan, scraping up browned bits as it boils. Raise heat and reduce slightly. Add cream and mix well. Taste for salt and add, if needed.

Place steaks on individual plates and spoon the sauce over them.

Helpful Hint

♦ *You may buy one small steak per person, or buy a larger steak and slice it before it is served. The cooking method is the same.*

Onion-Smothered Steak

Home-Baked Potato Chips

Thousand Island Salad

"I LIKE MY STEAK smothered in onions and served with French-fried potatoes, and Thousand Island dressing for my salad," a friend replied when I asked him to name his favorite meal for Father's Day. I created this menu for him so that he could enjoy it while reducing his fat intake. If pressed for time, use a nonfat bottled dressing for the salad.

Serves 4.

THIS MEAL CONTAINS A TOTAL OF 688 CALORIES PER SERVING WITH 29 PERCENT OF CALORIES FROM FAT.

⧗ Countdown

♦ *Preheat oven to 450 degrees F for potato chips.*
♦ *Start potatoes.*
♦ *Preheat gas grill, if using, for steak.*
♦ *While potatoes are baking, prepare onions and mushrooms for steak.*
♦ *If broiling steak, preheat broiler.*
♦ *Make salad.*
♦ *Grill or broil steak.*

HOME-BAKED POTATO CHIPS

I LIKE RED POTATOES for this recipe, but russet or Idaho will also work. The secret to these chips is slicing them thin and patting them dry with paper towels before baking. This is important: If they are not dry, the potatoes will steam rather than crisp when baking.

2   pounds red potatoes
     Vegetable-oil cooking spray
2   tablespoons butter or margarine
2   medium cloves garlic, crushed through a press
     Salt and freshly ground black pepper to taste

Preheat oven to 450 degrees F. Wash potatoes and slice ⅛ inch thick in a food processor fitted with a thin slicing blade or by hand. Place slices in a bowl of cold water. Drain and fill the bowl with cold water again. If the water is still cloudy, drain and fill the bowl one more time. Remove potatoes and pat dry with paper towels. Line 2 to 3 large baking trays with foil and spray with vegetable-oil

Shopping List

1¼ pounds steak (strip, rib eye, sirloin, skirt or flank)
½ pound mushrooms
1 head iceberg lettuce
2 tomatoes
1 bunch radishes
2 pounds red potatoes
1 small jar sweet pickle relish

Staples

onions (2)
garlic
sugar
butter or margarine
nonfat plain yogurt
Worcestershire sauce
ketchup
hot chili sauce, optional
chicken stock
vegetable-oil cooking spray
canola oil
salt
black peppercorns

Helpful Hints

♦ *Crushed garlic is used in both the potato and steak recipes. Crush all the garlic through a press and use one-fourth for the potatoes and the rest for the steak.*

♦ *Melt butter and garlic in a microwave on high for 1 minute to save time.*

(continued on page 177)

Lemon Peppered Chicken (PAGE 80)

Poached Salmon With Parsley Sauce (PAGE 129)

Normandy Veal (PAGE 232)
Oranges in Caramel (PAGE 252)

Balsamic Steak (PAGE 178)

Honey-Glazed Mahimahi (PAGE 136)

173

Hot & Spicy Stir-Fried Shrimp (PAGE 112)

Curried Chicken (PAGE 84)

Fragrant Fish Parcels (PAGE 145)
Pears in Red Wine (PAGE 250)

cooking spray. Place slices side by side on the trays. Do not overlap them. Melt butter with garlic and brush onto potatoes. Bake for 10 minutes. Check to see if they are crisp and golden. If not, bake another 5 minutes. Remove from the oven and season with salt and pepper to taste. Serve warm.

ONION-SMOTHERED STEAK

THIS IS A GREAT STEAK for Memorial Day, Fourth of July, Labor Day or any other time. The onions and mushrooms should completely cover the steak.

1¼	pounds strip, rib eye, sirloin, skirt or flank steak
1	teaspoon canola oil
1	tablespoon butter or margarine
1½	medium onions, sliced (about 3 cups)
½	cup defatted chicken stock
6	medium cloves garlic, crushed through a press
½	pound mushrooms, sliced (about 2 cups)
	Salt and freshly ground black pepper to taste

Brush steak with oil and set aside. Heat butter in a nonstick skillet and add onions. Sauté 1 minute. Add chicken stock, cover and cook on high for 3 minutes. Uncover and cook another minute, or until all the liquid has evaporated. Add garlic and mushrooms and sauté another 2 minutes. Add salt and pepper to taste.

Place steak on grill, sear for about 30 seconds and move steak a quarter turn. This will help keep it from sticking to the grates. Grill 4 minutes for a 1-inch-thick steak and about 2 minutes for a thinner one. Turn and add salt and pepper. Grill another 4 minutes for a thicker steak and 2 minutes for a thinner one. Steak can be cooked in a broiler the same way. Smother with onions and serve.

THOUSAND ISLAND SALAD

PEOPLE LIKE TO SPOON the dressing on generously.

½	head iceberg lettuce
2	medium tomatoes
16	radishes

DRESSING

1	cup nonfat plain yogurt
6	tablespoons ketchup
4	tablespoons sweet pickle relish
1	teaspoon Worcestershire sauce
2	teaspoons sugar
	Few drops hot chili sauce, *optional*

Wash and dry lettuce, wash and slice tomatoes and radishes. Toss together in salad bowl. Mix dressing ingredients together. Serve on salad.

Helpful Hints

♦ *Alter cooking times according to the thickness of the steak.*

♦ *If using a charcoal grill, light it first and let the coals heat for 30 minutes, or light a gas grill or broiler about 10 minutes before it is needed.*

♦ *Make sure the grill grates are clean, and spray them with a little vegetable-oil cooking spray to keep the steak from sticking.*

♦ *Slice onions and mushrooms in a food processor fitted with a thin slicing blade.*

Balsamic Steak

Rosemary Roasted Potatoes

Fresh Green Salad

See photograph, page 172.

WE ALWAYS THINK of steak and potatoes as a purely American dish, but Steak Frites (steak with French fries) is served at nearly every French brasserie. This is a modern version of this classic meal. If pressed for time, omit the salad and serve some carrot and celery sticks with or without the dressing.

Serves 4.

THIS MEAL CONTAINS A TOTAL OF 569 CALORIES PER SERVING WITH 28 PERCENT OF CALORIES FROM FAT.

⧗ Countdown

- *Preheat oven to 350 degrees F for potatoes.*
- *If grilling steak, preheat grill.*
- *Marinate steak.*
- *While steak is marinating, make potatoes.*
- *While potatoes bake, make salad.*
- *Grill or broil steak.*

BALSAMIC STEAK

SKIRT STEAK (also called beef plate) is one of my favorite cuts. It is full of flavor and cooks quickly. Balsamic vinegar tenderizes and flavors the meat without adding extra calories.

1¼	pounds skirt, flank or lean sirloin steak
1	cup balsamic vinegar
2	tablespoons chopped onion
	Salt and freshly ground black pepper to taste

Remove fat from meat. Place in a bowl or plastic bag with vinegar and onion. Let marinate 20 minutes. Drain and place on a hot grill or under a preheated broiler. For rare, cook 5 minutes if steak is thin or 8 minutes if thicker. Cook longer if you like it medium or well done. Remove to a cutting board, cover with foil and let rest 5 minutes. Slice on a diagonal against the grain.

Shopping List

*1¼ pounds skirt, flank or lean
  sirloin steak*
6 shallots
*3 small heads different types of
  lettuce*
*1 small bunch fresh chives or
  scallions*
*1 small bunch fresh rosemary or
  dried*
2 pounds russet or Idaho potatoes

Staples

onion
honey mustard
nonfat plain yogurt
butter or margarine
balsamic vinegar
sherry-wine vinegar
salt
black peppercorns

Helpful Hints

- *Preheat a gas grill or broiler for 10 minutes, or start a charcoal fire 30 minutes ahead.*

- *Slice skirt steak on a slant across the grain; otherwise it will be somewhat tough and stringy.*

ROSEMARY ROASTED POTATOES

FRESH ROSEMARY perfumes these potatoes, which are first sautéed to crisp them and then finished in the oven.

4   russet or Idaho potatoes (about 2 pounds)
2   tablespoons butter or margarine
6   shallots, chopped, or ½ small onion, chopped
2   sprigs fresh rosemary or 1 teaspoon dried

Preheat oven to 350 degrees F. Wash potatoes and cut into strips about ½ inch thick and 2 inches long. Heat butter in a nonstick ovenproof skillet large enough to hold potatoes in one layer. Add potatoes and shallots and sauté over medium heat for 15 minutes, shaking the pan or tossing potatoes every few minutes. Add rosemary and toss with potatoes. Bake in oven 10 minutes longer.

Helpful Hint

♦ *Use two skillets if you don't have one large enough to hold potatoes in a single layer.*

FRESH GREEN SALAD

SELECT THE LETTUCE that looks freshest in the market, choosing two or three different types for variety.

Several leaves from 3 small heads lettuce, about ⅓ head each

DRESSING
½   cup nonfat plain yogurt
2   teaspoons honey mustard
2   teaspoons sherry-wine vinegar
½   cup fresh chives or scallions, chopped

Cut lettuce heads in half and remove several inner and outer leaves from each one. Wash and drain well. Toss together with fresh chives.

For dressing: Whisk together yogurt, mustard and vinegar. Stir in chives. Toss with salad or serve on the side.

Helpful Hint

♦ *Cut lettuce heads in half in order to use some leaves from the center as well as those from the outside. This varies the color and texture.*

Beef Teriyaki

Stir-Fried Rice

Mushrooms & Onions

Shopping List

*1¼ pounds skirt, flank or lean
    sirloin steak*
½-inch piece fresh ginger
8 scallions
¾ pound mushrooms

Staples

onion
garlic
brown sugar
long-grain white rice
sesame oil
peanut oil
low-sodium soy sauce
dry sherry
salt
black peppercorns

TERIYAKI STEAK has been popularized in America by large Japanese restaurants that cook the meat on a hot griddle right at your table. My son chose just such a restaurant for dinner one evening. The flavors inspired me to develop this quick menu.

Serves 4.

THIS MEAL CONTAINS A TOTAL OF 651 CALORIES PER SERVING WITH 21 PERCENT OF CALORIES FROM FAT.

⧖ Countdown
♦ *Preheat grill or broiler for steak.*
♦ *Make teriyaki sauce and marinate steak.*
♦ *Cook rice.*
♦ *Cook mushrooms.*
♦ *Cook steak.*
♦ *Stir-fry rice.*

BEEF TERIYAKI

THE SECRET to a good teriyaki sauce is to cook it so a rich, glossy glaze coats the steak. Grilling ensures that the meat will sear, remaining juicy inside; you can also broil this steak.

¾	cup dry sherry
¼	cup brown sugar
½	tablespoon chopped fresh ginger
2	teaspoons minced garlic
½	cup low-sodium soy sauce
1¼	pounds skirt, flank or lean sirloin steak

Helpful Hints

♦ *Preheat a gas grill for 10 minutes, or start a charcoal fire 30 minutes ahead, or preheat the broiler so that the steak will be seared when placed under it.*

♦ *A quick way to chop ginger is to peel, cut into chunks and press through a garlic press with large holes.*

Heat sherry in a saucepan and add sugar, ginger and garlic. Simmer gently, covered, over low heat to dissolve sugar. Remove the lid and continue to cook until sauce thickens slightly, about 3 minutes. Add soy sauce. Cool several minutes. Trim fat from beef. With the point of a knife or skewer, make holes in steak at varying intervals so the sauce will penetrate the meat as it marinates. Place steak in a bowl just large enough to hold it or in a plastic bag. Pour marinade over steak. Marinate 10 minutes.

If grilling, remove steak from marinade and place on grill. Sear for 1 minute and turn to sear the other side. Move steak to the edge of the grill so that it is not directly over the fire and baste with marinade. Grill 5 more minutes, turn again and brush with marinade. Reserve remaining marinade for rice. Grill another 3 minutes for a 1½-inch-thick steak, less for thinner steaks. If you like your steak more well done, grill another 3 minutes, depending on thickness. If broiling, preheat broiler and broil steak in same manner. If using skirt or flank steak, slice across the grain, holding the knife on a slant to make diagonal cuts. If using sirloin steak, slice and serve.

STIR-FRIED RICE

IF YOU HAPPEN to have leftover rice on hand, use it and save time. Otherwise, boil the rice and let it drain while you make the mushrooms. It will stir-fry better when it is dry.

1	cup long-grain white rice
8	scallions, sliced
¼	cup teriyaki marinade from beef
	Salt and freshly ground black pepper to taste

Place rice in a strainer and wash under cold water. Fill a large pot with 3 to 4 quarts water and add rice. Bring water to a boil and gently boil rice, uncovered, for about 10 minutes. Test a few grains to see if they are cooked through but still firm. Drain into a colander and rinse with warm water. Set aside.

After you have made Mushrooms & Onions, stir-fry rice in the same wok or skillet without washing it; some of the sauce will remain in the pan. Draw rice to sides of pan and add beef teriyaki marinade to the center. Draw rice to the center and continue to stir-fry. Taste for seasoning. Add salt and pepper, if necessary.

MUSHROOMS & ONIONS

MAKE SURE YOUR wok or skillet is very hot so that the vegetables will be crisp. If the oil is not smoking, the vegetables will steam.

1	teaspoon peanut oil
1	medium onion, sliced (about 2 cups)
4	cloves garlic, crushed through a press
¾	pound mushrooms, thickly sliced (about 3¼ cups)
2	teaspoons sesame oil
	Salt and freshly ground black pepper to taste

Heat oil in a wok or skillet. Add onion and stir-fry for 3 minutes. Add garlic and cook another minute. Add mushrooms and continue to stir-fry for another minute. Sprinkle with sesame oil and add salt and pepper to taste.

Grilled Stuffed Steak

Pepper Jelly Succotash

Shopping List

1¼ pounds skirt, lean sirloin or
  flank steak
2 shallots
2 scallions
½ pound mushrooms
1 small bunch fresh parsley
1 small bunch fresh thyme or dried
3 cans or 3 packages frozen corn
  (11-ounce cans, 10-ounce
  packages)
2 packages frozen lima beans
  (14 ounces)
2 slices whole-wheat bread
1 small jar hot jalapeño pepper jelly

Staples

butter or margarine
chicken stock
vegetable-oil cooking spray
salt
black peppercorns
wooden toothpicks

Helpful Hints

♦ *If using a charcoal grill, light it
first. It will need 30 minutes to
heat. Light a gas grill or broiler for
at least 10 minutes before it is
needed.*

♦ *If using a stovetop grill, follow
the same cooking times.*

♦ *To save time, chop all the
ingredients in a food processor.
Start with the bread crumbs and
parsley, remove, do not rinse bowl,
and continue with the onions and
mushrooms.*

ONE YEAR Harrod's department store in London asked me to cook an American meal in their cookware department. I made this recipe on a stovetop grill, and it smelled so good that it lured customers and staff from all over the store. They insisted I come back the next day to cook it again.

Serves 4.

THIS MEAL CONTAINS A TOTAL OF 630 CALORIES PER SERVING WITH 21 PERCENT OF CALORIES FROM FAT.

⌛ Countdown

♦ *Preheat grill or broiler for steak.*
♦ *Make steak.*
♦ *Make succotash.*

GRILLED STUFFED STEAK

A MUSHROOM STUFFING perfumes the steak.

1¼	**pounds lean sirloin, skirt or flank steak, at least 1–1½ inches thick**
	Salt and freshly ground black pepper to taste
½	**tablespoon butter or margarine**
1	**medium shallot, chopped (about 1 tablespoon)**
½	**pound mushrooms, chopped (about 1 cup)**
2	**tablespoons chopped fresh parsley**
2	**tablespoons chopped fresh thyme or 1 tablespoon dried**
2	**tablespoons whole-wheat bread crumbs**
	Vegetable-oil cooking spray

Cut a pocket in steak by placing it on a counter and slicing it in half horizontally, carefully pulling back the top portion. (Do not cut all the way through.) Salt and pepper the inside. Melt butter in a small nonstick skillet and add shallot. Cook gently until transparent and golden, about 10 minutes. Add chopped mushrooms and a little salt and pepper. Cook until liquid has evaporated. Add parsley, thyme and bread crumbs. Taste for seasoning. Fill pocket of steak with stuffing. Close with toothpicks. Spray the outside with vegetable-oil cooking spray and place on a hot barbecue or under a broiler for 4 to 5 minutes on each side for rare, longer if you want the steak more well done.

Remove the toothpicks, slice and serve immediately.

PEPPER JELLY SUCCOTASH

AMERICAN Indians made dishes from the corn and beans they grew side by side in their fields. When they harvested the patch, they cooked the vegetables together and called it succotash, which is Indian for "hodgepodge." It was really a meal in itself, made with fresh vegetables in the summer and dried in the winter, with ham added. No wonder the early settlers took to it.

⅔ cup defatted chicken stock
3   11-ounce cans or 3 10-ounce packages frozen corn (about 3 cups)
3   cups frozen lima beans
6   tablespoons hot jalapeño pepper jelly
2   scallions, thinly sliced
    Salt to taste

Warm chicken stock in a large skillet. Add corn and lima beans and cook on medium heat until heated through, about 5 minutes if using canned vegetables or about 15 minutes if using frozen. Reduce to low heat and add jelly. Stir until jelly melts and coats vegetables. Add scallions and salt to taste.

Helpful Hints

♦ *Use fresh, frozen or canned corn and fresh or frozen lima beans for the succotash.*

♦ *Any type of hot pepper jelly will work.*

Vietnamese Stir-Fried Beef & Bok Choy

Crispy Noodle Cake

Shopping List

1 pound flank, skirt or lean sirloin steak

1 pound bok choy or Chinese cabbage

8 scallions

2 yellow, red or green bell peppers

1-inch piece fresh ginger

1 small jar Chinese chili paste with garlic or a mixture of garlic and hot pepper sauce

¾ pound angel-hair pasta or thin egg noodles

Staples

garlic
cornstarch
sugar
canola oil
low-sodium soy sauce
white vinegar
sesame oil
chicken stock
vegetable-oil cooking spray

Helpful Hint

♦ *The noodles will need to be turned. The easiest way to do this is to loosen them on the tray all around the edges, cut into 4 sections and, with a spatula, flip each section.*

EVERY TIME I go into my friend Binh Duong's Vietnamese restaurants, either in Hartford, Connecticut, or Boca Raton, Florida, he insists on making me his favorite dishes. Over the years, this one has become one of my favorites too. Crisp noodles are topped with fragrant stir-fried beef and vegetables. *See photograph, page 100.*

Serves 4.

THIS MEAL CONTAINS A TOTAL OF 596 CALORIES PER SERVING WITH 22 PERCENT OF CALORIES FROM FAT.

⧖ Countdown

♦ *Preheat broiler for noodles.*
♦ *Put water for noodles on to boil.*
♦ *Prepare noodles.*
♦ *Stir-fry beef.*

CRISPY NOODLE CAKE

COOKING THE NOODLES this way makes them pleasantly crunchy.

	Vegetable-oil cooking spray
¾	**pound angel-hair pasta or thin egg noodles**
2	**teaspoons canola oil**

Preheat broiler. Line a baking tray with foil and spray with vegetable-oil cooking spray. Bring a large pot of water to a boil. Add noodles. As soon as water returns to a boil, drain noodles and rinse under cold water. Shake dry and spread out evenly on the baking tray. Sprinkle oil over noodles and spray with vegetable-oil cooking spray. Place noodles on the middle rack of the oven. Keep an eye on them as you prepare the beef. When noodles are crisp, after about 10 minutes, remove and flip onto other side. Spray with oil again and return to broiler for another 5 minutes. To serve, cut noodles into 4 portions with a sharp scissors or a knife and transfer to individual plates. Cut each cake into 2-inch squares. Spoon beef, vegetables and sauce on top.

VIETNAMESE STIR-FRIED BEEF & BOK CHOY

Bok choy is related to the cabbage family. It looks a little like Swiss chard or an oversized leek with large green leaves at the top. It is available in most supermarkets. Chinese cabbage may be substituted. Buy presliced stir-fry beef if your market sells it.

Sauce

1	cup defatted chicken stock
½	cup low-sodium soy sauce
2	tablespoons sugar
1	tablespoon white vinegar
1	tablespoon cornstarch
2	teaspoons chili paste with garlic
1	teaspoon sesame oil

Beef & Bok Choy

1	pound flank, skirt or lean sirloin steak
1	pound bok choy (3 cups sliced)
8	scallions
1	teaspoon canola oil
4	medium cloves garlic, crushed through a press, *divided*
1	1-inch piece fresh ginger, chopped (about 1 tablespoon), *divided*
2	medium yellow, red or green bell peppers, sliced (about 2 cups)

For sauce: Mix all ingredients together.

For Beef & Bok Choy: Remove fat from beef. Slice into ½-inch-wide strips 2 to 3 inches long. Wash and dry bok choy. Slice on the diagonal into 1-inch pieces. Slice scallions on the diagonal.

Heat wok and add oil. Add half the garlic and half the ginger and fry until golden, about 30 seconds. Add bok choy, scallions and peppers and stir-fry until wilted, but still crunchy, about 2 minutes. Remove to a warm serving plate. Add remaining garlic and ginger and stir-fry until golden, about 30 seconds.

Add beef and stir-fry for 2 minutes. Remove to plate with vegetables. Add sauce to wok and stir to prevent lumping. Heat until sauce bubbles. Add vegetables and beef to sauce and toss several times. Remove wok from heat. Spoon over noodles and serve immediately.

Helpful Hints

♦ *Chili paste with garlic can be found in the Asian-products section of some supermarkets or in specialty food stores. Substitute an extra teaspoon crushed garlic and several drops of hot pepper sauce, if you cannot find it.*

♦ *Boneless, skinless chicken breast, shrimp or pork tenderloin may be substituted in this recipe.*

♦ *A quick way to chop ginger is to peel, cut into chunks and press through a garlic press with large holes.*

Mock Hungarian Goulash

Caraway Noodles

Shopping List

1¼ pounds skirt, flank or sirloin
* steak*
1 red bell pepper
2 large tomatoes
1 small bunch fresh parsley
1 small bunch fresh thyme or dried
1 small can or bottle imported
* Hungarian paprika or ordinary*
* paprika*
1 container nonfat sour cream
* (8 ounces)*
1 pound thin egg noodles or
* fettuccine*

Staples

garlic
onion
caraway seeds
bay leaves
1 tube tomato paste or 1 can
* (4½ ounces)*
all-purpose flour
butter or margarine
canola oil
chicken stock
salt
black peppercorns

Helpful Hints

♦ *If onions start to stick while they*
are cooking, add a little more
water to the pan.

♦ *It is worth buying good-quality*
imported Hungarian paprika.

IT'S DIFFICULT to find the time to make hearty stews, so I created this recipe, which gives the essence of a good thick goulash without the hours of preparation usually associated with the dish. Goulash, or *gulyas*, means herdsmen's stew. It is a perfect dinner for a winter's table. It also freezes well.

Serves 4.

THIS MEAL CONTAINS A TOTAL OF 765 CALORIES PER SERVING WITH 31 PERCENT OF CALORIES FROM FAT.

⌛ Countdown

♦ *Put water for noodles on to boil.*
♦ *Preheat broiler for steak.*
♦ *Make sauce.*
♦ *While sauce is cooking, broil steak.*

MOCK HUNGARIAN GOULASH

PAPRIKA IS THE Hungarian name both for sweet pepper and for the powder made from it. Ordinary paprika comes in varying degrees of flavor—from pungent to virtually tasteless. True Hungarian paprika may be hot or mild and can be found in most supermarkets. For an appealing presentation, place spoonfuls of sour cream around the goulash instead of mixing it into the sauce.

½	cup water
½	medium onion, chopped (about 1 cup)
2	tablespoons imported Hungarian paprika or 1½ tablespoons ordinary paprika
2	teaspoons all-purpose flour
1	cup defatted chicken stock
2	teaspoons tomato paste
2	teaspoons chopped fresh thyme or 1 teaspoon dried
2	bay leaves
2	sprigs fresh parsley
2	cloves garlic, crushed through a press
	Salt and freshly ground black pepper to taste
2	large tomatoes, *divided*
1	medium red bell pepper, diced (about 1 cup), *divided*
1¼	pounds skirt, flank or sirloin streak
2	teaspoons canola oil
4	tablespoons nonfat sour cream

Preheat broiler. Place water and onion in a large nonstick skillet. Cook for 10 minutes, or until onion is golden. Add paprika. Let cook for ½ minute to release flavor. Add flour and cook for another ½ minute. Add stock, tomato paste and herbs. Stir to blend ingredients. Add garlic and a little salt and pepper. Cover and simmer gently 15 minutes. Cut tomato into eighths. Then cut into 1-inch pieces and add half to sauce. Add half the diced red pepper to sauce and cook 5 minutes longer.

While sauce is cooking, brush steak with oil and place under the broiler. For a 1-inch-thick steak, broil 5 minutes. Salt and pepper the cooked side and turn. Broil 3 more minutes. (Reduce the cooking time if using a thinner piece of meat.) Slice steak about ¼ inch thick and add to sauce when it has finished cooking. Taste sauce and add salt and pepper if needed. Remove parsley sprig and bay leaves from sauce and spoon goulash onto a serving dish. Top with remaining tomatoes and red pepper. Place sour cream in spoonfuls around the platter. It will mix in as the sauce is served.

CARAWAY NOODLES

1 **pound thin egg noodles or fettuccine**
3 **tablespoons butter or margarine**
2 **tablespoons caraway seeds**
  Salt and freshly ground black pepper to taste

Bring a large pot with 3 to 4 quarts of water to a boil. Add noodles and boil about 10 minutes if dried or 3 minutes if fresh. Drain. Melt butter in a small saucepan and sauté caraway seeds for a few minutes. Place noodles in serving bowl and mix in caraway seeds and butter. Add salt and pepper to taste.

Steak in Red Wine Sauce

Sautéed Potatoes

French Green Salad

Shopping List

1¼ pounds lean sirloin steak
6 shallots
1 small bunch fresh parsley
1 small bunch fresh thyme or dried
1 small head romaine lettuce
1 small head red leaf lettuce
1 head Belgian endive
2 pounds red potatoes
½ pint heavy cream

Staples

lemon
bay leaves
butter or margarine
cornstarch
Dijon mustard
canola oil
dry red wine
brandy
chicken stock
vegetable-oil cooking spray
salt
black peppercorns

THIS DISH APPEARS on many French bistro menus. The steak sauce gets its tangy flavor from the shallots. It is often served with sautéed potatoes. If pressed for time, use a low-fat bottled salad dressing and any greens you have in the refrigerator.

Serves 4.

THIS MEAL CONTAINS A TOTAL OF 702 CALORIES PER SERVING WITH 29 PERCENT OF CALORIES FROM FAT.

⧗ Countdown

- ♦ *Preheat broiler or grill for steak.*
- ♦ *Make potatoes.*
- ♦ *Start steak sauce.*
- ♦ *Make salad.*
- ♦ *Broil steak.*

SAUTÉED POTATOES

THESE LITTLE POTATOES, known in France as *pommes château*, derive their name from another French dish, *châteaubriand*, the roasted beef tenderloin with which they are often served. For a quicker version of the traditional, I have used whole potatoes cut into 1-inch chunks with their skins left on.

> 2   pounds red potatoes
> 2   tablespoons butter or margarine
>   Salt and freshly ground black pepper to taste

Wash potatoes and cut into 1-inch chunks. Melt butter in a nonstick skillet large enough to hold potatoes in one layer. Raise heat to medium-high and add potatoes. Sauté, turning frequently, until they are golden brown outside. Lower heat and sauté until soft inside, about 20 to 25 minutes. Sprinkle with salt and pepper to taste.

STEAK IN RED WINE SAUCE

TRADITIONALLY THE STEAK is pan-fried, but in this recipe it is broiled to save time. The sauce can simmer while the meat cooks.

SAUCE

¼	cup defatted chicken stock
6	medium shallots, chopped (about ¾ cup)
1	cup dry red wine
2	bay leaves
2	sprigs fresh thyme or 2 teaspoons dried
½	cup brandy
1	teaspoon cornstarch
2	tablespoons heavy cream
	Salt and freshly ground black pepper to taste
1¼	pounds lean sirloin steak
	Vegetable-oil cooking spray
¼	cup chopped fresh parsley for garnish

Preheat broiler or grill.

For sauce: Place chicken stock and shallots in a nonstick skillet. Cook, uncovered, for 10 minutes, or until the liquid is absorbed and shallots are transparent. Add wine, bay leaves and thyme. Raise heat and cook sauce until reduced by half. Remove bay leaves and fresh thyme, if using. Add brandy and flambé: Warm brandy in sauce and, carefully averting face, tip pan to catch the flame on a gas stove or ignite with a match on an electric stove. Have a pot cover nearby to smother the flame if it gets out of hand. Mix cornstarch with cream and add to sauce. Simmer to thicken sauce. Add salt and pepper to taste. Keep warm.

Line a baking tray with foil and spray steak with vegetable-oil cooking spray. Place on tray. For a 1-inch-thick steak, broil 5 minutes and turn, then broil another 5 minutes for rare. Reduce time for thinner steak.

To serve: Place steak on a serving platter and slice. Spoon some sauce over the top and pass the rest. Garnish with parsley.

Helpful Hints

♦ *Preheat a gas grill or broiler for 10 minutes, or start a charcoal fire 30 minutes ahead.*

♦ *Chop parsley and shallots in a food processor to save time.*

FRENCH GREEN SALAD

Helpful Hint

♦ *I like to cut a head of lettuce in half and use the outer and inner leaves to vary the texture and color.*

ANY TYPE OF GREENS can be used for this salad.

1   small head each romaine lettuce, red leaf lettuce and endive

DRESSING

2   tablespoons fresh lemon juice
2   teaspoons Dijon mustard
¼   cup defatted chicken stock
2   teaspoons canola oil
    Salt and freshly ground black pepper to taste

Wash and dry greens. Tear into bite-size pieces. Whisk lemon juice and mustard together in a salad bowl. Whisk in chicken stock and oil. Add salt and pepper to taste. Add salad greens and toss together.

Beef Stroganoff

Buttered Egg Noodles

Quick Green Beans

THE RUSSIAN INFLUENCE in French cuisine was important long before the Russian Revolution sent the nobility scurrying to Paris for refuge. One of my favorite spots for lunch in Paris was the Conservatory of Music, where a charming old Russian couple served the most delicious examples of Russian food.

Serves 4.

THIS MEAL CONTAINS A TOTAL OF 645 CALORIES PER SERVING WITH 35 PERCENT OF CALORIES FROM FAT.

⧖ Countdown

- ♦ *Put water for noodles on to boil.*
- ♦ *Put water for beans on to boil.*
- ♦ *Make stroganoff.*
- ♦ *Cook noodles.*
- ♦ *Cook beans.*

BEEF STROGANOFF

THIS STROGANOFF is a mixture of Russian flavor and French ingenuity.

1¼	pounds flank, strip, rib eye, skirt or lean sirloin steak
1½	tablespoons canola oil
1	medium onion, chopped (about 2 cups)
1	pound mushrooms, sliced (about 4 cups)
1½	cups defatted chicken stock
4	tablespoons tomato paste
2	tablespoons Dijon mustard
½	teaspoon Worcestershire sauce
2	teaspoons sugar, *optional*
2	tablespoons heavy cream
	Salt and freshly ground black pepper to taste
¼	cup chopped fresh parsley for garnish, *optional*

Remove fat from meat and slice into thin strips about ¼ inch thick. If using flank steak, slice against the grain. Place ½ tablespoon oil in a nonstick skillet and brown a few slices at a time on high heat, adding more oil as needed. Do not overcook; the meat should be juicy and slightly rare. As soon as the meat is

Shopping List

1¼ pounds flank, strip, rib-eye, skirt or lean sirloin steak
1 pound mushrooms
1 pound green beans
1 small bunch fresh parsley, optional
1 tube or can tomato paste (4½ ounces)
½ pint heavy cream
½ pound egg noodles

Staples

onion
butter or margarine
sugar, optional
poppy seeds
Dijon mustard
Worcestershire sauce
canola oil
chicken stock
salt
black peppercorns

Helpful Hints

♦ *Brown a few pieces of meat at a time. If you brown all the meat at once, it will steam instead of browning.*

♦ *Make sure the onion is thoroughly cooked and golden. This helps flavor the sauce.*

♦ *Once the cream has been added, be careful not to boil the sauce.*

browned, remove from the pan. Continue to brown all meat slices in this manner. Add onions and sauté until transparent, about 10 minutes. If the pan seems too dry, add about ¼ cup water to prevent burning.

Add mushrooms and cook a few minutes. Pour in stock. Add tomato paste, mustard, Worcestershire, salt and pepper to taste. Mix thoroughly, scraping the bottom of the pan to incorporate all of the browned bits into the sauce. Cook for 5 to 6 minutes to reduce the sauce and slightly thicken it. Taste. You may need to add sugar and a little more Worcestershire sauce or mustard. There should be a delicate blend of flavors. Return meat to sauce and add cream. Cook for 2 to 3 minutes without boiling to rewarm meat. Taste for seasoning again.

To serve: Place cooked egg noodles on each plate and serve stroganoff over noodles. Sprinkle with parsley.

BUTTERED EGG NOODLES

WIDE EGG NOODLES are traditional for this dish, but any size pasta can be used.

- ½ **pound egg noodles**
- ½ **tablespoon butter or margarine**
- ¼ **cup defatted chicken stock**
- 1 **tablespoon poppy seeds**
  Salt and freshly ground black pepper to taste

Bring a large pot of water to a boil. Add noodles. Boil about 10 minutes. Drain in a colander. Melt butter with chicken stock, add poppy seeds and toss with noodles. Add salt and pepper to taste.

QUICK GREEN BEANS

SOME MARKETS sell the beans already trimmed for cooking. I buy these because I find it is worth the extra price to save some time in the kitchen.

- 1 **pound green beans, trimmed**
- ½ **tablespoon butter or margarine**
  Salt and freshly ground black pepper to taste

Cut beans into 2-inch pieces. Bring a medium-size pot of water to a boil. Add beans and boil for 2 to 3 minutes. Drain and mix with butter. Add salt and pepper to taste. Beans can also be cooked in the microwave. Wash the beans and place in a microwaveable bowl with butter. Microwave on high for 2 minutes. Test. If they are not done, cook another minute.

Chinese Garlic Steak

Oriental Peanut Noodles

EVERY NOW AND THEN, my family has a craving for spicy Chinese food. This dinner of garlic-flavored steak and peanuty noodles fits the bill.

Serves 4.

THIS MEAL CONTAINS A TOTAL OF 776 CALORIES PER SERVING WITH 30 PERCENT OF CALORIES FROM FAT.

⧖ Countdown

- *Marinate steak.*
- *Put water for noodles on to boil.*
- *While steak is marinating, make noodles.*
- *Cook steak.*

CHINESE GARLIC STEAK

THE ROMANS considered garlic an aphrodisiac. Homer praised it for its health-giving attributes, and the British used it to control infection during World War I. Whether or not garlic is a cure-all as its history suggests, it certainly produces magic in the kitchen.

1¼	pounds well-trimmed flank, tenderloin, sirloin or strip steak
½	cup low-sodium soy sauce
3	tablespoons brown sugar
6	medium cloves garlic, crushed through a press
2	teaspoons peanut oil

Cut steak into 1-inch strips. Mix soy sauce and sugar together. Stir to dissolve sugar. Add garlic. Place steak in a plastic bag or bowl and pour marinade over it. Let stand for 30 minutes, turning pieces after about 15 minutes.

Heat oil in a wok or frying pan. Remove meat from sauce. Drain and pat dry. When oil is smoking, add steak to the pan and toss for about 1 minute. Remove to individual plates. Add any remaining sauce and heat through. Spoon sauce over steak.

Shopping List

1¼ pounds well-trimmed flank, tenderloin, sirloin or strip steak
½ pound snow peas
½ pound fresh Chinese egg noodles or dried

Staples

garlic
brown sugar
crunchy peanut butter
sesame oil
low-sodium soy sauce
tea
rice-wine vinegar
peanut oil

Helpful Hints

- *Chicken may be used instead of beef.*

- *Cutting steak into strips helps to speed the marinating process. Buy precut stir-fry beef if your market has it.*

ORIENTAL PEANUT NOODLES

Helpful Hint

♦ *Fresh Chinese noodles can be bought in the cold case of the produce section of most supermarkets. Dried Chinese noodles, which may be substituted, can be found on the shelf in the Asian-products section.*

ALTHOUGH PEANUTS are usually considered as American as baseball, they have been very much a part of Asian cuisine since the 1500s, when the Spanish introduced this South American plant to the Malay Peninsula. Today, peanut butter has risen from its status as one of America's favorite lunch-box specials to the pantry of many famous restaurants. Thinning it with brewed tea gives this sauce an intriguing flavor.

½	**pound fresh Chinese egg noodles**
2	**teaspoons sesame oil,** *divided*
2	**cups snow peas, trimmed, halved if large**
3	**tablespoons crunchy peanut butter**
2	**tablespoons brewed tea**
2	**tablespoons low-sodium soy sauce**
2	**tablespoons rice-wine vinegar**
2	**medium cloves garlic, crushed through a press**

Bring a medium-size pot with 3 to 4 quarts of water to a boil and add noodles. Let boil about 1 minute. Drain immediately and run cold water through them and place in a large bowl. Toss in 1 teaspoon sesame oil. Bring a small pot of water to a boil and add snow peas. As soon as water returns to a boil, drain snow peas and rinse under cold water. Or microwave them on high for 1 minute. Add cooked snow peas to noodles.

In a small bowl, mix peanut butter and tea together to make a smooth sauce. Add remaining ingredients and stir in remaining teaspoon sesame oil. Toss sauce with noodles, making sure they are fully coated.

CHAPTER 5

Pork Dinners

Pork Dinners

◆

Cider Pork

Autumn Squash

Sautéed Green Beans

Shopping List

¾ pound pork tenderloin
½ pound green beans
1 small acorn squash
1 bunch fresh rosemary or dried
1 quart apple cider
1 small package walnuts
  (2½ ounces)

Staples

lemon
onion
raisins
butter or margarine
olive oil
salt
black peppercorns

Helpful Hint

♦ This recipe is for 2, but it can easily be doubled. Allot 15 minutes additional preparation time for peeling the squash if doubling the recipe.

♦ Sautéing onions until golden removes their bitter juices and caramelizes them.

I DECIDED to create this meal one fall day when the markets were filled with autumn colors and flavors: jugs of cider, green and orange squash and an array of nuts.

   Serves 2.

THIS MEAL CONTAINS A TOTAL OF 661 CALORIES PER SERVING WITH 24 PERCENT OF CALORIES FROM FAT.

⧗ Countdown

♦ Make squash.
♦ Make pork.
♦ While squash and pork cook, make beans.

AUTUMN SQUASH

THE SQUASH IS SAUTÉED and then left to finish cooking off the burner in the heat of the pan. This method allows it to soften while retaining its shape.

    1   tablespoon butter or margarine
    ½   medium onion, coarsely chopped (about 1 cup)
    2   cups cubed acorn squash, peeled and cut into ½-inch cubes
    ½   cup raisins
    1   tablespoon coarsely chopped walnuts
    3   tablespoons water
         Salt and freshly ground black pepper to taste

   Melt butter in a medium-size saucepan and gently sauté onion for 5 minutes until golden but not brown. Add squash and sauté another 2 minutes. Add raisins and walnuts and sauté 5 more minutes, stirring occasionally. Add water and salt and pepper to taste. Cover and remove from the heat. Let sit, covered, for 20 minutes, or until ready to serve.

CIDER PORK

THE PORK TENDERLOINS, which contain no bones and very little fat, are butterflied so that they will cook quickly.

¾ **pound pork tenderloin**
2 **tablespoons chopped fresh rosemary or 1 teaspoon dried**
1 **teaspoon olive oil**
1 **cup apple cider**
   Salt and freshly ground black pepper to taste

Trim fat from pork. Butterfly pork by pulling off the membrane until the tenderloin lies flat. Then cut pork in half horizontally and open it like a book. Do not cut all the way through. Sprinkle with rosemary. Heat oil in a nonstick skillet just large enough to hold pork snugly. Brown pork on all sides, about 5 minutes. Salt and pepper both sides. Add cider and bring to a simmer. Cover pan and cook on low heat for 10 minutes. Remove pork to a warm plate and cover with foil to keep warm. Raise heat and reduce liquid by half. Remove from the heat and spoon sauce over pork and serve.

SAUTÉED GREEN BEANS

THE AUTUMN PLATE of colors is finished with bright green beans. Blanching and cooling in cold water sets both their color and vitamins, and they only need a quick toss in hot oil to finish them. Alternatively, they can be cooked in a microwave oven.

1½ **cups green beans**
½   **teaspoon olive oil**
½   **tablespoon fresh lemon juice**
    Salt and freshly ground black pepper to taste

Wash and trim beans. Cut into 2-inch pieces. Bring a small saucepan of water to a boil. Add beans. When water returns to a boil, cook for 2 minutes. Drain and rinse under cold water. Heat oil in the same pan and add green beans. Toss in oil to warm through.

To cook in microwave: Place beans in a microwave-proof bowl, cover and cook on high for 5 minutes. Toss the beans in oil when they are cooked.

To finish, add lemon juice, salt and pepper to taste.

Helpful Hint

♦ *When the pork is cooked, it may be returned to the sauce to keep it warm while you finish the rest of the dinner.*

Whiskey Pork

Rosemary Lentils

Shopping List

4 pork chops (about 8 ounces each)
1 small bunch fresh rosemary or
*   dried*
1 small bunch fresh parsley
2-ounce piece lean ham
1 small package dried lentils

Staples

onion
garlic
bay leaves
Dijon mustard
cornstarch
brown sugar
olive oil
whiskey or apple juice
2 cans chicken stock (14½ ounces)
salt
black peppercorns

IN JANUARY, after the holiday rush, I usually feel a need to make a few meals that save pennies as well as calories. This is a hearty, low-budget meal, great for the winter months. Whiskey lends a subtle, intriguing flavor to the pork. Apple juice can be substituted.

Serves 4.

THIS MEAL CONTAINS A TOTAL OF 627 CALORIES PER SERVING WITH 23 PERCENT OF CALORIES FROM FAT.

⧗ Countdown

♦ *Make lentils.*
♦ *While lentils cook, make pork.*

ROSEMARY LENTILS

LENTILS ORIGINATED in central Asia, where they were cultivated in prehistoric times. They are rich in mineral salts and contain more protein than dried beans. For the busy cook, their chief virtue is that they don't need to be soaked and cook in about 30 minutes.

2	**cups defatted chicken stock**
2	**cups water**
1	**cup dried lentils**
½	**medium onion, chopped (about 1 cup)**
2	**bay leaves**
4	**teaspoons chopped fresh rosemary or 1½ teaspoons dried**
4	**medium cloves garlic, crushed through a press**
	Salt and freshly ground black pepper to taste
4	**tablespoons chopped fresh parsley**

Bring stock and water to a rolling boil. Place lentils in a strainer and rinse under cold water, picking out any stones. Add lentils, onion, bay leaves, rosemary and garlic to the water slowly so that it does not stop boiling. Reduce the heat, cover and simmer 20 minutes. Remove the lid and continue to cook on high to evaporate any remaining liquid. Season with salt and pepper to taste. Sprinkle with fresh parsley. Remove bay leaves before serving.

WHISKEY PORK

FLAMBÉING ALCOHOL has more purpose than just show. It evaporates the alcohol and caramelizes the sugars.

4	8 ounce pork chops
2	teaspoons olive oil
1	cup whiskey
½	cup defatted chicken stock
2	ounces chopped lean ham (½ cup)
2	tablespoons brown sugar
2	tablespoons Dijon mustard
1	teaspoon cornstarch
2	tablespoons water
	Salt and freshly ground black pepper to taste

Trim fat from chops. Heat oil in a large nonstick skillet and brown chops on both sides, about 2 minutes per side. Pour off any excess fat. Add whiskey and flambé. If cooking over gas, warm whisky in the pan for a few seconds and then tip the pan and let the flame ignite the liquid. Immediately remove from the heat and let the flame burn down. If you cook with electric heat, ignite with a match. Add stock. Cover the pan and lower the heat. Cook on low for 5 to 7 minutes, or until chops are cooked through. Remove the chops to a warm serving platter and cover with foil to keep warm.

Add ham, sugar and mustard and blend well together. Mix cornstarch and water together. Pour into sauce and cook, stirring, until it thickens. This will take about 1 minute. Add salt and pepper to taste. Pour some sauce over chops and serve the rest on the side.

Helpful Hints

♦ *Apple juice can be substituted for whiskey, if you prefer. In that case, reduce the juice over high heat to concentrate the flavors. It cannot be flambéed.*

♦ *For safety's sake when you flambé the whiskey, keep the pan lid nearby to snuff out the flame if necessary.*

♦ *Packaged presliced lean ham can be used, cut into squares.*

Barbecued Pork

Potato Salad

Sliced Tomatoes

Shopping List

1¼ pounds pork tenderloin
1 carrot
4 ripe tomatoes
1½ pounds red potatoes
1 bunch fresh chives or scallions
1 can tomato paste (8 ounces)

Staples

garlic
brown sugar
sugar
Dijon mustard
nonfat mayonnaise
Worcestershire sauce
Tabasco or other hot pepper sauce
white vinegar
canola oil
salt
black peppercorns

WHEN I ASKED my eldest son where he would like to go to celebrate after his graduation from law school, he said, "I want to have a relaxing dinner with everyone at home. How about barbecued pork and potato salad?" I created this menu so I could enjoy the day too. The potato salad, barbecue sauce and salad dressing can be made in advance, but this dinner can also be prepared easily in one step. Serve outdoors with some cold beer. The barbecue sauce is delicious, but if you are pressed for time, use your favorite bottled barbecue sauce.

Serves 4.

THIS MEAL CONTAINS A TOTAL OF 602 CALORIES PER SERVING WITH 17 PERCENT OF CALORIES FROM FAT.

⧗ Countdown

♦ *Preheat grill or broiler for pork.*
♦ *Cook potatoes.*
♦ *While potatoes boil, make pork.*
♦ *Finish potato salad and make tomatoes.*

POTATO SALAD

I LIKE RED POTATOES for this salad, but any type can be used. They will absorb more of the dressing flavors if you mix them together while they're still hot. Try to use fresh chives if you can.

1½	pounds red potatoes
3	tablespoons white vinegar
2–3	tablespoons Dijon mustard
2	tablespoons canola oil
⅓	cup chopped fresh chives or scallions
1	small carrot, peeled and diced
	Salt and freshly ground black pepper to taste

Helpful Hint

♦ *It's much easier to cut a bunch of chives with a scissors rather than chopping them in a food processor or with a knife.*

Wash potatoes and cut into 1-inch cubes. Place in a saucepan and add cold water to cover. Bring water to a boil and simmer for 20 minutes, or until cubes are cooked through. Mix vinegar, mustard and oil together in a serving bowl. Add chives and carrots. Drain potatoes and add to the bowl. Add salt and pepper to taste. Toss well, making sure potatoes are covered with sauce.

BARBECUED PORK

PORK TENDERLOIN not only cooks quickly but has very little fat. Brush the pork with the sauce before cooking it, then serve additional warmed sauce on the side so you can have as much or little as you like.

Helpful Hint

♦ *If using a charcoal grill, light it first and let the coals heat for 30 minutes, or light a gas grill or broiler about 10 minutes before it is needed.*

1¼	pounds pork tenderloin

BARBECUE SAUCE

1	cup tomato paste
⅓	cup Worcestershire sauce
⅓	cup brown sugar
¼	cup plus 4 teaspoons white vinegar
3	tablespoons Dijon mustard
8	medium cloves garlic, crushed through a press
2	teaspoons Tabasco or other hot pepper sauce

Trim fat from pork and poke holes in meat at varying intervals.

For barbecue sauce: Combine sauce ingredients and spoon or brush onto pork.

Place on a heated grill for 10 minutes. Turn and cook another 10 minutes. A thick tenderloin will take another 5 minutes. A meat thermometer inserted into the center should read 160 degrees F. Remove pork and let sit 5 minutes before carving. Meanwhile, warm remaining sauce. Carve pork, slicing the meat on an angle, and serve sauce on the side.

SLICED TOMATOES

THIS DRESSING takes only a few minutes to make, but if time is tight, you can slice some tomatoes and use a creamy low-fat bottled dressing instead.

4	ripe medium tomatoes
1	tablespoon nonfat mayonnaise
1	tablespoon white vinegar
½	teaspoon Dijon mustard
½	teaspoon sugar
	Salt and freshly ground black pepper to taste

Cut tomatoes into ¼-inch slices and place on serving platter. Mix mayonnaise, vinegar, mustard and sugar together. Add salt and pepper to taste. Spoon over tomatoes.

Italian Roast Pork

Herbed Garlic Lentils

Sautéed Green Beans & Tomatoes

PORK HAS BECOME one of the fastest-growing items on restaurant menus. Much of its newfound popularity has to do with the fact that it is now bred to be lean but remains as juicy and flavorful as ever. This hearty Italian dinner is perfect on a cold evening or great when you can grill the pork outside. If pressed for time, omit the beans and serve sliced tomatoes instead.

Serves 4.

THIS MEAL CONTAINS A TOTAL OF 651 CALORIES PER SERVING WITH 17 PERCENT OF CALORIES FROM FAT.

⧖ Countdown

- ◆ *Put chicken stock and water for lentils on to boil.*
- ◆ *Preheat oven to 400 degrees F for pork.*
- ◆ *Make lentils.*
- ◆ *Roast pork.*
- ◆ *While lentils and pork cook, make beans.*

HERBED GARLIC LENTILS

I USE LENTILS when I am in a hurry because they don't need soaking. In this recipe, they cook unattended while you prepare the rest of the meal.

2¼	cups defatted chicken stock, *divided*
2	cups water
1	cup dried lentils
2	bay leaves
4	teaspoons chopped fresh rosemary or 2 teaspoons dried
4	medium cloves garlic, crushed through a press
½	medium onion, chopped (about 1 cup)
2	teaspoons cider vinegar
2	teaspoons olive oil
	Salt and freshly ground black pepper to taste

Put 2 cups chicken stock and 2 cups water on to boil. Place lentils in a strainer and discard any stones that you find. Rinse and drain. When liquid is boiling rapidly, pour lentils into the pot slowly so that the water does not stop boiling. Add bay leaves, rosemary and garlic. Reduce the heat slightly and

Shopping List

1¼ pounds pork tenderloin
½ pound green beans
2 tomatoes
1 small bunch fresh rosemary
*   or dried*
1 small bunch fresh sage or dried
1 package lentils (12 ounces)
2 cans chicken stock
*   (14½ ounces each)*

Staples

onion
garlic
bay leaves
cider vinegar
olive oil
salt
black peppercorns

Helpful Hint

◆ *Chopped onion is used here and in the beans. Chop all of it together in a food processor and reserve ¼ cup for the beans.*

simmer 20 minutes. Meanwhile, heat ¼ cup chicken stock in a small nonstick skillet and add onion. Cover and cook until onion is transparent, adding more stock or water if onion starts to burn. Onion should be golden, not brown. Add onion to lentils as soon as they are cooked. After lentils have cooked 20 minutes, remove the lid, add vinegar and continue to cook on high to evaporate any remaining liquid, about 10 minutes. Stir in oil and season with salt and pepper to taste. Place on individual plates and arrange sliced pork on top.

ITALIAN ROAST PORK

THIS SIMPLE PORK needs about 25 minutes baking time to keep it juicy and flavorful. If it is cooked too long, it will become dry and toughen.

1¼	pounds pork tenderloin
2	medium cloves garlic, crushed through a press
2	tablespoons chopped fresh sage or 2 teaspoons rubbed dried sage
2	teaspoons olive oil
	Salt and freshly ground black pepper to taste

Helpful Hint
♦ *Use fresh sage if you can. It is available in supermarkets and has a much sweeter flavor than the dried.*

Preheat oven to 400 degrees F. Line a baking pan with foil. Remove fat from pork. Mix garlic and sage together. With a sharp knife, make several deep incisions in pork and insert a little of the garlic-sage mixture in each one. Brush meat with olive oil and place on the baking pan in the oven. Roast for 25 minutes, or until a meat thermometer reaches 160 degrees F. Remove, cover with foil and let stand a few minutes. Slice and serve over the lentils.

SAUTÉED GREEN BEANS & TOMATOES

ALTHOUGH THIS RECIPE calls for fresh tomatoes, when I have opened cans of tomatoes or tomato sauce in the refrigerator, I use them up in this dish. The measurements don't have to be exact; use about 1 cup of sauce for the recipe.

½	pound green beans, trimmed
1	teaspoon olive oil
¼	cup chopped onion
2	tomatoes, cut into ½-inch pieces
	Salt and freshly ground black pepper to taste

String green beans if they are large and cut into 1-inch pieces. Heat oil in a small nonstick skillet. Add beans, onion and tomatoes. Cover and simmer for 5 minutes. Beans will be a little crisp. Add salt and pepper to taste.

Pork Lo Mein

Spicy Cucumber Salad

EVER SINCE my college days in Boston, which has a wonderful Chinatown, one of my favorite dishes has been Lo Mein, probably because it was one of the few meals I could afford to eat in a restaurant. If pressed for time, omit the cucumbers.

Serves 4.

THIS MEAL CONTAINS A TOTAL OF 522 CALORIES PER SERVING WITH 20 PERCENT OF CALORIES FROM FAT.

⧗ Countdown

♦ *Put water for noodles on to boil.*
♦ *Make lo mein.*
♦ *Make cucumbers.*

PORK LO MEIN

LO MEIN IS an easily made dish containing boiled noodles that are then stir-fried. A little sesame oil mixed in just before serving heightens the flavor.

1	tablespoon cornstarch
2	tablespoons water
¾	pound pork tenderloin
¾	pound fresh Chinese egg noodles or dried
½	pound snow peas, trimmed
½	cup defatted chicken stock
2	tablespoons dry sherry
2	teaspoons oyster sauce
2	teaspoons peanut oil
½	medium onion, sliced (about 1 cup)
¼	pound broccoli florets (1½ cups)
2	teaspoons chopped fresh ginger
2	medium cloves garlic, crushed through a press
½	pound fresh bean sprouts (about 2 cups)
¼	pound mushrooms, sliced
2	tablespoons sesame oil
	Salt and freshly ground black pepper to taste

Mix 1 tablespoon cornstarch with water. Trim fat from pork. Cut pork into small cubes and toss in cornstarch mixture. Bring a large pot of 3 to 4 quarts water to a boil and add fresh noodles. As soon as water returns to a boil, drain

---

Shopping List

¾ *pound pork tenderloin*
¼ *pound mushrooms*
2 cucumbers
¼ *pound broccoli florets*
1-inch piece fresh ginger
½ *pound snow peas*
½ *pound fresh bean sprouts*
¾ *pound fresh Chinese noodles*
1 small bottle oyster sauce

Staples

onion
garlic
sugar
Tabasco or other hot pepper sauce
cornstarch
rice vinegar
sesame oil
peanut oil
dry sherry
chicken stock
salt
black peppercorns

Helpful Hints

♦ *This recipe calls for pork, but you may use beef, chicken or shrimp. The method is the same.*

♦ *Fresh Chinese noodles are available in the refrigerated section of most supermarkets, usually near the produce area.*

♦ *To save time chopping ginger, I peel the skin, cut ginger into small pieces and place in a garlic press with large holes. Hold it over the marinade to catch the juices.*

noodles. If using dried noodles, follow package instructions, cooking for about 3 minutes. Cut snow peas into 1-inch pieces. Mix chicken stock, sherry and oyster sauce together in a small bowl.

Place a wok or skillet over a high flame or heat and add peanut oil. Add onion and broccoli and stir-fry 2 minutes, tossing ingredients constantly. Add ginger and garlic, then add pork and cook 1 minute. Add snow peas, bean sprouts and mushrooms. Toss about 1 minute and add noodles. Stir-fry for about 2 to 3 minutes. Add oyster sauce mixture to the pan. Continue tossing for 2 more minutes. Add sesame oil, salt and pepper. Taste for seasoning and add more if necessary. Serve immediately.

♦ *Slice mushrooms in a food processor fitted with a thick slicing blade.*

♦ *Prepare all ingredients before starting to stir-fry. Arrange them on a chopping board or plate in order of cooking, so you won't have to refer to the recipe as you stir-fry.*

SPICY CUCUMBER SALAD

THE CRUNCHY, spicy salad adds a refreshing touch to the meal. Rice vinegar is weak and sweet. If you don't have any, add about 1 ounce water and ¼ teaspoon sugar to ¼ cup distilled vinegar.

⅓	cup rice vinegar
4	teaspoons sugar
½	teaspoon salt
¼	teaspoon freshly ground black pepper
4–6	drops Tabasco or other hot pepper sauce
2	cucumbers

Mix vinegar, sugar, salt, pepper and Tabasco together in a glass or nonaluminum bowl. Peel cucumbers and cut in half lengthwise. Scrape out seeds with a teaspoon. Slice and toss in dressing. Serve with lo mein.

CHAPTER 6

Lamb Dinners

Lamb Dinners

◆

Florentine Lamb Chops

Herbed Spinach

Minted Potatoes

Shopping List

4 loin lamb chops
*   (about 7 ounces each)*
4 shallots
2 pounds small red potatoes
1 small bunch fresh mint
1 small bunch fresh chives or
*   scallions*
1 small bunch fresh tarragon or
*   dried*
1 small bunch fresh rosemary or
*   dried*
2 packages frozen chopped spinach
*   (10 ounces each)*

Staples

garlic
canola oil
butter or margarine
dry sherry
chicken stock
salt
black peppercorns

To celebrate the new produce that arrives in the spring, I like to serve this dinner. Rosemary and garlic bring out the full flavor of the lamb, which is served over spinach seasoned with shallots and rosemary. The potatoes are tossed in a delicate mint butter.

    Serves 4.

This meal contains a total of 660 calories per serving with 32 percent of calories from fat.

⧗ Countdown

♦ *Preheat oven to 350 degrees F for lamb.*
♦ *Make potatoes.*
♦ *While potatoes cook, make spinach.*
♦ *While spinach cooks, begin cooking lamb.*
♦ *Finish lamb and spinach.*

MINTED POTATOES

Use whichever fresh herbs your market has. For example, basil or dill is a delicious alternative to the mint.

2	**pounds small red potatoes**
2	**tablespoons butter or margarine**
½	**cup chopped fresh mint**
	Salt and freshly ground black pepper to taste

    Wash potatoes and place in a large saucepan. Cover with cold water. Cover pan with a lid and bring water to a boil. Cook potatoes until soft, about 20 to 25 minutes. Drain. Melt butter in the same pan and add mint. Toss drained potatoes in the pan. Add salt and pepper to taste and serve.

HERBED SPINACH

Cultivated by the Persians around the sixth century, spinach figures prominently in spring and holiday dishes.

2	**10-ounce packages frozen chopped spinach**

1 tablespoon butter or margarine
4 medium shallots, chopped (about ¼ cup)
4 tablespoons chopped fresh chives or scallions
4 teaspoons chopped fresh tarragon or 2 teaspoons dried
   Salt and freshly ground black pepper to taste

Place frozen spinach in a saucepan and cover. Cook until spinach is defrosted, about 7 to 10 minutes. Remove the cover and raise the heat to remove all the moisture from spinach.

When it is ready, move spinach to the sides of the pan and add butter and shallots. Sauté about 1 to 2 minutes and mix with spinach. If using onion, sauté 5 minutes. Add chives, tarragon, salt and pepper to taste. Cover until ready to serve.

FLORENTINE LAMB CHOPS

IN THE PAST, springtime meant lambing season, and new or baby lamb became traditional fare in April. Today, good lamb is available year-round, but it remains a favorite dinner in the spring.

4 7-ounce loin lamb chops
1 tablespoon chopped fresh rosemary or ½ tablespoon dried
4 medium cloves garlic, crushed through a press
½ tablespoon canola oil
½ tablespoon butter or margarine
   Salt and freshly ground black pepper to taste
½ cup dry sherry
¼ cup defatted chicken stock

Preheat oven to 350 degrees F. Line a baking sheet with foil. Trim fat from chops. Rub chops with rosemary and crushed garlic. Heat oil in a nonstick skillet just large enough to hold the lamb chops in one layer. Add butter. When it is sizzling, add chops. When they are browned, turn them. Salt and pepper the cooked side. Remove to the baking sheet and place in oven for 15 minutes to finish cooking. Pour off fat from the skillet and add sherry, and boil, stirring and scraping up all the browned bits. Boil until reduced by half. Add chicken stock and reduce by half again.

When chops are finished, place spinach on individual plates and place the lamb on top. Spoon sauce over chops and spinach.

Helpful Hints

♦ *For ease, I have used frozen chopped spinach. It will take about 10 minutes to defrost, so start it cooking and then continue with the chops.*

♦ *A quarter of a medium onion can be substituted for the shallots.*

Helpful Hint

♦ *Loin lamb chops weigh between 5 and 7 ounces each. If your lamb chops are small, buy 2 per person and reduce the cooking time to 7 minutes.*

Spiced Lamb Chops

Green Pepper Couscous

Mint & Tomato Salad

Shopping List

4 loin lamb chops
  (about 7 ounces each)
2 medium green bell peppers
4 medium tomatoes
1 small bunch fresh mint
1 package precooked couscous
  (10 ounces)

Staples

onion
garlic
nonfat plain yogurt
butter or margarine
canola oil
ground allspice
dry white wine
salt
black peppercorns

SLOW-COOKED LAMB STEW AND COUSCOUS are traditional North African dishes. Here, the combination lives on in a time-saving version. Quick-cooking loin lamb chops in a light wine sauce are served over the couscous. A Middle Eastern salad of mint, tomato and yogurt provides refreshing contrast.

   Serves 4.

THIS MEAL CONTAINS A TOTAL OF 546 CALORIES PER SERVING WITH 28 PERCENT OF CALORIES FROM FAT.

⧖ Countdown

♦ *Make couscous.*
♦ *Make lamb.*
♦ *While lamb cooks, make tomatoes.*

GREEN PEPPER COUSCOUS

COUSCOUS DATES FROM earliest times and is really another form of pasta, made by moistening hard durum wheat and rolling it in flour to form tiny pellets. An authentic Moroccan couscous takes about an hour to make and requires three steamings in a couscoussière. Happily for us, precooked couscous, the kind found in supermarkets, takes only about 5 minutes to make.

1	tablespoon butter or margarine
½	medium onion, sliced (about 1 cup)
2	medium green bell peppers, diced (about 2 cups)
4	medium cloves garlic, crushed through a press
1½	cups water
1	cup precooked couscous
	Salt and freshly ground black pepper to taste

Helpful Hints

♦ *Make sure the couscous is marked "precooked." Check the description on the package.*

Melt butter in a nonstick saucepan and add onion. Sauté gently for about 10 minutes, or until onion is golden. Add green peppers and garlic and sauté another 5 minutes. Add water and bring to a boil. Stir in couscous, cover, and remove from the heat. Let stand 5 minutes. Fluff with a fork and add salt and pepper to taste.

SPICED LAMB CHOPS

THESE LAMB CHOPS are sprinkled with allspice and finished with a little white wine.

  1   teaspoon canola oil
  4   7-ounce loin lamb chops
  2   teaspoons ground allspice
      Salt and freshly ground black pepper to taste
  1   cup dry white wine

Heat oil in a large nonstick skillet. Sprinkle lamb chops with allspice. When oil is sizzling, add chops. Brown 1 minute and turn to brown the other side. Sprinkle cooked sides with salt and pepper to taste. Lower heat and cook for 10 minutes. Remove from pan and cover with foil to keep warm.

Pour excess fat from pan. Place back on the heat and add wine. Increase heat to boil, stirring to scrape up all the browned bits, and reduce wine by half. Place chops on individual plates and pour sauce over them.

MINT & TOMATO SALAD

RIPE, FRESH TOMATOES with a mint-yogurt dressing make a colorful finish to this quick Mediterranean dinner.

  4   ripe medium tomatoes
  ½   cup nonfat plain yogurt
  ½   cup chopped fresh mint
      Salt and freshly ground black pepper to taste

Cut tomatoes into bite-size wedges. Mix yogurt and mint together. Sprinkle tomatoes with salt and pepper to taste. Toss with yogurt dressing. Serve with couscous and lamb.

Lamb With Lemon Sauce

Roasted French Fries

Green Beans Vinaigrette

Shopping List

1¼ pounds boneless loin of lamb or 4 loin chops (about 7 ounces each)
2 lemons
1 pound small green beans
1 small bunch fresh rosemary or dried
1 red onion
2 pounds red potatoes
1 small jar red currant jelly

Staples

lemons (2)
garlic
onion
all-purpose flour
Dijon mustard
butter or margarine
canola oil
vegetable-oil cooking spray
chicken stock
salt
black peppercorns

WHEN ENGLISH RANCHERS tried to introduce lamb to the western United States, beef won the battle. I'll never forget one evening when we were having dinner in a Houston restaurant with some friends. After Betty ordered lamb, her very Texan husband turned to her saying, "Deah, have you forgotten this is beef country?" Today, however, most Americans are finally beginning to appreciate lamb the way the French and English have for centuries. It's tender and needs very little cooking. The sauce for this lamb is slightly sweet and gives a rich-flavored coating. It comes with oven-crisped French fries and a green bean salad. If pressed for time, omit the beans and make a tossed salad with whatever greens you have on hand and use low-fat bottled salad dressing.

Serves 4.

THIS MEAL CONTAINS A TOTAL OF 618 CALORIES PER SERVING WITH 31 PERCENT OF CALORIES FROM FAT.

⧖ Countdown

♦ *Preheat oven to 450 degrees F for potatoes.*
♦ *Make potatoes.*
♦ *Put water for beans on to boil.*
♦ *Make lamb.*
♦ *While lamb is cooking, make beans.*
♦ *Finish lamb.*

ROASTED FRENCH FRIES

ROASTING FRENCH FRIES in the oven crisps them outside, while cooking them to tenderness inside.

> **Vegetable-oil cooking spray**
> 2 **pounds red potatoes**
> 2 **tablespoons butter or margarine**
> 4 **medium cloves garlic, crushed through a press**
> **Salt and freshly ground black pepper to taste**

Preheat oven to 450 degrees F. Line a baking sheet or roasting pan with foil and spray with vegetable-oil cooking spray. Wash and slice potatoes in half lengthwise. Slice each in half lengthwise again. Cut each slice into ¼-inch-thick

Helpful Hint

♦ *Make sure the pan is large enough to accommodate the potatoes in a single layer so they will become crisp.*

strips. Melt butter and garlic together. This can be done in the microwave. Scatter potato strips in one layer on the baking sheet and brush melted butter mixture over them. Toss to make sure all potatoes are completely coated. Place on the middle shelf in the oven for 15 minutes. Remove and turn strips and roast for another 15 minutes. When potatoes are finished, remove and salt and pepper them.

LAMB WITH LEMON SAUCE

You MAY NEED to ask the butcher for lamb loin, for it is not usually on display in the supermarket. Substitute lamb loin chops, if necessary. Brown and cook the chops using the same method.

Helpful Hint

♦ *You may also use 8 smaller chops, adjusting the cooking time accordingly.*

1¼	pounds boneless loin of lamb or 4 chops, about 7 ounces each
2	medium cloves garlic, crushed through a press
2	teaspoons chopped fresh rosemary or 1 teaspoon dried
2	teaspoons canola oil
½	medium red onion, sliced (about 1 cup)
1	cup defatted chicken stock, *divided*
1	tablespoon all-purpose flour
2	tablespoons red currant jelly
2	tablespoons fresh lemon juice
	Salt and freshly ground black pepper to taste

Trim fat from lamb. Roll lamb in garlic and rosemary. Heat oil in a large nonstick skillet. Place meat in pan and brown on all sides. Lower the heat, cover and cook 15 minutes, turning once during the cooking. For chops, cook 5 to 7 minutes, turning once.

Remove to a plate and cover with foil to keep warm. Tip any fat out of the pan. There will be very little. Add onion and ¼ cup chicken stock. Cook over medium heat until onion is golden, about 5 minutes. Sprinkle in flour and cook, stirring, for 1 minute. Add remaining ¾ cup stock and let sauce cook so it reduces slightly. Stir jelly well so there are no lumps and add to sauce. Add lemon juice, salt and pepper. Taste and add more salt and pepper, if needed. Strain sauce. Slice lamb and spoon sauce over it.

GREEN BEANS VINAIGRETTE

SMALL, THIN GREEN BEANS, called *haricots verts* or French green beans, are now available in some supermarkets. They're tender, sweet and perfect for this dinner. Substitute regular green beans, trimmed and cut into 2-inch lengths, if small ones prove difficult to find.

1	pound small green beans, trimmed

Vinaigrette Dressing
½ tablespoon fresh lemon juice
2 teaspoons Dijon mustard
1 tablespoon defatted chicken stock
1 teaspoon corn or canola oil
   Salt and freshly ground black pepper to taste

Bring a small saucepan of water to a boil and add green beans. If using small beans, drain as soon as water returns to a boil. For larger beans, boil 3 to 4 minutes and drain. Refresh under ice-cold water. Or, to microwave: Cook, covered, on high for 4 minutes for small beans, 7 minutes for larger ones.

For vinaigrette dressing: Whisk lemon juice and mustard together until smooth. Whisk in chicken stock and oil. Season with salt and pepper. Toss with green beans.

Middle Eastern Meatballs

Zucchini Salad

IN CREATING the following recipes, I have tried to capture the delicate flavor and excitement of the original while minimizing preparation time. The meatballs combine ground lamb and beef, flavored with cinnamon. They are broiled and placed in warm pita bread pockets, which catch the tasty juices. Some freshly chopped parsley, onion and a little yogurt are spooned into the bread for a hot sandwich.

Serves 4.

THIS MEAL CONTAINS A TOTAL OF 652 CALORIES PER SERVING WITH 12 PERCENT OF CALORIES FROM FAT.

⧗ Countdown

- *Preheat broiler for meatballs.*
- *Put a pot of water on to boil for zucchini.*
- *Form meatballs.*
- *Make salad.*
- *Broil meatballs, and while they are cooking, warm pitas.*

MIDDLE EASTERN MEATBALLS

THE MEATBALLS can also be served over a bed of fluffy rice with some chopped parsley and onions sprinkled on top.

½	cup raisins
¾	pound ground lamb
½	pound ground round beef
2	medium onions, chopped (about 2 cups), *divided*
2	teaspoons ground cinnamon
2	teaspoons salt
6	pita breads, halved
1	cup chopped fresh parsley
¼	cup nonfat plain yogurt or more to taste

Preheat broiler. Place raisins in a strainer and rinse under cold water to plump them up. Drain. Thoroughly mix lamb, beef, 1 cup chopped onion, raisins, cinnamon and salt together. To test for seasoning, take a little bit of the mixture and either sauté it in a skillet or cook it in the microwave for a few seconds, then taste. Add more cinnamon or salt, if necessary. Roll into meatballs about 1 inch in diameter. Place meatballs on a tray lined with foil. Broil for 5 minutes and turn meatballs over. Broil for another 3 to 4 minutes. If you like

Shopping List

¾ pound ground lamb
½ pound ground round beef
4 scallions
1 pound zucchini
1 medium head lettuce
1 bunch fresh parsley
6 pita breads

Staples

lemon
onions (2)
garlic
raisins
ground cinnamon
nonfat plain yogurt
olive oil
chicken stock
salt
black peppercorns

Helpful Hint

- *The meat should be finely ground and extra lean. Ask the meat department to grind it for you.*

your meatballs well done, cook 3 to 4 minutes longer.

While meat is cooking, place pita breads on a low rack for 5 minutes to warm through.

To serve: Open pita breads and divide meatballs among them. Sprinkle parsley and remaining onion on top and add a spoonful of yogurt. Serve immediately.

ZUCCHINI SALAD

EVERY MIDDLE EASTERN meal includes at least one salad. Here, the zucchini is cooked lightly and tossed with garlic-lemon dressing.

2	**tablespoons fresh lemon juice**
4	**medium cloves garlic, crushed through a press**
¼	**cup defatted chicken stock**
4	**teaspoons olive oil**
4	**scallions, trimmed and sliced**
	Salt and freshly ground black pepper to taste
1	**pound zucchini, sliced (about 4 cups)**
	Several lettuce leaves, washed

Bring a pot of water to boil. Mix together lemon juice and garlic. Whisk in stock and oil. Add scallions, salt and pepper to taste. Add zucchini to water. Let water return to a boil and simmer for 1 to 2 minutes, uncovered. Or cook zucchini in microwave, covered, on high for 5 minutes. Drain and toss in the dressing. Serve on a bed of lettuce leaves.

Lamb & Eggplant Kabobs
Mint Pesto Linguine

SERVING LAMB with mint pesto linguine gives a new twist to the usual combination of lamb and mint sauce. I came upon this recipe for pesto while exploring the shops and small restaurants in the Italian area of Providence, Rhode Island. The mint makes a wonderful alternative to basil in a fresh pesto. *See photograph on the cover.*

   Serves 4.

THIS MEAL CONTAINS A TOTAL OF 607 CALORIES PER SERVING WITH 32 PERCENT OF CALORIES FROM FAT.

⌛ Countdown
♦ *Put water for pasta on to boil.*
♦ *Preheat grill or broiler for lamb.*
♦ *Wash and drain mint for pesto.*
♦ *Marinate lamb.*
♦ *While lamb marinates, make pesto sauce.*
♦ *Assemble kabobs and cook meat kabobs.*
♦ *Cook vegetable kabobs.*
♦ *Cook pasta.*

LAMB & EGGPLANT KABOBS

ALTHOUGH the colorful array of vegetables and meat in kabobs is attractive, I find that the meat and vegetables often don't cook in the same amount of time, with the vegetables usually falling off the skewer before the meat is cooked. Here, the lamb and eggplant are threaded on one set of skewers and the peppers and tomatoes on the other, giving them all a chance to cook evenly in their own time. I sometimes remove meat and vegetables from the skewers and serve them on a platter.

MARINADE
¼	cup fresh lemon juice
2	tablespoons chopped onion
4	teaspoons brown sugar
4	medium cloves garlic, crushed through a press
2	teaspoons chopped fresh rosemary or 1 teaspoon dried

KABOBS
1¼	pounds lamb cubes, cut from leg into 1¼-inch cubes
½	pound eggplant, unpeeled
2	medium green bell peppers

Shopping List

1¼ pounds lamb cubes, cut from leg
½ pound eggplant
2 green bell peppers
8 cherry tomatoes
3 lemons
1 small bunch fresh rosemary or dried
2 bunches fresh mint
1 small jar pine nuts (1¾ ounces)
2-ounce piece Parmesan cheese
½ pound linguine

Staples

garlic
onion
brown sugar
olive oil
salt
black peppercorns
8 kabob skewers
   (at least 10 inches long)

Helpful Hints

♦ *Kabobs can be cooked either on the grill or under the broiler. Preheat a gas grill or broiler for 10 minutes, or start a charcoal fire 30 minutes ahead. The new smokeless indoor stovetop grills are a great alternative if you don't have an outdoor grill. Make sure the grill grates are clean.*

♦ *Lemon and crushed garlic are used both here and in the pesto. Squeeze all the lemon juice and crush all the garlic at one time; reserve 1 tablespoon lemon juice and 2 teaspoons garlic for the pesto.*

8	cherry tomatoes or 2 tomatoes, quartered
2	teaspoons olive oil

Preheat broiler or grill. If using wooden skewers, soak in water.

For marinade: Mix marinade ingredients together and add lamb cubes. Marinate 20 minutes, turning cubes once during this time. Wash eggplant and cut into 1-inch cubes. Wash and seed pepper and cut into large pieces about 2 inches square. Remove lamb from marinade and pat dry.

For kabobs: Place lamb cubes and eggplant on 4 skewers, alternating them on the skewers. If your skewers are small, you may need extra ones. Place green peppers and tomatoes on 4 other skewers, alternating them. Brush vegetables with oil.

Grill lamb and eggplant for 15 minutes, turning once during grilling. After the first 5 minutes, place green peppers and tomatoes on the grill for 10 minutes, turning once after 5 minutes. Or, if using the broiler, line a baking tray with foil and place kabobs on the tray. Broil for the same length of time.

To serve: Remove vegetables and lamb from the skewers and place on a serving plate.

MINT PESTO LINGUINE

THE TRADITIONAL WAY of making pesto is to pound and mash fresh garlic and pine nuts in a mortar and pestle into a fragrant paste that is used to dress up pasta, potatoes, pizzas and sandwiches. Thanks to the food processor and blender, it has become a quick and easy sauce to make. In this version, only a little oil is added.

Helpful Hint

♦ *Any kind of fresh mint may be used.*

4	cups fresh mint leaves, loosely packed
⅓	cup water
4	medium cloves garlic, crushed through a press
1	tablespoon fresh lemon juice
2	teaspoons olive oil
½	cup freshly grated Parmesan cheese
2	tablespoons pine nuts
	Salt and freshly ground black pepper to taste
½	pound linguine

Bring a large pot with 3 to 4 quarts of water to a boil. Carefully wash and dry mint leaves. Place in the bowl of a food processor. Add water, garlic, lemon juice and oil. Process until the mixture reaches sauce consistency. Spoon into a bowl large enough to serve pasta. Fold in cheese and pine nuts. Add salt and pepper to taste. When water is boiling, add pasta and cook about 10 minutes. Drain linguine and toss in pesto sauce.

CHAPTER 7

Veal Dinners

Veal Dinners

◆

Veal Meat Loaf

Mashed Potatoes

THIS IS A DELICIOUS, modern version of an old childhood favorite: meat loaf and mashed potatoes. The meat loaf is made with veal, rather than beef and pork, giving it a lighter taste. It is so simple that you may want to double it and freeze half. Pureed celery flavors the potatoes.

Serves 4.

THIS MEAL CONTAINS A TOTAL OF 459 CALORIES PER SERVING WITH 25 PERCENT OF CALORIES FROM FAT.

⧗ Countdown

- ♦ *Preheat oven to 400 degrees F for meat loaf.*
- ♦ *Put potatoes and celery on to cook.*
- ♦ *Make meat loaf.*
- ♦ *While meat loaf cooks, finish potatoes.*

MASHED POTATOES

IN THE CONTEST between smooth and lumpy mashed potatoes, my vote goes to lumpy. I mash the potatoes in a food processor using the plastic blade. Be careful not to overprocess, or they will become gluey. A food mill or potato ricer can also be used.

1½	**pounds red potatoes**
8	**medium stalks celery, diced (about 4 cups)**
1	**ounce grating cheese: Cheddar, Jarlsburg or gruyère (about ¼ cup grated)**
⅔	**cup skim milk**
	Salt and freshly ground black pepper to taste

Wash potatoes but do not peel. Place potatoes and celery in a saucepan and cover with cold water. Cover with a lid and bring to a boil. Boil 30 minutes, or until the potatoes are cooked through.

Drain thoroughly and cut potatoes in quarters. Process potatoes and celery in a food processor fitted with a plastic or dough blade for 3 to 5 seconds. Or mash through a food mill or potato ricer. Mix in cheese, milk, salt and pepper to taste. Serve with juices from the meat loaf poured over top.

Shopping List

1¼ pounds ground veal
1 medium bunch celery
1 carrot
6 ounces mushrooms
1 bunch fresh parsley
1½ pounds red potatoes
1-ounce piece grating cheese (Cheddar, Jarlsburg or gruyère)

Staples

onion
whole or ground nutmeg
skim milk
bread crumbs
olive oil
salt
black peppercorns

Helpful Hint

♦ *Leave the skins on the potatoes. This way, they won't absorb water while they're cooking. The skins add color and texture to the finished dish.*

VEAL MEAT LOAF

To speed baking time, I form my meat loaf into loaves on a baking sheet rather than in a loaf pan. Freshly grated nutmeg gives this meat loaf its special flavor. I prefer to spend a couple of extra minutes and grate my own since it gives a sweeter, fuller flavor than ground nutmeg, but you can, of course, use the ground. If you do, make sure it is no more than 6 months old, or it will overpower the flavor of the veal.

2	teaspoons olive oil
½	medium onion, diced (1 cup)
1	medium stalk celery, diced (about ½ cup)
1	medium carrot, diced (about ½ cup)
6	ounces mushrooms, diced (about 1 cup)
1¼	pounds ground veal
1	cup chopped fresh parsley
½	cup bread crumbs
1	teaspoon freshly grated nutmeg or ½ teaspoon ground
1	teaspoon salt
	Freshly ground black pepper to taste

Preheat oven to 400 degrees F. Heat oil in a small nonstick skillet and add onion. Sauté for 3 minutes and add celery, carrot and mushrooms. Sauté for 5 minutes over medium-high heat. Mix vegetables into ground veal. Add parsley, bread crumbs, nutmeg, salt and pepper. Mix well.

Line a baking sheet with foil. Divide mixture into 4 parts and mold into 4 small loaves on the sheet. Place in the oven for 15 to 20 minutes, or until the loaves are slightly pink in the middle. Serve immediately.

Sautéed Veal With Leeks

Lemon-Parsley Rice

Shopping List

1¼ pounds stewing veal
4 medium leeks
1 bunch fresh parsley
2 lemons
bouquet garni (fresh parsley,
   bay leaves, fresh thyme)

Staples

butter or margarine
skim milk
long-grain white rice
raisins
dry white wine
canola oil
1 can chicken stock (14½ ounces)
salt
black peppercorns

Helpful Hints

♦ *Buy stewing veal that is cut into at least 1-inch squares without a lot of gristle. Larger pieces will cook more evenly and remain juicy.*

♦ *This dish freezes well. If you have time, double the recipe and freeze half.*

♦ *Wash leeks by cutting them in half lengthwise and in half again and running them under cold water. They can be sliced in a food processor fitted with a thin slicing blade.*

WHEN I WANT a hearty dinner, I make this recipe. The leeks, lemon juice and raisins give this provincial French dish a slightly Middle Eastern flavor.
   Serves 4.

THIS MEAL CONTAINS A TOTAL OF 618 CALORIES PER SERVING WITH 15 PERCENT OF CALORIES FROM FAT.

⧗ Countdown
♦ *Make veal.*
♦ *Make rice.*

SAUTÉED VEAL WITH LEEKS

STEWING VEAL is cut from either the shoulder or parts of the leg that are not used for more expensive scaloppine. In most supermarkets, it can be found already cut into cubes, but if not, ask the butcher to prepare it while you shop. The recipe calls for a bouquet garni, a bundle of fresh herbs. It's easy to make one. Simply tie some parsley, thyme sprigs and a bay leaf together with some kitchen string and add it to the pan with the other ingredients. If you don't have time for that, at least throw some fresh parsley and a bay leaf into the sauce and fish them out just before serving.

1¼	**pounds stewing veal**
2	**teaspoons canola oil**
4	**medium leeks**
½	**cup dry white wine**
½	**cup skim milk**
	Bouquet garni (2 sprigs parsley, 2 bay leaves, 2 sprigs thyme)
	Salt and freshly ground black pepper to taste
¼	**cup raisins**
2	**tablespoons fresh lemon juice**

   Trim fat from veal and cut into 1-inch cubes. If veal is already cubed, trim any fat and gristle that remains. Heat oil on medium-high heat in a large nonstick skillet and add veal. Sauté veal on all sides until golden brown, about 5 minutes. Meanwhile, trim any dark or damaged leaves from leeks and wash. Thinly slice and add to the skillet with meat. Add wine, milk and bouquet garni. Add a little salt and pepper. Cover and simmer gently for about 20 minutes. Remove bouquet garni and add raisins and lemon juice. Cook another 5 minutes. Taste for seasoning. Add more salt and pepper, if necessary.

LEMON-PARSLEY RICE

LEMON ADDS a refreshing touch to many dishes. Here, it flavors the rice, blending well with the veal sauce.

1   cup long-grain white rice
1   tablespoon butter or margarine
2   cups defatted chicken stock
    Grated rind of 2 lemons
2   tablespoons fresh lemon juice
½   cup chopped fresh parsley
    Salt and freshly ground black pepper to taste

Place rice in a colander and rinse under cold water. Heat butter in a small heavy-bottomed skillet and sauté rice for 1 minute. Add chicken stock, grated lemon rind and lemon juice. Bring to a boil, reduce heat and cook, covered, for 15 minutes, or until liquid is absorbed and rice is cooked through. If rice begins to stick to the pan before it is done, add a little more chicken stock. Add parsley and toss well. Add salt and pepper to taste.

Herbed Grilled Veal

Sautéed Green Beans & Ham

Tomato-Basil Pasta

Shopping List

1½ pounds tenderloin of veal or 4 veal loin chops (7 ounces each)
1¼ pounds ripe tomatoes or 1 can crushed tomatoes (28 ounces)
1 small bunch fresh basil or 1 bunch fresh parsley
1 small bunch fresh oregano or dried
1 small bunch fresh rosemary or dried
¾ pound fresh green beans
2-ounce piece lean low-sodium ham
2-ounce piece Parmesan cheese
¾ pound spaghettini

Staples

garlic
butter or margarine
ground cayenne
tomato paste
olive oil
salt
black peppercorns

Helpful Hint

♦ *Preheat a gas grill for 10 minutes, or start a charcoal fire 30 minutes ahead, or preheat oven to 400 degrees F.*

A SIMPLE GRILLED VEAL TENDERLOIN flavored with oregano and rosemary is served with green beans that have been sautéed with ham. The tomato sauce on the accompanying pasta has become one of my favorites because it is so easy. It is prepared in seconds in a food processor. *See photograph, page 98.*

    Serves 4.

THIS MEAL CONTAINS A TOTAL OF 754 CALORIES PER SERVING WITH 30 PERCENT OF CALORIES FROM FAT.

⌛ Countdown

♦ *Put water for pasta on to boil.*
♦ *Preheat grill or oven to 400 degrees F for veal.*
♦ *Cook veal.*
♦ *Cook beans.*
♦ *Make sauce for pasta.*
♦ *Cook pasta.*

HERBED GRILLED VEAL

TENDERLOIN OF VEAL is available in most supermarkets, but you may have to ask the butcher for it. You can substitute veal loin chops. This dish is delicious hot or cold. It takes only 20 minutes to roast or grill, even less time if chops are used.

1½	pounds veal tenderloin or 4 veal loin chops, about 7 ounces each
2	teaspoons olive oil
1	teaspoon chopped fresh oregano or ½ teaspoon dried
1	teaspoon chopped fresh rosemary or ½ teaspoon dried
	Salt and freshly ground black pepper to taste

Preheat grill. Trim fat from veal and brush it with oil. Sprinkle oregano and rosemary on top. Grill veal for 10 minutes, or about 5 minutes for chops. Turn and cook 10 more minutes, about 5 more for chops. The meat will be seared outside and rare and juicy inside. Leave on the grill 5 more minutes if you prefer it more well done. Remove from grill and add salt and pepper to taste. Cover with foil and let stand 5 minutes. Slice thinly and serve with the pasta. If using an oven, place veal on a rack in a roasting pan and roast for the same length of time. For chops, grill or broil 4 minutes, turn and cook another 4 minutes.

SAUTÉED GREEN BEANS & HAM

LEAN HAM adds flavor to these beans.

¾	pounds fresh green beans
1	tablespoon butter or margarine
2	medium cloves garlic, crushed through a press
½	cup lean, low-sodium ham, cut into small cubes (2 ounces)
	Salt and freshly ground black pepper to taste

Bring a pot of water to a boil. Trim beans and cut into 2-inch lengths. Add beans to boiling water. As soon as water returns to a boil, drain beans, or if you prefer, cook 5 minutes longer to desired tenderness. Refresh under cold water. Or, beans can be blanched in a microwave oven: Sprinkle with water and cook on high for 5 minutes.

Melt butter in a skillet and add garlic. Add beans and ham to the skillet. Toss and warm through, about 2 minutes. Add salt and pepper to taste.

Helpful Hint

♦ *Packaged presliced ham cut into squares can be substituted.*

TOMATO-BASIL PASTA

JOY AND STANLEY, friends who live nearby, stopped in one night while I was making this sauce. They prefer their food with as little fat as possible, so I made a second batch without oil and we tasted them side by side. Joy voted for the no-oil sauce and Stanley for the one with oil. My husband thought it was delicious both ways. The sauce should be ready to pour over the pasta as soon as it is drained. The heat of the pasta will cook it.

1¼	pounds tomatoes (about 4 medium) or 2½ cups canned whole tomatoes
¾	cup chopped fresh basil
3	tablespoons tomato paste
1½	tablespoons olive oil
4	medium cloves garlic, crushed through a press
¼	teaspoon ground cayenne
	Salt and freshly ground black pepper to taste
¾	pound spaghettini
½	cup freshly grated Parmesan cheese

Bring a large pot with 3 to 4 quarts of water to a boil. Wash tomatoes and remove stems. Cut into quarters and place in a food processor with basil, tomato paste, oil and garlic. Process the mixture until it reaches sauce consistency. Add cayenne, salt and pepper. Taste for seasoning and add more, if necessary. Add pasta to boiling water. When water returns to a boil, cook for 8 minutes, or until pasta is tender but firm. Drain and place in a serving bowl. Pour tomato sauce over the top and mix thoroughly. Serve immediately. Pass Parmesan to sprinkle on top.

Helpful Hints

♦ *Use canned crushed tomatoes if ripe ones are unavailable. They're picked at their peak and make an excellent sauce. Follow the same method.*

♦ *This sauce can also be served on meat or in any recipe requiring tomato sauce.*

♦ *Fresh basil makes a difference. If you can't find it, use fresh parsley with a teaspoon of dried oregano.*

Normandy Veal

Orzo With Caraway Seeds

Steamed Broccoli

Shopping List

4 veal rib chops (about 5 ounces each)
2 Granny Smith apples
1 leek
1 pound broccoli florets
1 quart apple juice
1 small box orzo (8 ounces)
whole caraway seeds
2 ounces Calvados, apple brandy or regular brandy

Staples

lemon
butter or margarine
olive oil
salt
black peppercorns

Helpful Hints

♦ *Veal loin chops can also be used.*

♦ *The veal will give off some fat as it browns, so no oil or butter is necessary.*

♦ *Granny Smith apples are juicy but hold their shape well when cooked.*

♦ *Slice apples and leeks in a food processor fitted with a thin slicing blade.*

WHILE LIVING IN PARIS, we spent many weekends in Normandy. It's French apple country, and apples play in important role in the cuisine there. In this dinner, tender veal chops are served in a rich sauce of apple, brandy and leeks and served over orzo, with broccoli as an accompaniment. *See photograph, page 171.*
     Serves 4.

THIS MEAL CONTAINS A TOTAL OF 555 CALORIES PER SERVING WITH 21 PERCENT OF CALORIES FROM FAT.

⧖ Countdown

♦ *Put water for orzo on to boil.*
♦ *Make veal.*
♦ *Cook orzo.*
♦ *While orzo is boiling, steam broccoli.*

NORMANDY VEAL

AMERICAN APPLE BRANDY can be substituted for Calvados. It tends to be less sweet. Taste the sauce and add a teaspoon of sugar if necessary. Or use ordinary brandy.

4	**5 ounce veal rib chops**
	Salt and freshly ground black pepper to taste
1	**medium leek, sliced (about 2 cups)**
2	**Granny Smith apples**
¼	**cup Calvados (apple brandy) or ordinary brandy**
1¾	**cups apple juice**

Heat a nonstick skillet just large enough to hold the veal in one layer for a few seconds. Add chops and brown 2 minutes per side. Salt and pepper the cooked side. Lower the heat and cook about 4 minutes, depending on the thickness of the chops. Remove to a plate and cover with foil to keep warm. Add leek and sauté for 5 minutes, without browning, adding a tablespoon or so of apple juice if leeks begin to stick. Cut apples into quarters and core. Slice into ¼-inch pieces and add to leek. Sauté for 3 minutes, turning them with a fork to prevent breaking. Add Calvados to the pan, stirring to scrape up the browned bits. Cook 2 minutes. Add apple juice, increase heat and boil to reduce liquid by about half, about 7 to 10 minutes. It should become thicker and a little syrupy. Return veal to sauce to warm through, about 1 minute. Serve the veal over a bed of orzo with apples, leeks and sauce spooned on top.

ORZO WITH CARAWAY SEEDS

ORZO IS A rice-shaped pasta sold in most supermarkets. It is small, has a firm texture and easily absorbs the flavor of the sauce.

- 1½ **cups orzo**
- 4 **teaspoons whole caraway seeds**
- 1 **tablespoon butter or margarine**
  Salt and freshly ground black pepper to taste

Bring a large pot with 3 to 4 quarts of water to a boil and add orzo. Cook for about 10 minutes, or until orzo is cooked through but still firm. Drain. Mix caraway seeds and butter into the hot orzo. Add salt and pepper to taste.

STEAMED BROCCOLI

MANY MARKETS carry precut broccoli florets either in the produce section or on the salad bar. Buy these if you want to save time.

- 1 **pound broccoli florets**
- 2 **teaspoons olive oil**
- 1 **tablespoon fresh lemon juice**
  Salt and freshly ground black pepper to taste

Place broccoli in a steaming basket. Place over ½ inch water. Cover and bring to a boil. Steam 5 minutes. Or to microwave: Place in microwave-safe serving bowl, cover and cook on high for 5 minutes. Sprinkle cooked broccoli with oil. Toss with lemon juice, salt and pepper.

Quick-Fried Diced Veal

Simple Fried Rice

Shopping List

1¼ pounds veal cutlets
1 cucumber
¾ pound green beans
1 package frozen peas (10-ounce package)
1 small bottle hoisin sauce
1 small bottle low-sodium tamari or low-sodium soy sauce
¼ pound lean ham

Staples

onion
garlic
cornstarch
long-grain white rice
sugar
peanut oil
dry sherry
black peppercorns

WOK COOKING is a good way to use up any leftover rice, meat or vegetables. These recipes for an inventive veal stir-fry with beans and cucumbers and fried rice are based on a menu that cookbook author Kenneth Lo made at my cooking school in London. Lo arrived for the class wearing a beautiful powder-blue cashmere sweater. When I offered him an apron, he refused, saying, "This dish is so easy, I won't make a mess." And he didn't.

Serves 4.

THIS MEAL CONTAINS A TOTAL OF 625 CALORIES PER SERVING WITH 18 PERCENT OF CALORIES FROM FAT.

⧗ Countdown

♦ *Put water for rice on to boil.*
♦ *Marinate veal.*
♦ *Make rice.*
♦ *Make veal in same wok.*

SIMPLE FRIED RICE

IF YOU HAVE leftover rice, use it. You will need about 3 cups cooked.

1	cup uncooked long-grain white rice (3 cups cooked)
1	tablespoon peanut oil
1	medium onion, diced (about 1 cup)
¼	pound lean roasted ham (⅔ cup diced)
½	cup frozen peas
1	tablespoon low-sodium tamari or low-sodium soy sauce
	Freshly ground black pepper to taste

Helpful Hints

♦ *Don't bother washing the wok after the rice is cooked; you can cook the veal in it immediately after.*

♦ *Like soy sauce, tamari is made from soybeans, but it is thicker, with a milder flavor. Low-sodium soy sauce can be substituted.*

If using uncooked rice, place in a strainer and wash. Put a large pot with 3 to 4 quarts of water on to boil. Add rice to boiling water. Cook, uncovered, for 10 minutes. Test a few grains. They should be soft throughout but still firm. Drain.

Heat oil in a wok or skillet. Add onion and cook for 1 minute. Add ham and cook 2 minutes, then add peas. Add cooked rice and cook 2 minutes. Add tamari and cook 1 minute, tossing to blend with the other ingredients.

QUICK-FRIED DICED VEAL

MOST OF YOUR TIME preparing this dish will be spent cutting up the ingredients.

¼   cup dry sherry
2   teaspoons sugar
4   medium cloves garlic, crushed through a press
1¼ pounds veal cutlets
1   tablespoon cornstarch
1   tablespoon low-sodium tamari or low-sodium soy sauce
1   tablespoon hoisin sauce
2   tablespoons peanut oil, *divided*
¾   pound green beans, trimmed and cut into 1-inch lengths
1   cucumber, unpeeled, cut into cubes (about 2 cups)

In a medium-size bowl, mix sherry, sugar and garlic together. Cut veal into bite-size pieces and marinate in sherry mixture for 10 minutes. Remove from mixture, reserving marinade. Sprinkle cornstarch over veal and toss. Set aside.

Mix tamari and hoisin together and add to marinade. Mix well. Heat 1 tablespoon oil in wok and add veal. Stir-fry for 30 seconds. Remove veal. Add remaining 1 tablespoon oil and heat. Add beans and stir-fry for 1 minute, or until crisp-tender. Remove beans to plate with veal. Pour marinade into wok and add remaining tablespoon oil to make a creamy sauce. When sauce is bubbling, return veal and beans to wok. Stir-fry for 1 minute. Add cucumber and toss for 1 minute. Spoon over rice.

Helpful Hint

♦ *Have all ingredients cut before you start to cook and arrange them in order of use on a plate so you won't have to refer to the recipe while you cook.*

Veal Gorgonzola

Italian Rice & Peas

Radicchio & Radish Salad

Shopping List

4 veal chops (about 5 ounces each)
1 large head radicchio lettuce
10 radishes
1 small bunch fresh parsley
2 packages frozen baby peas (10 ounces each)
2-ounce piece gorgonzola cheese
1 pint half-and-half
6 ounces Arborio or Valencia-style rice

Staples

onion
cornstarch
all-purpose flour
skim milk
balsamic vinegar
olive oil
brandy
chicken stock
salt
black peppercorns

I ENJOY SERVING this elegant and colorful menu from Lombardy in northern Italy for a special occasion. The tangy gorgonzola sauce complements the sautéed chops. If pressed for time, omit the salad or use whatever greens you have on hand.

Serves 4.

THIS MEAL CONTAINS A TOTAL OF 732 CALORIES PER SERVING WITH 22 PERCENT OF CALORIES FROM FAT.

⧗ Countdown

♦ *Make rice.*
♦ *While rice cooks, make veal.*
♦ *Make salad.*

ITALIAN RICE & PEAS

ARBORIO OR ANY OTHER short-grain rice is best. If you can't find one of these, use long-grain white rice instead.

2	teaspoons olive oil
½	medium onion, chopped (about 1 cup)
2	10-ounce packages frozen baby peas
2	tablespoons chopped fresh parsley
1	cup defatted chicken stock
⅔	cup Arborio or Valencia-style rice
	Salt and freshly ground black pepper to taste

Place oil in a large nonstick skillet and gently sauté onion for 5 minutes, without browning. Add frozen peas, parsley and chicken stock. Bring to a boil and add rice. Cover and simmer for 10 to 15 minutes, stirring once during that time. The rice should be tender, but slightly firm. Add salt and pepper to taste.

VEAL GORGONZOLA

GORGONZOLA is a blue-veined cheese that takes its name from the town in Lombardy.

Helpful Hints

♦ *An inexpensive brandy will do.*

♦ *Domestic gorgonzola may be used.*

4	5-ounce veal chops
2	tablespoons all-purpose flour
	Salt and freshly ground black pepper to taste
1	teaspoon olive oil
½	cup brandy
½	cup crumbled gorgonzola cheese
¼	cup skim milk
¼	cup half-and-half
1	teaspoon cornstarch
1	tablespoon water

Dredge chops in flour seasoned with a little salt and pepper. Heat oil in a nonstick skillet over medium-high heat and add veal chops. Turn after 2 minutes and brown the second side for about 2 minutes. Transfer chops to a serving dish. Place a piece of foil over meat to keep warm. Pour brandy into the skillet, raise the heat to high and boil, stirring and scraping up the browned bits from the bottom. Reduce brandy by half, about 3 to 4 minutes. Reduce heat and stir gorgonzola cheese into the sauce. Add milk and half-and-half. Cook for a minute. Taste for seasoning. Add pepper if needed. The cheese should provide enough salt. Return chops to the pan and simmer gently, 5 to 7 minutes for rare, or 7 to 10 minutes for well done. Remove chops to a serving platter. Mix cornstarch and water together and stir into sauce. Bring to a boil to thicken. Spoon over veal chops.

RADICCHIO & RADISH SALAD

THE FLAVORS OF radicchio and radish are delicious with only a touch of balsamic vinegar for a dressing.

1	large head radicchio lettuce
10	radishes
2	tablespoons good-quality balsamic vinegar

Wash and dry lettuce and tear into bite-size pieces. Wash and slice radishes. Toss together. Sprinkle with vinegar and toss again.

Veal Marsala

Pasta With Mushrooms

Parmesan Green Beans

Shopping List

4 veal scaloppine (about 5 ounces each)
1 pound fresh small or regular green beans
1 ounce dried porcini mushrooms or other dried mushrooms
1-ounce piece Parmesan cheese
½ pound fettuccine
8 ounces dry Marsala wine or medium sherry

Staples

all-purpose flour
butter or margarine
olive oil
salt
black peppercorns

VEAL IS SOMETIMES CALLED "the chameleon of the kitchen," a saying attributed to Grimod de la Reynière, an eighteenth-century gourmand. In fact, the charm of veal is its ability to go with many flavors. In this menu, it picks up the sweet flavors of the Marsala wine, making an elegant Italian dish.

Serves 4.

THIS MEAL CONTAINS A TOTAL OF 725 CALORIES PER SERVING WITH 27 PERCENT OF CALORIES FROM FAT.

Countdown

- *Put water for pasta on to boil.*
- *Boil water for dried mushrooms and soak them.*
- *Make veal.*
- *Make pasta.*
- *Make beans.*

VEAL MARSALA

MARSALA WINE is named after the town in Sicily where it is made. It is a fortified white wine that does not deteriorate after opening. Use dry Marsala, or if you can't find it, substitute medium sherry.

4	5-ounce veal scaloppine
4	tablespoons all-purpose flour
1	tablespoon olive oil
1	cup dry Marsala wine
	Salt and freshly ground black pepper to taste

Ask your butcher to flatten veal, or do it yourself by placing it between 2 pieces of wax paper and pounding with a wooden mallet or the bottom of a heavy skillet, using a sliding motion. Place flour on a plate and dredge veal. Shake off any excess flour. Heat oil in a nonstick skillet. When oil is sizzling, add veal. Brown both sides, in batches if necessary, about 2 minutes. Remove to a warm plate and salt and pepper cooked meat. Cover with foil to keep warm. Pour off excess fat and turn up the heat. Add Marsala to the pan and boil, stirring to scrape up the browned bits. Add juices from the plate of veal to the pan. Reduce heat and let simmer for 1 minute. Taste the sauce for seasoning and add more, if necessary. Cover with foil to keep warm while you finish making the rest of the meal. Spoon sauce over veal and serve with pasta.

PARMESAN GREEN BEANS

SMALL FRENCH GREEN BEANS, sold in some supermarkets, are sweet and good. Use them if you find them, but regular green beans will be fine.

1	pound fresh small green beans or regular green beans, trimmed
2	tablespoons butter or margarine
¼	cup freshly grated Parmesan cheese
	Salt and freshly ground black pepper to taste

Helpful Hint

♦ *Buy good-quality Parmesan cheese and ask your market to grate it for you, or cut it into small pieces and chop it in the food processor. Freeze extra for quick use.*

Bring a pot with 1 to 2 quarts of water to a boil. If beans are large, remove their strings. Blanch beans by adding them to the boiling water. Cook small beans for 1 minute, larger beans for 3 minutes. They should be tender, but crisp. Drain and refresh beans under cold water. Or, to cook in a microwave oven, sprinkle with water and cook small beans, covered, on high for 3 minutes, or 6 minutes for larger beans.

Heat butter in a saucepan. Toss beans in butter. Add Parmesan cheese and continue to stir beans in the butter for 2 to 3 minutes. Add salt and pepper to taste.

PASTA WITH MUSHROOMS

IN ITALY, the pasta would be served as a first course rather than with the veal and beans. For this dinner, however, I have chosen a very simple sauce for the pasta that goes well with the veal.

1	ounce dried porcini mushrooms or any dried mushrooms
4	tablespoons butter
½	pound fettuccine
	Salt and freshly ground black pepper to taste

Place dried porcini in boiling water. Let soak for 10 minutes. Bring a large pot with 3 to 4 quarts of water to a boil. Drain porcini. Melt butter in a saucepan or in a microwave oven on high for 1 minute; add porcini. Set aside. When water is boiling rapidly, add fettuccine. Boil for about 10 minutes, or until tender but firm. Drain and place in a serving bowl. Immediately pour drained porcini and butter over pasta and toss. Season with salt and pepper.

Veal Medallions in Madeira Sauce

Kumquats & Rice

Shopping List

1¼ pounds veal tenderloin or 4 boneless loin chops (about 5 ounces each)
¼ pound kumquats or ½ pint orange juice
1 small bunch watercress
4 scallions
1 small jar orange marmalade
4 ounces medium-sweet Madeira wine or medium sherry

Staples

onion
all-purpose flour
long-grain white rice
sugar
olive oil
1 can chicken stock (14½ ounces)
salt
black peppercorns

THIS IS A MEAL for a special occasion. Madeira wine has a nutty, slightly sweet flavor, and it makes a sophisticated sauce for veal. The slightly sour, orange-like fruit of the kumquats adds an unusual touch to the rice, but orange juice can be used instead when kumquats are not available.

Serves 4.

THIS MEAL CONTAINS A TOTAL OF 646 CALORIES PER SERVING WITH 18 PERCENT OF CALORIES FROM FAT.

⧗ Countdown

♦ *Put water for rice on to boil.*
♦ *Prepare veal for cooking.*
♦ *Cook rice.*
♦ *While rice is cooking, make veal.*

VEAL MEDALLIONS IN MADEIRA SAUCE

MEDALLIONS ARE small steaks cut from the tenderloin. You may need to ask the meat department for this particular cut since it may not be displayed. Loin chops or boneless, skinless chicken breasts can be substituted.

1¼	pounds veal tenderloin or 4 boneless loin chops, about 5 ounces each
¼	cup all-purpose flour
	Salt and freshly ground black pepper to taste
2	teaspoons olive oil
1	medium onion, finely chopped (about 1 cup)
¾	cup defatted chicken stock, *divided*
½	cup medium-sweet Madeira wine
2	tablespoons orange marmalade
	Several sprigs watercress for garnish, *optional*

Trim fat and sinew from veal tenderloin and cut into medallions, about 1½ inches thick. To do this, start at thick end of the tenderloin, measure about 1½ inches and slice through meat. Continue cutting steaks until you reach tail. This piece will be somewhat thinner than the others and should be removed from the pan a little before the larger pieces. Place flour on a dish and add a little salt and pepper. Dredge medallions in flour seasoned with salt and pepper.

Heat oil in a large nonstick skillet and brown veal about 2½ minutes on each

Helpful Hint

♦ *Madeira wine is sold in some supermarkets. A medium sherry can be used instead.*

side. Remove from pan and lightly salt and pepper medallions. Add onion and 2 tablespoons chicken stock to the pan, stirring to scrape up any browned bits. Lower the heat and cover. Cook gently for 5 minutes, or until onion is soft and transparent. Add Madeira, remaining chicken stock and orange marmalade to onion. Raise the heat and reduce liquid by about one-third. Lower the heat and return veal to sauce and cook 1 to 2 minutes. Serve medallions on individual plates and spoon sauce over them. Wash and dry watercress and add to the plates as garnish.

KUMQUATS & RICE

KUMQUATS CAN BE EATEN like grapes and have a sweet skin with a slightly sour pulp. In season from December to March, they add color and flavor to the rice while complementing the Madeira wine sauce for the veal. If they're not available, use only 2 cups chicken stock and add ½ cup orange juice and only 2 teaspoons sugar.

2½	cups defatted chicken stock
4	teaspoons sugar
¼	pound kumquats, washed and diced (about 8)
1	cup long-grain white rice
4	scallions, washed and sliced
2	teaspoons olive oil
	Salt and freshly ground black pepper to taste

Bring stock and sugar to a boil and add kumquats. Simmer 5 minutes and add rice and scallions. Lower heat, cover and simmer for 20 minutes, or until rice is cooked and liquid has been absorbed. Add oil and toss. Add salt and pepper to taste.

CHAPTER 8

Desserts

Desserts

◆

Harlequin
Fruit Platter

Shopping List

3 kiwi fruit
5 tangerines
½ pineapple
1½ pounds black or purple grapes,
  seedless if possible
1 pint strawberries
3 Cortland apples
1 pomegranate

Staples

lemon
nonfat plain yogurt
honey
ground cinnamon

Helpful Hints

♦ *Choose any fruit readily available in the market.*

♦ *Use Cortland apples, if available. They will stay white for a day after cutting.*

♦ *Make the dressing first and grate tangerine rind before peeling the tangerines.*

♦ *To open a pomegranate, cut off pointed or blossom end. Score the skin in quarters from stem to blossom end. Break fruit in half and break again along scored lines. Bend each quarter inside out and remove the seeds.*

A COLORFUL FRUIT PLATTER served with a quick dip can provide the centerpiece for your table. It's a pretty alternative to a bowl of fruit salad.

Serves 6.

THIS DESSERT CONTAINS A TOTAL OF 215 CALORIES PER SERVING WITH 4 PERCENT OF CALORIES FROM FAT.

DRESSING

1	cup nonfat plain yogurt
2	tablespoons honey
1	tablespoon finely grated tangerine zest
½	teaspoon ground cinnamon

FRUIT

5	tangerines
3	Cortland apples
3	kiwi fruit
½	pineapple
1½	pounds black or purple grapes, seedless if possible
1	lemon
1	pomegranate
1	pint strawberries

For dressing: Mix dressing ingredients together and taste. Add more honey or cinnamon if necessary. Serve in bowl next to fruit platter.

For fruit: Choose a small attractive tray or serving platter. Peel tangerines and divide into sections. Wash, quarter and core apples and cut into slices. Squeeze lemon and toss apples slices in juice. Peel and slice kiwis. Peel and core pineapple and cut into large chunks. Wash grapes and divide into small bunches. Hull strawberries. Open pomegranate and remove seeds.

To assemble: Place fruit in diagonal lines on the tray. Start in upper left corner and place tangerines in a line reaching to lower right corner. Place a line of apples on one side and a line of kiwis on the other. Place a line of pineapple next to kiwis and a line of black grapes next to apples. Place a line of strawberries next to apples. Continue placing fruit in diagonal lines to fill tray. Any combination may be used. Simply alternate vibrant and light colors. Sprinkle pomegranate seeds around tray on top of fruit to add color.

Marinated Orange Slices

THIS ATTRACTIVE DISH is a perfect light finale to any dinner, especially around Christmas and New Year's, when oranges are in season.

Serves 4.

THIS DESSERT CONTAINS A TOTAL OF 146 CALORIES PER SERVING WITH 0 PERCENT OF CALORIES FROM FAT.

4	**large navel oranges,** *divided*
1	**large lemon**
4	**tablespoons sugar**
4	**tablespoons Strega or Grand Marnier,** *optional*

Peel 3 oranges over a bowl, collecting the juice. Remove white pith. Slice oranges crosswise and remove seeds. Place slices in a bowl and grate lemon rind over them. Juice remaining orange and lemon and pour the juice over slices. Sprinkle sugar over top. Add liqueur and refrigerate until needed.

Shopping List

4 large navel oranges
4 ounces Strega or Grand Marnier, optional

Staples

lemon
sugar

Helpful Hint

♦ *Strega or Grand Marnier gives the dish extra flavor but this addition is not necessary. If I don't have one of these liqueurs on hand, I buy a miniature bottle. Strega is an Italian liqueur that has a slightly flowery taste.*

Peaches With
Raspberry Sauce

Shopping List

4 ripe peaches
½ pint raspberries (8 ounces)
1 small bunch fresh mint
1 small bottle kirsch (1½ ounces),
* optional*

Staples

confectioners' sugar

Helpful Hints

♦ *Use the raspberry sauce over any type of ice cream, cake or fruit.*

♦ *You can use any soft, ripe fruit or a mixture of fruits.*

♦ *If fresh raspberries are unavailable, use frozen.*

♦ *Straining the raspberry puree gives you a smooth sauce. If you don't mind raspberry seeds, omit this step.*

♦ *Kirsch is a liqueur made from pits and juice of cherries. The best kirsch or kirschwasser comes from the Black Forest in Germany. It can be omitted.*

♦ *The sauce will keep for a week refrigerated.*

SUMMER BERRIES and stone fruits such as peaches, apricots and nectarines are favorites of mine. Serve this dessert whenever ripe fruit is available.

Serves 4.

THIS DESSERT CONTAINS A TOTAL OF 140 CALORIES PER SERVING WITH 3 PERCENT OF CALORIES FROM FAT.

4	**ripe peaches**

SAUCE

½	**pint raspberries (8 ounces)**
¼	**cup confectioners' sugar**
3	**tablespoons kirsch,** *optional*
4	**sprigs fresh mint**

Bring a pot of water to a boil. Add peaches. Remove after 20 seconds and dip immediately into cold water to stop the cooking. Peel them. Cut in half, remove pits and slice. Place slices in a semicircle on 4 individual plates.

For sauce: Puree raspberries either in a food processor or food mill or press through a sieve. Add sugar and kirsch. The amount of sugar depends on the ripeness of the raspberries. Taste puree. More sugar may be necessary. Pass sauce through a strainer to remove seeds. Spoon over peaches and garnish each plate with a sprig of mint.

Peaches
in White Wine

THIS REFRESHING COMBINATION is drink and dessert all in one. First you eat the peaches, then you drink the wine.

Serves 4.

THIS DESSERT CONTAINS A TOTAL OF 157 CALORIES PER SERVING WITH 0 PERCENT OF CALORIES FROM FAT.

Shopping List

4 large ripe peaches
white wine (Sancerre or Riesling)

4   **large ripe peaches**
4   **glasses half filled with chilled white wine (Sancerre or Riesling)**

Bring a pot of water to a boil. Add peaches. Remove after 20 seconds and dip immediately in cold water to stop the cooking. Peel. Cut in half and remove pits. Slice peaches. Add 1 sliced peach to each glass of chilled wine. Serve immediately with spoons.

Pears
in Red Wine

Shopping List

4 ripe pears
1 small package sliced almonds
    (1½ ounces)

Staples

lemon
dry red wine (6 ounces)
cinnamon stick
sugar

Helpful Hints

♦ *This recipe can be made ahead and frozen.*

♦ *Be careful not to mark or bruise the pears when turning them during cooking. Use the backs of two spoons to turn them gently.*

THESE DELICATELY POACHED pears are a light, pretty end to a meal. *See photograph, page 176.*

    Serves 4.

THIS DESSERT CONTAINS A TOTAL OF 275 CALORIES PER SERVING WITH 7 PERCENT OF CALORIES FROM FAT.

⅔	**cup dry red wine**
⅔	**cup water**
¾	**cup sugar**
1	**strip lemon rind**
1	**cinnamon stick**
4	**ripe pears**
¾	**tablespoon sliced almonds for garnish**

Place wine, water, sugar, lemon rind and cinnamon stick in a saucepan large enough to fit pears snugly. Cook over medium heat until sugar is completely dissolved. Bring to a boil for 3 minutes. Peel pears, leaving stems on. Place in liquid and poach until soft. Pears must poach for at least 30 minutes to ensure that the flavor reaches the middle. During poaching time, turn pears very gently.

When pears are cooked, remove them from the liquid. Boil liquid until thick and syrupy. Preheat oven to 350 degrees F. Place pears in a shallow serving bowl or in individual fruit dishes and spoon syrup over them.

To garnish, toast almonds on a baking pan in the oven for 5 minutes, until golden and slightly brown on edges. Place at varying intervals on pears. Almonds will stick to syrup.

Tipsy Fruit Salad

I CAN ALWAYS TELL when it starts to get cold up north: My phone starts to ring and friends and family appear for a few days of sun. I love seeing them, but I'd rather spend my time visiting with them than in the kitchen. This dessert came to my rescue for one Sunday brunch.

It begins with fruit salad bought from a salad bar or deli.

Serves 4.

THIS DESSERT CONTAINS A TOTAL OF 139 CALORIES PER SERVING WITH 0 PERCENT OF CALORIES FROM FAT.

2	pounds store-bought fruit salad
2	tablespoons Grand Marnier or other orange liqueur
1	tablespoon fresh lemon juice
3	carambolas, 1 peeled and cored pineapple, 2 kiwis, 1 pint fresh berries, or other colorful fruit not already in salad; alone or in combination
¼	cup chopped fresh mint

Drain fruit salad, reserving liquid. Gently mix in remaining ingredients. Add 1 to 2 tablespoons of the reserved liquid.

Shopping List

2 pounds fruit salad
3 carambolas, 1 peeled and cored pineapple, 2 kiwis, 1 pint fresh berries, or other colorful fruit not already in salad; alone or in combination
1 small bunch fresh mint
1 ounce Grand Marnier or other orange liqueur

Staples

lemon

Helpful Hints

♦ *Serve on its own or with cookies, or over fruit breads, bread puddings, rice pudding, unfrosted cakes, plain cheesecake or ice cream.*

♦ *This recipe is best with fresh fruit salad. If using canned, add some freshly cut apples and pineapple to it.*

Oranges in Caramel

Shopping List

4 navel oranges
extra-fine granulated sugar

COLORFUL WHOLE ORANGES in a golden sauce bring sparkle to the table. *See photograph, page 171.*

Serves 4.

THIS DESSERT CONTAINS A TOTAL OF 195 CALORIES PER SERVING WITH 0 PERCENT OF CALORIES FROM FAT.

Rind from 4 oranges for garnish
¾ **cup extra-fine granulated sugar**
⅔ **cup cold water**
1 **cup warm water**
4 **whole navel oranges**

Helpful Hint

♦ *The sugar syrup can be made ahead and the oranges prepared just before serving.*

Carefully peel off pieces of orange skin with a vegetable peeler. Try not to take any white pith. Cut into needle-thin shreds and blanch in boiling water for 1 minute. Rinse in cold water. Wrap in a damp paper towel until needed. Shreds will keep overnight if placed in a towel in a plastic bag.

Dissolve sugar in ⅔ cup cold water over a low heat. Be sure water does not boil before all sugar is dissolved. Bring liquid to a boil and cook until it is a light caramel color or golden brown. Remove from heat and immediately pour 1 cup warm water into caramel. Return the pan to the heat and stir to dissolve hardened particles. Cool.

Remove skin from oranges with a serrated knife, cutting with a sawing motion between skin and flesh of the orange. Continue around in circles until skin is removed. Try not to leave any pith.

To serve: With a serrated knife, partially slice oranges into 6 slices across the membranes: Make 1 slice nearly through orange to the center, 2 slices nearly through to the right of the center slice, and 2 to the left, leaving slices still attached. Stand each orange on its end and pierce with a toothpick to hold together. Stand oranges in a serving bowl or 4 individual dessert bowls and sprinkle with orange rind. Spoon the caramelized sugar syrup over them.

All-American Blueberry Pie

WHEN THE FIRST BLUEBERRIES start to appear, I know summer isn't far behind. This is my favorite way to serve them. They remain whole, juicy and firm because half of them are not cooked, while the other half are briefly simmered.

Serves 10.

THIS DESSERT CONTAINS A TOTAL OF 239 CALORIES PER SERVING WITH 31 PERCENT OF CALORIES FROM FAT.

1	9-inch pie crust, *recipe follows*
2	pints blueberries (about 5 cups)
1	cup sugar
¼	cup cornstarch
1	cup water

Prepare pie crust. Wash and drain blueberries. Remove stems, if necessary. Reserve 2 cups berries for sauce and fill prebaked pie shell with remaining berries. Combine sugar and cornstarch in a saucepan. Add water and bring to a simmer. Cook until liquid thickens, about 3 minutes. Add reserved berries and simmer 5 minutes, stirring constantly, or until sauce is thick and clear, not cloudy. Spoon over blueberries in pie shell. Place in refrigerator to set.

PIE CRUST

1	cup all-purpose flour
6	tablespoons butter or margarine
2	ounces low-fat cream cheese (¼ cup)
3	tablespoons ice water

Sift flour into a bowl. Cut butter and cream cheese into 1-inch pieces. Cut into pastry with a pastry cutter or 2 knives. Rub in fat with your fingertips so there are no large lumps. Mixture should resemble bread crumbs. Make a well in the center of mixture and add a little water. Mix it in with a knife or fork and add more water. When mixture starts to come together in a ball, knead slightly with your hands. Don't overknead. Cover and place in refrigerator to rest for about 20 minutes. Preheat oven to 350 degrees F.

Flour countertop and roll out pastry and line pie plate with it. Place foil or parchment paper over dough and add dried beans, rice, stale bread or anything else that will serve to weigh down pastry. Bake 15 minutes. Take out of oven and remove filling and foil. Return pastry to oven and cook 10 more minutes to complete baking. Remove from oven. Fill with blueberries as directed above.

Shopping List

2 pints blueberries
  (about 14 ounces)
1 package low-fat cream cheese
  (3 ounces)

Staples

cornstarch
all-purpose flour
butter or margarine
sugar

Helpful Hints

♦ Raspberries or strawberries can be used for this pie.

♦ Buy a ready-made pie crust, if you are pressed for time.

Glazed Apple Tart

Shopping List

*2 pounds Granny Smith apples
(about 6)
1 small jar apricot jam*

Staples

*ground cinnamon
brown sugar
sugar
all-purpose flour
unsalted butter
canola oil*

Helpful Hints

♦ *Slice apples in a food processor to save time.*

♦ *The pie crust does not need rolling out. Simply push into a pie plate with fingers.*

I LOVE TO SMELL APPLES with cinnamon baking in the oven. They give the entire house a warm and inviting aroma. This tart is very simple to make, but it will need 45 minutes to bake and 5 more minutes to glaze. It is a combination of an American apple crumble and a French apple tart. If pressed for time, buy a ready-made crust.

Serves 10.

THIS DESSERT CONTAINS A TOTAL OF 256 CALORIES PER SERVING WITH 12 PERCENT OF CALORIES FROM FAT.

CRUST

1	cup all-purpose flour
½	cup brown sugar
1	teaspoon ground cinnamon
1	teaspoon unsalted butter
2	tablespoons canola oil

FILLING

2	pounds Granny Smith apples
1	tablespoon sugar

GLAZE

1	cup apricot jam
2	tablespoons water

Preheat oven to 350 degrees F.

For crust: Mix flour, brown sugar and cinnamon together. Add butter and oil and cut in with pastry cutter or rub in with fingers. Gently press into a 9-inch pie plate.

For filling: Peel, core and slice apples lengthwise into ¼-inch slices. Set aside one-third of the best-looking apple slices. Spoon remaining apples into pie plate. Spread evenly over crust. Place the best apples slices in circles over top of pie, overlapping each slice. Sprinkle with sugar. Bake 45 minutes.

For glaze: Heat jam and water in a saucepan without boiling. Strain and brush over top layer of apples after the pie is baked.

Light
Key Lime Cake

KEY LIMES AND KEY LIME PIE are an important part of cooking in the Florida Keys. This light cake made with Key lime juice will take 45 minutes to bake plus 15 minutes to assemble. Although the preparation is longer than that of the other desserts, I have included it because it is so delicious and can be made a day ahead or frozen.

Serves 16.

THIS DESSERT CONTAINS A TOTAL OF 200 CALORIES PER SERVING WITH 23 PERCENT OF CALORIES FROM FAT.

	Vegetable-oil cooking spray
1¾	**cups all-purpose white flour**
2	**teaspoons baking powder**
½	**teaspoon salt**
6	**tablespoons unsalted butter or margarine**
1	**cup sugar**
2	**large eggs**
1½	**teaspoons grated Key lime or regular lime zest**
1	**tablespoon Key lime juice or regular lime juice**
⅔	**cup buttermilk**

SYRUP

1	**cup sifted confectioners' sugar**
½	**cup Key lime or regular lime juice**
2	**tablespoons confectioners' sugar for sprinkling over cake**

Preheat oven to 350 degrees F. Spray the inside of a 6-cup Bundt pan or 9-inch springform mold with vegetable-oil cooking spray. Set aside. Stir flour, baking powder and salt together in a small mixing bowl. In a large bowl, beat butter until softened and gradually add sugar. Beat in eggs very gradually, then lime zest and juice. Alternately stir in dry ingredients and buttermilk, beginning and ending with flour mixture. Spoon into the prepared cake pan and bake 45 minutes, or until a cake tester inserted into the center comes out clean and cake starts to pull away from the sides of the pan. Cool 10 minutes, then loosen edges and invert onto a wire rack set over a plate.

For syrup: Whisk confectioners' sugar and lime juice together, making sure there are no lumps. While cake is still warm, poke holes in it using a skewer or cake tester. Slowly spoon lime syrup over cake. Spoon any syrup that seeps onto the plate over cake. Let cool completely.

To garnish, sprinkle confectioners' sugar over top just before serving.

Shopping List

1 bottle Key lime juice (16 ounces)
1 quart buttermilk

Staples

vegetable-oil cooking spray
baking powder
salt
all-purpose flour
unsalted butter or margarine
eggs
sugar
confectioners' sugar

Helpful Hint

♦ *Key limes can be difficult to find. Use bottled Key lime juice or Persian (regular) limes instead.*

Rich & Creamy Homemade Chocolate Sauce

Shopping List

6 ounces good-quality semisweet chocolate

Staples

sugar
vanilla extract

Helpful Hint

♦ *Be careful when melting chocolate. It can be temperamental. Don't let it boil. The cocoa fat will separate and you won't have a smooth sauce.*

I LIKE TO MAKE this sauce ahead and keep it in the refrigerator or freezer. The velvety chocolate texture and flavor can turn ice cream, fruit or store-bought cake into something special.

Serves 10.

THIS DESSERT CONTAINS A TOTAL OF 125 CALORIES PER SERVING WITH 65 PERCENT OF CALORIES FROM FAT.

6	ounces good-quality semisweet chocolate
½	cup sugar
2	teaspoons vanilla extract
1	cup water

Cut chocolate into small pieces and place in a heavy-bottomed saucepan with sugar, vanilla and water. Melt chocolate over very low heat. When it is melted and sugar is dissolved, mix well. Bring to a very low simmer and cook gently for 10 to 15 minutes, or until sauce is thick. Serve over peeled peaches, ripe pears, brownies, cake or ice cream.

Rum Mango Sauce

Try this sauce on a cold evening over frozen yogurt or fresh fruit and think warm thoughts of the Caribbean. Or serve it at a summer party.

Serves 4.

This dessert contains a total of 189 calories per serving with 5 percent of calories from fat.

Sauce

1¾	cups peeled, cubed ripe fresh mango
⅔	cup sweetened condensed milk
3	tablespoons light rum
2	tablespoons brown sugar
1½	teaspoons fresh lime juice
4	cups peeled, cubed ripe fresh mango

For sauce: Place mango, condensed milk, rum, brown sugar and lime juice in a food processor. Process until smooth.

Place mango cubes in 4 fruit bowls and spoon sauce over fruit.

Shopping List

4–5 large ripe mangoes
1 can sweetened condensed milk (14 ounces)
1 fresh lime
light rum

Staples

brown sugar

Helpful Hint

♦ *Mangoes are available almost year-round in most supermarkets. To cut mango cubes quickly, slice off each side of the mango as close to the seed as possible. Take the mango half in your hand, skin-side down. Score the fruit in a cross-hatch pattern through to the skin. Bend the skin backwards so the cubes pop up. Slice the cubes away from the skin. Score and slice any fruit left on the pit.*

Raspberry Sorbet

Shopping List

5 half-pint baskets fresh raspberries
kirsch or rum

Staples

sugar

Helpful Hints

♦ *1 pound unsweetened frozen raspberries or other berries can be used.*

♦ *This can be made in about 30 minutes if you have an ice cream maker. Otherwise, it will take 5 minutes to prepare and will need to sit at least 4 hours in the freezer.*

♦ *This is best served within 2 days of making it. If frozen longer, remove from the freezer about 12 hours in advance. Let stand 5 minutes and whirl in a food processor, then refreeze.*

♦ *Place serving plate and dessert dishes in the freezer about 15 minutes before needed. Because there are no preservatives or emulsifiers in homemade sorbets, the edges of the sorbet will melt if it is unmolded onto room-temperature plates.*

THIS IS A DESSERT for a special occasion. It can be made several days ahead. Serve with the raspberry sauce from Peaches With Raspberry Sauce (page 248), or with fresh raspberries or other soft fruit.

Serves 8.

THIS DESSERT CONTAINS A TOTAL OF 198 CALORIES PER SERVING WITH 0 PERCENT OF CALORIES FROM FAT.

1½	**cups water**
1⅔	**cups sugar**
5	**half-pint baskets fresh raspberries**
2	**tablespoons kirsch or rum**

Place water in a heavy-bottomed saucepan. Sprinkle sugar on top. Heat to dissolve sugar, but do not boil. When sugar is completely dissolved, about 5 minutes, bring to a boil. Remove from heat as soon as a full boil is reached. Cool.

Puree raspberries and strain. This can be done in one step with a food mill. Or use a food processor and then strain or mash through a sieve. Mix in 2 cups of the cooled sugar syrup and kirsch. Refrigerate until cold, and freeze in an ice cream maker following manufacturer's instructions.

If you do not have an ice cream maker, place in a metal bowl in your freezer. Take out and whisk after 2 hours when sorbet is beginning to freeze. Replace and freeze another 2 hours or longer. Whisk one more time.

To finish: Frozen sorbet may be scooped into bowls. Or line an ice cream mold or bread loaf pan with plastic wrap. When the sorbet begins to hold its shape, spoon it into the mold. Cover tightly and place in the freezer.

To serve: Take sorbet out of freezer 5 to 10 minutes before serving. Run a knife along sides of mold to loosen sorbet and then turn over onto a cold serving plate. Remove plastic wrap and serve.

Mocha Granita

THE ITALIANS LOVE a good coffee granita, especially after a large dinner. Granita is like a sorbet; it does not contain egg whites or cream, so its texture is slightly grainy.

This can be made in about 30 minutes if you have an ice cream maker. Otherwise, it will take 5 minutes to prepare and will need to sit for least 2 hours in the freezer.

Serves 4.

THIS DESSERT CONTAINS A TOTAL OF 105 CALORIES PER SERVING WITH 0 PERCENT OF CALORIES FROM FAT.

3½	cups prepared espresso coffee or double-strength regular coffee
1	cup sugar
1	vanilla bean or 2 teaspoons vanilla extract
2	teaspoons unsweetened cocoa powder

Place coffee, sugar and vanilla bean (if using vanilla extract, add later) in a saucepan and heat until sugar is completely dissolved. Do not boil liquid. Add cocoa and vanilla extract, if using, and mix thoroughly. Pour into a metal bowl and cool. Freeze in an ice cream machine. Or, pour hot mixture into a roasting pan or large metal bowl to cool and place in the freezer for 1½ hours. When it has started to freeze, remove and beat with a whisk. Return to the freezer for another ½ hour.

Shopping List

1 jar instant espresso coffee or regular coffee

Staples

unsweetened cocoa powder
sugar
vanilla bean or vanilla extract

Helpful Hints

♦ *Use either good espresso coffee or double-strength regular coffee. Instant coffee works very well.*

♦ *A metal bowl will cool the mixture faster, but any type of bowl can be used.*

Index

P

Whiskey pork, 201
White beans
    cannellini
        and romaine salad, 35
        rosemary, 81
    and tuna salad, Tuscan,
     134
    vichysoisse, 32
White wine
    mussels in, 125
    peaches in, 249
    sauce, scallops in, 123
Wine. *See also* Red wine;
  White wine

recommendations for
    different meals, 23–24
Wok cooking, 22

Y

Yam slices, roasted, 82

Z

Zucchini
    gratinéed, 143

salad, 220
sticks, steamed carrots
  and, 81
and tomato salad, 135